THE FEDERAL RESERVE SYSTEM

THE FEDERAL RESERVE SYSTEM

A History of the First 75 Years

by

CARL H. MOORE

McFarland & Company, Inc., Publishers
Jefferson, North Carolina, and London

British Library Cataloguing-in-Publication data are available

Library of Congress Cataloguing-in-Publication Data

Moore, Carl H., 1916–
    The Federal Reserve System : a history of the first 75 years / by
Carl H. Moore.
    p. cm.
    Includes bibliographical references and index.
    ISBN 0-89950-503-1 (lib. bdg. : 50# alk. paper) ∞
    1. Board of Governors of the Federal Reserve System (U.S.)—
History. 2. Monetary policy—United States—History. I. Title.
HG2563.M68 1990
332.1'1'0973—dc20   89-43660
                                            CIP

Manufactured in the United States of America

McFarland & Company, Inc., Publishers
 Box 611, Jefferson, North Carolina 28640

Table of Contents

Acknowledgments

As with any historical research, many people have contributed ideas, facts and suggestions. Authors writing during the early years of the Federal Reserve System compiled volumes of detail that served to give a picture of the early days of the Fed. Parker Willis, Carter Glass and Paul Warburg probably made the greatest contribution in this area. Personnel at all of the Federal Reserve banks, especially the San Antonio office, and at the Board of Governors were invaluable in assembling historical as well as current data. Michael Whitehouse at the Board of Governors; Rosemary Lazenby, Chief of the Central Records and Archives at the New York Fed; and Jane Freeman, Research Librarian at the Dallas Fed, were especially helpful in supplying vital material. Parts of the manuscript were reviewed by former chairman William McChesney Martin; Robert Boykin, President of the Federal Reserve Bank of Dallas; and Tom Frost, Chairman of the Board of the Frost National Bank. I am particularly grateful to Joseph Coyne, Assistant to the Board of Governors, for reading the entire manuscript and making valuable suggestions for its improvement. To my wife, Sue, goes my special appreciation for her help, encouragement, tolerance of my obsession with work on "The Book" and her reading of chapters for continuity.

My thanks to each one who had a part in putting together this review of the first 75 years of our central banking system.

Acknowledgments

Preface

It is said that in the days of kings and emperors history was rewritten by each new realm. Since histories are written by human beings, it follows that any history must bear some bias and reflect to a degree the feelings of the author.

My attempt at writing a history of the Federal Reserve System is from a background of first, a farm boy exposed to the problems of a midwestern farm during the 1920s and 1930s; second, a study of economics; and third, 32 years with the Federal Reserve Bank of Dallas as an economist and a vice president in charge of operations. Whatever "coloring" this adds to this history, so be it.

Volumes have been written on the details of the struggle to bring the Federal Reserve Act into law. I will leave those details and heated discussions to writers such as Paul Warburg and Carter Glass, who were present and participated in the discussions. Their books are ample coverage of the events.

I have put most of the statistical material in appendices so that the more casual reader will not have to struggle through the maze of statistics and thus miss the continuity of the history.

It would be unfair to the reader to omit some of the vigorous and at times humorous conversations during the debates, so to add spice for the reader, I have included some of these. They are a part of the history of this banking system that has withstood two world wars, the Great Depression of the 1930s and a move from a debtor nation to a creditor and back to a debtor nation.

It seemed reasonable to approach this history by using calendar dates. While the major events of such a history do not always fit neatly into such a package, they do provide convenient "handles" and reference points both for the reader and the author.

One more comment. This is intended to be a history of the events and action of the Federal Reserve System. It is not an attempt to discuss the pros and cons of monetary policy or the various theories of economics. I must confess to an occasional editorial comment and my personal prejudices will no doubt show at times. But it is not my purpose to cover ground that so many fine authors have covered in expounding the intricacies of monetary management or international transactions. Wherever possible, facts have been gleaned from public documents. It is my hope that the reader of this history will find it interesting and in it a story of our republic government in action. Institutions have a way of changing to meet challenging conditions and I believe the history of our central banking system reflects that ability to meet new challenges.

A word of caution to readers of the statistical tables. Assembling data over a period of 75 years involves some difficulty in obtaining comparable data. Definitions used for items are changed or modified. Some series are discontinued and others started. Although every attempt has been made to provide reliable and comparable statistics, the reader should exercise caution in drawing firm conclusion based on the data. Data for more recent years are, as expected, more reliable but may not always be strictly comparable with earlier series.

Chapter 1
The Climax of a Long Struggle

It was one minute before six o'clock in the evening, December 23, 1913. President Woodrow Wilson sat at his desk in the Executive Office of the White House. Legislative leaders, cabinet members and the press stood by to witness a momentous step in the history of the United States.

Looking around the group, President Wilson noticed that his friend and chairman of the House Banking Committee, Representative Carter Glass (D–VA) was in the back of the room. This man, who had spent years of patient and vigorous toil to bring this bill to this point, was worthy of recognition, and the president asked him to join him at his desk with Senator Robert Owen (R–OK), chairman of the Senate Banking and Currency Committee and sponsor of the bill in the Senate. The occasion was the signing into law of the bill creating the Federal Reserve System.

Four gold pens were given to the president for signing the bill, and at 6:02 P.M., December 23, 1913, he began signing the Federal Reserve Act into law. With the first pen he wrote, "Approved, 23 Dec. 1913," and gave the pen to Congressman Glass. With the second he wrote, "Wood," and gave the pen to Senator Owen. With the third he wrote, "row," and gave the pen to Secretary of the Treasury William G. McAdoo. With the fourth he wrote, "Wilson," and directed that it be given to Senator William D. Chilton (D–WV), who had sent the pen to the White House and asked that it be used in signing the bill.

In a speech following the signing of the bill, President Wilson said the new law was a "constitution of peace for the business interest of the United States." He expressed his pleasure in completing a work he believed would be of lasting benefit to the business of the nation. While the president did not say so in so many words, he made it plain that it was his belief that the new law would quicken the activities of trade and commerce. Mr. Wilson said he was surprised at the sudden acceptance of the measure by public opinion everywhere. Businessmen, he said, had opened their eyes to find the measure, which they supposed to be hostile, a serviceable friend.

Thus ended more than 100 years of debate — often bitter — of how the United States should handle its monetary affairs.

1

Carter Glass, sponsor of the bill in the House of Representatives to create the Federal Reserve System. Sometimes called the "father" of the Federal Reserve System. Later served as secretary of the treasury and also as senator from Virginia. Courtesy Board of Governors, Federal Reserve System.

AUTHORSHIP OF THE ACT

Who wrote the Federal Reserve Act has little significance and is probably of no interest to students of the system in the 1990s. The question was important in the early days of the system not so much as to why it was written as to the fact that when it became law and appeared to be a successful venture, not a few wanted to claim credit for writing it. Parker Willis, in his review of the history of the system, said in part, "The question of the authorship of the Federal Reserve Act has been many times referred to during the eight years which have passed since its adoption, and it has already become the center of a multitude of erroneous statements. The authorship of any large piece of work which has engaged the attention, first and last, of many minds is always open to some doubt and differences of opinion. It is, moreover, usually a matter about which controversy is ungraceful and should, if possible, be avoided.... Authorship has been variously ascribed to members of the so-called money trusts and to a group of "Hebrew bankers."

Willis proceeds to review the many men who had a hand in the framing of the Federal Reserve Act. Congressman Carter Glass and Senator Robert Owen unquestionably had a large hand in its development as well as its passage by Congress. Ideas were contributed over the years preceding the writing of the act by men such as Paul Warburg, Senator Nelson W. Aldrich (R–RI) and a host of other men interested in correcting the inefficient banking system of the country. Mr. Willis points out that attributing any credit to a Colonel House, an assistant to President Wilson, is probably in error as the colonel's main contribution was to criticize the act. While Professor J. Lawrence Laughlin and the National Citizens League (discussed later) undoubtedly played a role in gaining acceptance of the act by the rank and file of businessmen and bankers his contribution to the actual writing of the act was minimal.

It is not exaggerating to say the debate on what kind of banking structure was needed has gone on since men began to participate in commerce and business. In more recent years it is often called the struggle between the "haves" and the "have nots." It has been a part of the political struggle in the United States since the founding of our government with the "Populists" fighting for low interest rates and easy money. On the other hand, the so-called conservatives firmly believed in a more open, competitive society with the market setting interest rates and prices. Another basic issue was whether a country should have a strong central government regulating the economy or most of the powers should be given to the outlying areas (in the United States to the states) and the role of the central government kept to a minimum.

As the leaders of the 13 colonies struggled to form a government after defeating the British and gaining their independence, Alexander Hamilton and Thomas Jefferson were the champions for the two sides; Hamilton for a strong central government and Jefferson for more power to the states. For the next 100 years the issue would be debated, and the topics debated would include the issuing of currency, setting tariffs, slavery, regulation of banks, railroads and trucks, and a host of other issues.

FIRST UNITED STATES BANK

Early in our history, Hamilton was able to secure the establishment of a strong bank that gave stability to currency for a time. In 1791, the First United States Bank was authorized and gave stability to our currency for 20 years. But a bill to renew its charter in 1811 was defeated by one vote both in the House and the Senate. Chaos broke out, and in 1816 the Second Bank of the United States was authorized by a large margin in both houses.

Again, the charter was for 20 years, and when it came up for renewal in 1836, politics prevailed and the charter expired. There followed 27 years of an unstable currency, the birth of "wildcat" banks, dozens of different banks issuing their own currency, loss of confidence in the banking industry and great difficulty in financing the Civil War. A major milestone in bringing some sense of stability to the currency issue took place in 1863 with the passage of the National Banking Act.

PROBLEMS PERSISTED

The National Banking Act brought major improvements to the banking industry. But banks in the agricultural areas often could not obtain enough credit or currency to supply the seasonal needs of their customers. After the harvest season, any surplus funds at country banks were sent to the money center banks in the large cities — mainly New York — where they earned interest. The money center banks loaned the funds out to speculators in the stock market and when they needed the money and called the loans, money panics often resulted.

The inelasticity of the currency, an archaic system of bank reserves and the lack of a "lender of last resort" for the banks contributed to feast and famine in the financial community. Script was often used when currency was not available. Currency issued by banks not known to the customers was often discounted.

Here is a summary of the problems as expressed by Carter Glass in his book *An Adventure in Constructive Finance.*

> For fifty years prior to the enactment of the Federal Reserve Act, the United States endured the handicap of an unscientific currency system. Again and again it was pronounced by textbook writers and experienced bankers the most barbarous system on earth. The defects were so glaring and the failure to remedy them fraught with such ill consequences as to constitute a positive indictment of the statesmanship of the nation. For a part of the time, we rested in the imaginary security of ignorance; for another part, we seemed indifferent to our plight, and for the remainder of the time were afraid to apply the remedy lest we interfere with the processes and profits of a privileged class. For no protracted period were we without warning. At nearly every decennial the fateful malady manifested itself in violent financial disturbance which swept the country from Dan to Beersheba. Catastrophe had overtaken us five times within thirty years right in the midst of great prosperity. Strange to say, prosperity, under the then-prevailing currency system, was actually conducive to disaster.
>
> The Siamese twins of disorder were an inelastic currency and a fictitious reserve system. The banks and politicians were perfectly willing to tackle the task of readjusting the currency; but the bankers, through sheer acquisitiveness, objected to interference with their reserve arrangement, and the politicians, through fear of the bankers, were averse to stirring up enmities among men of power.

Colorful language but a problem well stated.

CHECK COLLECTION A PROBLEM

Another problem prior to the Federal Reserve Act involved the collection of checks. Because of a network of interbank relations, a check might move around the country from bank to bank for weeks before arriving at the bank on which it was drawn. Bad checks were everywhere, and even legitimate transactions might take weeks to complete.

A SEARCH FOR SOLUTIONS

Struggling to find a solution to the problems, politicians and bankers debated several suggested programs. The severe money panic of 1907 dramatized the urgency of finding a solution. In 1908 Congress passed the Aldrich-Vreeland Act, which among other things called for a national clearinghouse and created the National Monetary Commission. The purpose of the commission was to study the various central banking systems of the world—mainly in Europe—and report back to Congress. The National Clearinghouse never got off the ground, and following the report of the commission, Senator Theodore E. Burton (R–OH) introduced a bill calling for the organization of a National Reserve Association. This was to be run by bankers and supervised by the government.

DEMOCRATS COME TO POWER

The bill was well on its way to becoming law when the election of 1912 swept the Democrats into power for the first time in 50 years. (The four-year term of Cleveland was an exception, but he was as conservative as any Republican.) No good Democrat would support a bill devised by Republicans, so nothing became of Senator Burton's bill. Instead, the Democrats and many independent economists and politicians began to work for the passage of a bill that would bring about an elastic currency, more effective collection of checks, a "lender of last resort" for the banking system and a modern reserve system.

Carter Glass (D–VA), had been serving on the House Banking and Currency Committee, and following the report of the National Monetary Commission, he was assigned the chairmanship of a subcommittee of the House Committee with instructions to devise a reserve banking scheme. The chairman of the Committee, Representative Arsene J. Pujo (D–LA) was to assume the task of investigating the "Money Trust."

Parenthetically, the struggle for power was still very evident, and the division of loyalty between a strong central power and the "common people" continued unabated. Few trusted the "bankers," and the "bankers" felt they alone had the knowledge to run the "money system." This battle continued throughout the debate in Congress, in the press and among supporters of both sides. All did agree that something must be done. The discussion of what that something was caused tempers to flare and strong words to echo in the halls of Congress while heated discussions took place in the classrooms of universities, in the national press and in smoke-filled rooms. And as is often the case, the solution was not entirely pleasing to anyone, but it was acceptable to most.

IDEAS SHARPLY DIVIDED

Some of the comments in the Congress shed light on the intensity of the debate. Speaking about the Burton bill, Congressman Glass objected to the Treasury being involved. James B. Forgan, from Illinois and then president of the American Bankers Association, also in opposition, said, "[T]he issue of anything that could bear such an infernal name as emergency currency puts the Federal government in the picayune and incongruous business of discounting commercial paper."

Congressman John G. McHenry (D–PA) was even more vigorous in his comments. "The bill enables Wall Street to turn panics off and on at will. The Secretary of the Treasury would become the 'hired man' of Wall Street. Shall we close, as a fitting climax to this billion-dollar Republican Congress, by crowning our masters, King Morgan and King Rockefeller, the heroes of the last panic, or shall it be King Taft, Wall Street's hired man?"

Perhaps more perceptive was the comment of Senator Burton. "The time is coming when that general principle of currency issue commensurate with business volume is going to be adopted either through a central bank or by other means."

Debate on Congressman Glass's bill to create the Federal Reserve System invoked emotional and testy comments on the floor of the House and the Senate. In support of the bill, Congressman Glass extolled the virtue of the central board (the Federal Reserve Board), saying, "No financial interest can pervert or control the Board. It is an altruistic institution, a part of Government itself, representing the American people, with such powers as no man would dare misuse."

At one point in the debate it was proposed that there be as few as three and not more than five regional banks. Opponents quickly saw that this would mean one in each of the money center cities and that, they said, would put it under the dominance of "selfish bankers."

In the Senate, Senator James Lewis (D–IL) responded to a critic as follows:

> What does my distinguished friend expect in a political government? The Senator (who raised the question) is right. The bill is political, political to the extent that it voices the political ideas of the people of the country, political in that it expresses the platform of the (Democratic party).... All things must be guided, honorable sir. To some men each system must be entrusted.

A QUICK SUMMARY OF THE ACT

In the preamble to the act its purpose is stated as "An Act: To provide for the establishment of Federal reserve banks, to furnish an elastic currency, to afford means of rediscounting commercial paper, to establish a more effective supervision of banking in the United States and for other purposes." The act provided for two basic structures: a central body to be known as the Federal Reserve Board and not more than 12 Reserve banks to be located throughout the country as determined by the Organization Committee. The duties and responsibilities of each were not clearly defined (which led to some problems) but were stated in general terms.

The central board was to be composed of seven men, five of which were to be appointed by the president and confirmed by the Senate. The secretary of the treasury and the comptroller of the currency were to serve as *ex officio* members, but the secretary of the treasury was to act as chairman when he was present. The board was to have the power to receive its funds for operations from the Reserve banks. Neither the board nor the banks were to receive any appropriated funds. The board was to exercise general supervision over the Reserve banks and was to make a full report to the Speaker of the House of Representatives annually. (Other duties of the Board and its organization will be discussed in subsequent chapters.)

The Reserve banks were to operate under the direction of a board of directors who were to be elected in a very specific manner. Three of the directors were to be appointed by the Federal Reserve Board, and one would be designated as chairman and Federal Reserve Agent. In addition to the usual powers of a corporation, the Reserve banks were empowered to

- "receive from any of its member banks, and from the United States, deposits of current funds in lawful money, national bank notes, Federal reserve notes, or checks and drafts upon solvent member banks, payable upon presentation; or, solely for exchange purposes, may receive from other Federal reserve banks deposits in current funds in lawful money, national bank notes, or checks and drafts upon solvent member banks, payable upon presentation";
- "discount notes, drafts, and bills of exchange arising out of actual commercial transactions";
- purchase and sell in the open market, at home or abroad, either to or from domestic or foreign banks, firms, corporations or individuals, cable transfers and banker's acceptances and bills of exchange;
- deal in gold coin and bullion;
- buy and sell United States government securities;
- establish from time to time, subject to review and determination of the Federal Reserve Board, rates of discount;
- establish accounts with other Federal Reserve banks;
- issue Federal Reserve notes, obligations of the United States Government.

This is not intended to be a comprehensive summary of the act. Discussions in later chapters will enlarge upon various sections as different parts are explored and their impact discussed. The act contains more than 15,000 words and contains much legal language which is important to a careful interpretation but not critical to our story of the history of the system. (A copy is in the Appendix for those who wish to study it in more detail.)

FEDERAL ADVISORY COUNCIL

Throughout the debate on the Glass bill and in other discussions of "banking" problems, commercial banking interests of the nation insisted that only bankers could effectively and efficiently operate any organization given responsibility for handling monetary and currency affairs. President Wilson was adamant that bankers should not have control of the system. In fact, he insisted that the Federal Reserve Board be appointed by the administration.

As a concession to the banking interests, the final Federal Reserve Act included provision for a Federal Advisory Council. This was to be composed of one representative from each Federal Reserve District. Section 12 of the act says in part, "Each Federal Reserve bank by its board of directors shall annually select from its own federal reserve district one member of said council.... Meetings of said council shall be held at Washington, District of Columbia, at least four times each year. The [council] may in addition ... hold such other meetings ... as it may deem necessary,... may select its own officers and adopt its own methods of procedure.... It [the council] shall have power ... to confer directly with the Federal Reserve Board ... to make recommendations in regard to the operations of the Board and Federal Reserve Banks" (quote omits some wording in the interest of space).

Thus, as President Wilson on that December evening signed the Federal Reserve bill into law, a new "creature" was born. A unique creature, it was neither government nor private but part of both. Created by Congress, organized with private capital, most of its employees would not be considered "government" employees, but the system would set up its own salary schedules and retirement plan. Only the salary of the members of the Federal Reserve Board were set by Congress. Required to earn their own funds to cover expenses (no appropriation from Congress), the Fed banks had to be profitable. Yet, they were to be not-for-profit organizations operating in the public interest. Moreover, any profit beyond bringing their surplus capital account equal to paid in capital, was given to the U.S. Treasury's general account.

Congressman Glass summed up the benefits of the new law as follows: "The Federal Reserve Act revolutionized this wretched system (of banking) by providing a reserve bank currency based on sound, liquid commercial paper, responsive at all times and to the fullest extent to every reasonable demand of legitimate business.... At the same time it wrecked the old system of reserve deposits which was a breeder of panics."

The Federal Reserve System was the result of much debate and compromise. But it was a major step in the establishment of a stable currency. In the years to come it would be a powerful guide in the financial affairs of the nation. Assailed from many sides during the next 75 years, the system would be modified, added to, changed, would struggle for its very existence at times, but through it all it would survive.

Chapter 2

Getting Organized

Hooray! Our work is done! The new banking act is passed, signed by President Wilson, and now it is the law of the land. The debate is over and the battle won!

Not quite. A document setting forth the new banking organization that was to solve the problems of finance once and for all represented a fine piece of legislation. But now the work of implementing the act began, and those who had lost the fight in the halls of Congress were ready to press their point as the Federal Reserve Act was being put in place.

HOW MANY FED BANKS?

Remember, the act said there would be not fewer than 8 nor more than 12 Reserve banks. One group representing the leading banking interests assumed that certainly not more than 8 would be established. And surely by far the largest would be in New York City. However, the rural areas were equally sure there could not be fewer than 12, and they did not want New York City to dominate the system. So the battle continued.

Enter the Organization Committee. Section 2 of the Federal Reserve Act said,

> As soon as practicable, the Secretary of the Treasury, the Secretary of Agriculture and the Comptroller of the Currency, acting as "The Reserve Bank Organization Committee," shall designate not less than eight nor more than twelve cities to be known as Federal Reserve cities....

In addition, when the cities had been selected, the nation was to be divided into the same number of districts as there were Reserve cities and with only one Reserve bank in each district. Once this was done, the Organization Committee was to certify to the comptroller of the currency the outline of the districts. It was then the comptroller's duty to notify all national banks that they should subscribe to the capital of the Reserve bank in their district.

SUBSCRIBING CAPITAL STOCK

Before the Reserve banks could open for business, the national and other eligible banks in each district had to subscribe a minimum of $4 million to

10

the capital of their Reserve bank. Aside from this action each national bank and eligible nonnational bank was to certify to the comptroller their acceptance of the provisions of the act within 60 days after the passage of the act. When the Organization Committee had designated the cities in which Federal Reserve banks were to be organized and fixed the limits of each Federal Reserve District, each national bank was required within 30 days to subscribe for stock in their Reserve bank in an amount equal to 6 percent of their own capital accounts. One percent was callable by the Organization Committee or the Federal Reserve bank; an additional 1 percent was callable within three months and another 1 percent within six months. The remaining 3 percent was subject to the call of the committee or the Federal Reserve Board. (It has never been necessary to call this last 3 percent.)

The act further provided that if the banks in the district did not provide the necessary $4 million in capital, the stock would be offered to the public and if that did not raise the minimum amount the U.S. Treasury would provide the balance. Only the stock subscribed by the banks would be voting stock.

HURRY UP!

Not only was there much work to be done but it was supposed to be done quickly and without making a lot of enemies. The number one item to handle was the selection of the Reserve cities. The act gave little direction. It just said that the division of the nation into Federal Reserve Districts should be done "with due regard to the convenience and customary course of business and shall not necessarily be coterminous with any state or states." Perhaps one of the most helpful suggestions was given by Senator John Shafroth (D–CO) during the debate on the proposed bill. Senator Shafroth said:

> No bank should be more than one night's train ride from its Federal Reserve bank. In cases of a run on his bank, a banker could gather up his commercial paper with maturities of thirty, sixty and ninety days, catch the train and be at the Federal Reserve Bank by morning, discount his notes and wire his bank that there was plenty of money to pay depositors. To place Reserve banks more than a night's train ride from the member banks it served would make it impossible to meet one of the very needs for which it was designed.

To complicate matters for the Organization Committee, President Wilson's nominee for comptroller of the currency would not be confirmed for several weeks, so in effect, it was a two-man committee—Secretary of the Treasury William McAdoo and Secretary of Agriculture David Houston, who began the work of the committee.

Imagine you and one friend are handed this difficult assignment and told to hurry up and get it organized so the Reserve banks can open. You are well aware of the conflicts of ideas, and pressure quickly builds from groups with very definite opinions as what your decision should be. To the credit of the writers of the act, your decisions are subject only to the review of the Federal Reserve Board.

Secretary McAdoo had played a major role in developing the legislation that became the Federal Reserve Act, so he was familiar with the various viewpoints and arguments. He was a native of Georgia and had been a prominent attorney in New York City. Appointed by President Wilson, he also was involved in the spring of 1914 in courting and marrying President Wilson's younger daughter. He was an extremely able person, hardworking and probably the dominant member of the president's cabinet.

Secretary Houston was a brilliant classical economist. He had served as president of Washington University in St. Louis before coming to Washington in 1913 to serve in President Wilson's cabinet.

John Skelton Williams, President Wilson's nominee for comptroller of the currency, was president of the Bank of Richmond (Virginia). Also, he had organized and served as president of the Seaboard Airline Railroad, a line that served much of the Atlantic coast. He joined the committee toward the end of final deliberations.

PRELIMINARY ORGANIZATION COMMITTEE
Realizing the great amount of detailed planning necessary for the opening of the Fed banks, Secretary McAdoo, early in January 1914, appointed Henry Parker Willis, editor, *New York Journal of Commerce* and professor of banking at Columbia University, chairman of a committee to develop guidelines for the operation of the new Fed banks (officially, it was the Committee of Financial Experts but was generally known as the Preliminary or Technical Organization Committee). This committee was charged with the responsibility of setting guidelines for the operation of the Fed banks. Members of the committee included Joseph A. Broderick, member, State Banking Department of New York; O. Howard Wolfe, secretary of the Clearing House Committee of the American Bankers Association; Edmund D. Fisher, deputy comptroller of New York; Ralph Dawson, officer with Guaranty Trust Company of New York; and Andrew H. Benton, of the firm of Marwick, Mitchell, and Company. Also assisting the committee were Harry Ward and C.C. Robinson with Irving National Bank of New York.

The work of this committee was invaluable to the newly organized Fed banks as it gave guidance in making policy decisions on discounting paper and set out a uniform accounting system that among other things, provided for a method of settling accounts between Fed banks. Also, it set up a uniform method of reporting activities.

SURVEYING OPINIONS
In the language of the 1980s, the two-man Organization Committee "hit the ground running." The first item of business had to be the selection of the

Reserve cities. Parker Willis, in his book *The Federal Reserve System,* points out that the decisions faced in this respect by the committee were a microcosm of the debate that had raged in the Congress. "On no point," he states, "had there been sharper controversy than as to the issue whether banks (Reserve banks) should be four, eight, twelve or some other number." New York bankers were adamant that New York City should have the largest bank and that it should dominate other banks. In effect, they wanted one or maybe two large banks – the other one in Chicago – and no more. They said that other countries would not want to deal with several banks and certainly not with a "small" one. McAdoo and Houston believed that relations with other central banks should be with the "system" and not with any one bank. Outside of New York City there was strong sentiment for downplaying the size and importance of the New York bank. Country banks and politicians from rural areas, especially from the South and West, still feared dominance by "Wall Street" and the "moneyed interests."

Wisely, McAdoo and Houston tackled first the question of the New York bank. No one ever doubted that there would be a Reserve bank in New York City. During the first week of January 1914, Secretaries McAdoo and Houston journeyed to New York City and conducted four days of hearings. They heard arguments by the city's financial leaders, including J.P. Morgan. The point was made that the New York Fed must be dominant to ensure respect of other central banks. They wanted their district to include all of New England and the states to the south of New York. It was even suggested that it extend west to include Ohio and south to Washington D.C. If the financial leaders of New York prevailed, the New York Fed would include nearly half of the total capitalization of the entire system. (A suggestion from outside New York was to give the New York Fed only lower Manhattan.)

McAdoo and Houston were not impressed. The *New York Times* is quoted as reporting that "the present disposition of the organizers is to hobble New York." The secretaries insisted that their purpose was to construct a coordinated system and that the central banks of Europe would have to deal with the system as a whole rather than with just one of its parts.

LOCAL ISSUES IMPORTANT –
LET'S HEAR FROM THE "GRASS ROOTS"

Next stop Boston. Parts of New England adjacent to New York wished to be in the New York district. In fact, the Clearing House Association in Hartford, Connecticut, declined the invitation of the Boston Chamber of Commerce to appear in support of a Reserve bank in Boston. However, in Boston McAdoo and Houston heard the first expressions of civic pride and the advantage of Reserve banks being closer to the banks and businesses they would serve. Community leaders, while admitting the value of a "large" bank, believed this advantage was more than offset by the fact that a local organization would be more familiar with and sympathetic to local and regional problems. The secretaries were to hear this argument echoed in city after city as they toured the nation holding hearings in nearly 50 cities.

Following the hearings in Boston, McAdoo and Houston returned to Washington D.C. and invited representatives from other eastern cities to express their oinions as to the location of Federal Reserve cities. Knowing that the New York people wanted to include Philadelphia in the New York district, a delegation from Philadelphia went to Washington to press for a Reserve bank in their city. Richmond, Virginia, and Baltimore, Maryland, also made a pitch for their town.

Now it was time to head west and south. No jet airplanes to whisk them from city to city. So get out the train schedule and make as many as possible in the time allotted. On January 18, McAdoo and Houston started on a 10,000 mile cross-country tour that took them to Chicago, St. Louis, Kansas City, Lincoln, Denver, Seattle, Portland, San Francisco, Los Angeles, El Paso, Austin, New Orleans, Atlanta, Cincinnati and Cleveland. At each stop business and financial leaders were invited to express their opinions as to where the Reserve cities should be located. Community leaders from nearby cities were encouraged to come to the hearings and many did. From the vantage point of the 1990s it might be questioned why they did not also visit Dallas, Houston, Detroit and even Memphis. Perhaps train schedules were not convenient, and no doubt those cities did make their voice heard either by correspondence or in person.

The theme heard first in Boston that local and regional interests were vital and that "big New York" should not dominate the system was heard over and over. Every city felt they were most important and that a Federal Reserve bank in their city would best serve the area. Houston and McAdoo repeatedly tried to downplay the importance of the bank in their city, saying that economic and business growth was much more dependent on other factors. Nonetheless, history was to demonstrate that it did have an impact on the cities chosen. One illustration: For most of the first 65 years of the system's operation, payment for checks sent by the Fed banks to member banks had to be paid for either by a draft on the bank's reserve account at the Fed or on a commercial bank located in the same city as the Fed bank. Thus, the Fed could obtain immediate funds in payment for the checks. It also meant that it would be to the advantage of outlying banks to have an account with the bank located in the city where its Federal Reserve bank was located. Later, payment by a charge on any member bank was made possible through the extensive wire-transfer facilities.

Most cities tooted their own horn but on the West Coast, Seattle, Portland and Los Angeles deferred to San Francisco as the choice location for their Fed. A quote from the *New York Times* reveals the feeling of the "eastern crowd." "The hearings of the reserve bank organizers, generally speaking, have been more remarkable for the local jealousies they have disclosed than for the perception that there was anything of national significance in the new departure."

DECISION TIME

Returning to Washington, Houston and McAdoo sat down to digest what they had learned. One question still remained unanswered: Would a large number of national banks which had opposed mandatory membership in the system elect to give up their national charter rather than support the new system? Discussion in the Congress and in hearings before congressional committees had been loud and clear in opposition to mandatory membership. In an attempt to sound out the feeling of national banks on this issue, the committee polled all national banks asking for their preference for a Federal Reserve city with which they would be affiliated. They were asked to name a first, second and third choice. Since the Federal Reserve cities had not yet been chosen, some banks named cities not in their final district. In fact, a few West Coast banks named New York as their first choice. Many analysts believe this was the most important factor in determining which cities would be chosen. Also, it gave the committee confidence that national banks were ready to accept the idea of the Federal Reserve System.

On April 2, 1914, 100 days after President Wilson signed the Federal Reserve bill into law, the Organization Committee released its report. It named the following sites as Federal Reserve cities in which a Federal Reserve bank would be organized: Boston, New York, Philadelphia, Richmond, Atlanta, Cleveland, Chicago, St. Louis, Dallas, Minneapolis, Kansas City and San Francisco. The nation was divided into 12 Reserve districts around those 12 cities. Within a year a branch of the Atlanta bank was opened in New Orleans. By 1920 branches were opened in Birmingham, Alabama; Jacksonville, Florida; Nashville, Tennessee; Detroit, Michigan; Cincinnati, Ohio; Pittsburgh, Pennsylvania; El Paso and Houston, Texas; Omaha, Nebraska; Denver, Colorado; Buffalo, New York; Baltimore, Maryland; Louisville, Kentucky; Memphis, Tennessee; Little Rock, Arkansas; Seattle and Spokane, Washington; Portland, Oregon; Salt Lake City, Utah; and Los Angeles, California.

EVERYONE HAPPY? NO WAY!

A difficult job well done. Now everyone can settle down to the task of organizing the 12 banks. And of course, everyone was happy. Not quite. New York was unhappy because there were 12 districts. The committee was criticized for putting a bank in St. Louis and in Kansas City—two in the same state. Baltimore could not believe they were in the Richmond district. And New Orleans yelled louder than anyone because surely they should have had a Reserve bank, not Atlanta. Cincinnati and Pittsburgh had received more support than Cleveland. A charge of "politics" was leveled at the committee for the selection of two cities in Missouri. Missouri was

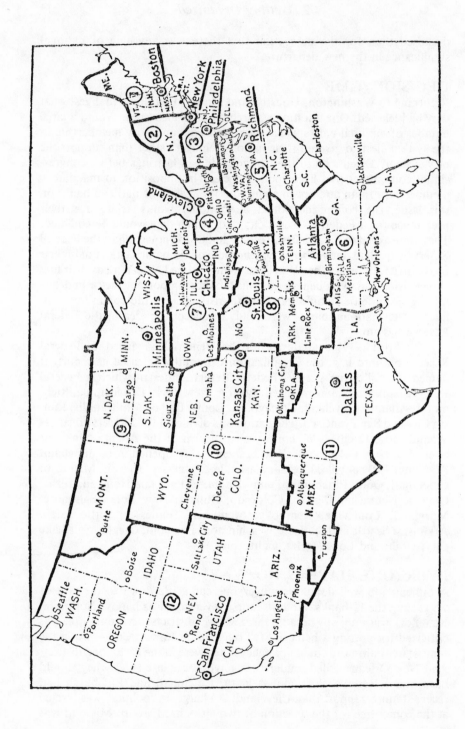

a strong Democrat state, and David Houston was from St. Louis. McAdoo was from Richmond, so he was accused of favoritism in the selection of that city. President Wilson defended the committee but denied that he had made any suggestions to the committee. The depth of feeling in some cities is illustrated by the mass protest in the city of New Orleans on April 5 and a demand that the decision be reconsidered. In Baltimore on April 15, financial and business leaders, civic leadership and hundreds of others jammed the Lyric Theater and heard the mayor of Baltimore and the governor of Maryland denounce the committee's decision to pass over their city and name Richmond.

Responding to the criticism, the committee released the results of its poll of national banks and their preference for Reserve cities. It also released a statement showing the basic criteria used in its final decision. These were:

1. The ability of member banks within a district to provide the necessary capital.
2. The mercantile, industrial and financial connections existing within each district.
3. The probable ability of the Federal Reserve bank in each district to meet the legitimate business demands placed upon it.
4. The fair and equitable division of the available capital for the Federal Reserve banks among the districts.
5. Geographic factors, and the existing network of transportation and communication. (John Safroth's one-night train ride)
6. Population, area and prevalent business activities of the districts.

This quieted some of the criticism, but cities like Cincinnati, Pittsburgh, Baltimore and New Orleans were not convinced. Even 75 years later there remains some feeling of being left out in some of these cities. On the other hand, cities like Dallas, Kansas City and Richmond were delighted. They found their status in the banking community greatly enhanced. It is reported that a prominent Kansas City business leader told Secretary McAdoo, "I have always said that you and Houston were great men. Now there isn't a man in Kansas City to dispute it."

In the spring of 1915, the Federal Reserve Board appointed a committee to investigate and evaluate requests that had been presented to the board for changes in the boundaries of several districts. The committee was to investigate the whole question of possible changes in boundaries and possible changes in location of reserve banks and even elimination of some districts. The broader question of changing Reserve cities and eliminating Reserve districts would be settled later by an opinion of the attorney general saying the board did not have the authority to make such changes but could make

Opposite: **Map showing the location of the 12 Federal Reserve banks and the boundaries of the 12 Federal Reserve districts, as determined by the Reserve Bank Organization Committee. Courtesy Board of Governors, Federal Reserve System.**

minor changes in boundaries. (See Chapter 3 for attorney general's ruling.) Requests had come from banks in the Atlanta, Dallas, Kansas City, New York, Chicago and Minnesota Districts.

A few minor modifications in district lines were made but only when it was evident that the flow of business activity made it desirable. Fairfield County, Connecticut, was moved from the Boston District to New York, and the northern New Jersey counties from Philadelphia to New York. Several counties in Oklahoma were moved from the Dallas District to Kansas City. After World War II the southeastern counties of Oklahoma were moved from the Dallas District to the Kansas City District and the southern counties of Arizona from the Dallas District to the San Francisco District. The validity of the committee's original judgment in defining the boundaries of the districts is reflected in the fact that after 75 years the Reserve cities and the district boundaries remain essentially intact. Even with the change from rail to air transportation the outline of the districts has proven to be very workable. (A list of the counties in each district as of September 1917 is shown in the Appendix.)

The wide range in the size of the districts and the strength of the commercial banks in the districts are illustrated by the following table. A tabulation of population shows a similar pattern. Note the shift in relative position of the Fed banks by 1980.

District	Number of national banks	Six percent of capital of the national banks	Rank 1914	Rank 1988
Boston (1-A)	445	$ 9,924,543	5	10
New York (2-B)	447	20,621,606	1	1
Philadelphia (3-C)	747	12,488,138	3	8
Cleveland (4-D)	767	12,007,384	4	7
Richmond (5-E)	475	6,303,301	7	6
Atlanta (6-F)	372	4,641,193	11	4
Chicago (7-G)	952	12,479,876	2	3
St. Louis (8-H)	458	4,990,761	8	12
Minneapolis (9-I)	687	4,702,925	12	11
Kansas City (10-J)	836	5,590,015	10	9
Dallas (11-K)	731	5,540,020	9	5
San Francisco (12-L)	514	7,825,375	6	2

Note: Numbers and letters following the names of the districts are used to designate the district. They appear on all Federal Reserve notes indicating the bank of issue.

Source: H. Parker Willis, The Federal Reserve System, Annual Report of the Board of Governors, 1988.

NAMING THE FEDERAL RESERVE BOARD

As soon as the Organization Committee had certified the outline of the districts, President Wilson began the task of selecting his nominees for the Federal Reserve Board, which he would then submit to the Senate for confirmation. Imagine the following conversation as the president sought to find board members.

"Hello. This is President Wilson. I would like to place your name in nomination to the newly created Federal Reserve Board."

"Yes, Mr. President. Just what is this new board?"

"It's the board that was created by the Federal Reserve Act."

"Oh, yes. I remember now. Mr. President, I need to think about it. Could you send me some information regarding the duties of members of the board and how long the commitment would be. I'm honored that you have considered me, but I really need to know more about the position. Can I call you back?"

Sounds like a silly conversation, doesn't it? But in the spring of 1914 it might well have happened. The nature of the Federal Reserve Act was not well known. And the duties of the Federal Reserve Board were only vaguely spelled out by the act. President Wilson's first attempts to fill the board were met with some hesitancy.

The secretary of the treasury and the comptroller of the currency were named as *ex officio* members of the board by the act. Five additional persons (no—the act said "men") were to be nominated by the president and confirmed by the Senate. There could be only one from any one Federal Reserve District, and in making his selection, the act said that the "president shall have due regard to a fair representation of the different commercial, industrial and geographic divisions of the country" (Sec. 10, par. 1). The members of the board were to devote all of their time to the work of the board and originally were to receive a salary of $12,000 annually, payable monthly, plus actual necessary travel expenses.

Whom would President Wilson name? Every interest group had their ideas. It was expected, by those knowledgeable about the act, that it would be a position of cabinet level. The salary was adequate and as President Wilson announced this board could be called "the Supreme Court of Finance." The banking community expected the board to have a great deal of influence. And surely the president would nominate some bankers. Others believed one should be a businessman, another a lawyer; still others wanted an economist named. The names submitted by the president suggest that he wanted a fairly wide range of interests represented on the board.

One of the first businessmen contacted was W.D. Simmons of St. Louis, a merchant of well-known standing in the midwest. When he was unable to accept, Harry A. Wheeler of Chicago, vice president of a trust company, was contacted, and he agreed to have his name submitted.

Here are the five names sent to the Senate on May 4, 1914: Richard Olney, a conservative Boston lawyer and secretary of state under President Grover Cleveland; Harry A. Wheeler, Chicago businessman and former president of the United States Chamber of Commerce; Paul A. Warburg, partner in the Wall Street investment firm of Kuhn, Loeb & Company;

Adolph C. Miller, a former professor of economics at the University of California; William P.G. Harding, president of the First National Bank of Birmingham, Alabama.

POLITICS AGAIN

As might be expected in politics, no sooner had these names been submitted than the "roof fell in" on President Wilson. The well-known Mr. Olney was turned down because of his previous connection with stewardship of the State Department earlier. Also, he was considered "too old." Mr. Wheeler turned down the offer of appointment because of the restrictions placed on members of the board after serving their term (no banking activity for two years). Mr. Wheeler was replaced by Thomas Jones of Chicago. The Senate committee didn't like Mr. Jones because of his association with the International Harvester Company, which was not popular in the midwest and was being investigated by the Justice Department. Charles Hamlin, a businessman from Boston, was named in place of Mr. Olney, who withdrew his name.

Now the conservatives concentrated on shooting down Jones and Warburg, the latter because he represented "Wall Street." President Wilson decided to fight to have his men confirmed. He was even ready to take the fight to the floor of the Senate. But when it was evident that he would lose on the floor in the fight to name Jones, he asked his friend to withdraw his name, which he gladly did, not having been eager to serve in the first place.

Warburg had declined to appear before the Senate committee hearings, fearing harassment similar to what Jones had experienced. He even asked to have his name withdrawn, but friends finally persuaded him to appear before the committee. Apparently, the committee had vented their resentment on Jones, and Warburg was easily confirmed. Jones was replaced by Frederick A. Delano of Chicago, president of the Monon Railroad. Finally, Hamlin, Delano, Warburg, Harding and Miller were confirmed. On August 10, 1914, the Federal Reserve Board was officially sworn in, with Hamlin named as "Governor" and Delano as "Vice Governor."

WAR BREAKS OUT

Nine days before the board members were sworn in, Germany declared war on Russia and two days later declared war on France, and the following day Great Britain declared war on Germany. World War I was a reality. Most U.S. citizens noted little impact on their day-to-day operations. But

Opposite: **Members of the first Federal Reserve Board.** *Left to right:* **Parker Willis, secretary to the board; W.P.G. Harding; Paul Warburg; William McAdoo, secretary of the treasury and *ex officio* member; Adolph G. Miller; John Skelton Williams, comptroller of the currency and *ex officio* member; Charles S. Hamlin and Frederick A. Delano. Courtesy Board of Governors of Federal Reserve System.**

the wartime atmosphere and the implications of reduced communications between the United States and Europe raised many questions about the opening of the newly created Federal Reserve banks. The Federal Reserve Board was in place and could act, but the reformed banking structure created by the Federal Reserve Act was far from being ready for action.

Almost immediately trade with Europe came to a standstill. Goods at ports ready for shipment were immobilized. The U.S. cotton crop about to be harvested was expected to be the largest on record, and Europe was one of the largest importers of raw cotton. Moreover, the war stopped shipments to other countries not directly involved in the fighting. The situation was further complicated by the fact that immediate payment was demanded of many debts owed to European entities. The board's Annual Report for 1914 gives some details of the problems facing the nation.

> The condition with which the Board was confronted when it began its work on the 10th of August had such a considerable bearing upon the policy pursued that it is well worthy of further notice. Seldom, if ever, has the banking and business community of the country found itself in a situation of such uncertainty and perplexity. The outbreak of hostilities in Europe led immediately to a serious rupture of international financial relationships, not only in the affected areas of Europe but throughout the whole commercial world. The United States was directly and profoundly affected by the suspension of communications with Europe, involving as its most serious consequences the temporary breaking down of the export trade and the collapse of the financial markets, with resulting shock to the credit system. There had been extraordinary efforts on the part of European holders of American securities to realize by sales in the New York market. The securities markets were badly demoralized, prices fell with alarming rapidity, and the country was exposed to a serious and disastrous drain of gold.
>
> The whole situation demonstrated afresh, and to a striking degree the dependence of our banking system upon the call-loan market because of the large proportion of the country's banking reserves which were invested in call loans protected by stock-exchange collateral. Stock exchanges throughout the country closed, and call loans were thus made unavailable. Emergency currency was issued by the Secretary of the Treasury and clearing-house certificates in large volume were issued by clearing-house associations in the principal financial centers. Moreover, the tendency to hoard cash, frequently experienced in former periods of stringency, was again being manifested by country banks, some of which curtailed accommodation to an extreme degree, thereby adding greatly to the embarrassment of their customers and city correspondents. Much doubt was expressed as to the ability of borrowers to meet their maturing obligations, securities of high grade were unmarketable, while a situation existed in the foreign-exchange markets which was altogether unprecedented. The conditions thus briefly outlined created an impression of profound alarm throughout the business community and gave rise to frequent expression of belief that the organization of the reserve system should be deferred until the return of more normal conditions, both for the success of the system

and in order that the existing situation might not be complicated and aggravated by the injection of new and incalculable elements into it.

Recognizing that the situation called for action and that the Federal Reserve System was not in place and would not be for a while, the secretary of the treasury requested an amendment to the Federal Reserve Act to provide for the issuing of emergency currency. This was done by incorporating into Section 27 phraseology from the Aldrich-Vreeland Act of May 30, 1908, which was due to expire June 30, 1914. The amendment was for one year and permitted national banks to expand their issuing of currency and with the suspension of certain tax provisions on the new issues. The bill was quickly passed by Congress on August 4, 1914. Although additional currency could have been provided, the crisis passed, and as confidence was restored, only a portion of the addition issue was needed.

In still another area the newly created Federal Reserve Board faced a hard question. The situation in Europe posed a threat to the gold supply of the nation, and the board chose to participate in the development of a Gold Exchange Fund of $108,000,000. Pledges were obtained from banks for that amount which it was thought adequate to protect against claims of foreign countries in the amount of about $100,000,000.

In addition, the board lent its support to the building of a Cotton Loan Fund to provide relief to cotton farmers as they faced loss of markets and the closing of cotton exchanges. Again banks of the country pledged money to this fund, but the members of the Federal Reserve Board added their personal support to the effort to raise about $200,000,000 for the Cotton Loan Fund.

Referring to these two funds, Parker Willis states:

> Full credit should be given to the beneficial results of these two outstanding plans for emergency relief, and it should be recognized that, as matters stood at the time, it was practically out of the question for the Federal Reserve Board to have proceeded with its work in reserve bank organization had it not disposed of all possible claims upon it, originating either with the Treasury or the community in the belief that real and immediate help could be given. It should, however, be always be borne in mind that what was thus done produced a psychological rather than a material effect. Operations under the gold exchange fund were small and under the cotton loan fund practically zero.

The board and leaders in banking, business and the Congress were divided on the question of whether or not to proceed with the organization of the Reserve banks. As mentioned, some believed it would be best to wait for more "normal" conditions. In an effort to proceed with at least the technical work needed to open the banks, the board called a meeting of the entire directorates and officers of the Reserve banks and a few outside experts in Washington D.C. to discuss the practical problems in opening the

Reserve banks. Dividing the group into four committees, work was begun on the proposed bylaws, accounting methods, check clearing and other nitty-gritty work of a bank. According to Willis, who attended the meeting, two points of view quickly became evident. One, that the Federal Reserve agents and the board should be kept as far away as possible from the practical work of the banks. The other point of view was that the board through its agents should be closely and constantly in touch with the operations of the banks. Finally, the banks reluctantly accepted a more or less uniform set of bylaws but reserved the right to amend them if necessary.

Resolving differences on accounting methods was not as easily done. Men who had had practical bank-operating experience were quick to see that uniform accounting was essential. Others who were not familiar with the day-to-day operations saw the uniform accounting as a means of controlling even the details of operations of the banks.

This latter point of view was not in the best interest of the system, and it was agreed that the board would immediately order the necessary accounting forms and send a supply to the banks which could then have additional supply prepared in their districts.

The question of when to open the banks was not resolved, and strong opinions were held on the subject. Some felt that to open the banks with conditions so unsettled would insure that they would fail as they would rediscount more paper than they could support. Conditions in the markets desperately needed the stability that the Reserve banks might bring to the nation. Currency was very inflated with the $400,000,000 emergency notes issued under the extension of the Aldrich-Vreeland law. Stock exchanges continued closed, and confidence had not returned to the nation.

FED BANK DIRECTORS

Opening the Reserve banks also required that each bank have a board of directors — not just any board, but one elected and appointed by an exact procedure set forth in the act. The board was to consist of nine members. Three were to be appointed by the Federal Reserve Board, and one of these three was to be designated by the board as chairman of the board of directors and "Federal Reserve Agent" and one as deputy chairman and "Deputy Federal Reserve Agent." These three appointed by the Federal Reserve Board were to be known as "Class C" directors. They had to be "for at least two years residents of the district for which they are appointed." The director designated as Federal Reserve agent shall be "a person of tested banking experience." As soon as the members of the Federal Reserve Board were sworn in, they began the process of naming the Class C directors.

Six directors were to be elected by the member banks in each district. Again, it was not a simple election. Three of the six could not be an officer, director or employee of any bank. These were called Class B directors and had to be "actively engaged in their district in commerce, agriculture or some other industrial pursuit." The remaining three could be officers or directors of a bank, and they usually were.

Here is how the election of the six directors was to be conducted.

- First, the chairman of the board of the Reserve bank was to classify all member banks into three groups, and each group should contain, as nearly as possible, the same number of member banks and as nearly as possible, the banks in each group shall be of similar capitalization.
- Second, at a regularly called meeting of the board of directors of each member bank it was to elect by ballot a "District Reserve Elector." His name was to be certified to the chairman of the board of directors of the Federal Reserve district. The chairman would then make a list of the electors by banks and furnish each member bank a list of those in its group.
- Then each member bank could nominate one candidate for Class A director and one candidate for Class B director.
- The chairman of the Fed bank then would compile a list of those nominated indicating by whom nominated and within 15 days after its completion furnish a copy to each elector in the member banks.
- Every elector within 15 days after receiving the list was to indicate his first, second, and third choice upon a preferential ballot furnished by the chairman of the Fed bank by placing a cross opposite the name of his first, second and third choice (how about that for detail?).
- Any candidate receiving a majority of votes in the column of first choice would be declared elected. If no candidate had a majority of votes in the first column, then the votes in the first and second columns would be added together, and if this gave a nominee a majority, he would be declared elected. If no candidate received a majority, then the votes in columns one, two, and three would be added together, and the candidate having the highest number of votes declared elected. An immediate report of the election was to be declared. (The act doesn't say to whom or in what manner. After all of this detail on how the election was to be run, a reader might expect some detail on how the results were to be announced.)

The term of all directors, elected or appointed, was to be for a term of three years. Vacancies would be filled in the same manner as provided for the original selection and replacement directors would serve for the unexpired term of their predecessors. At the first meeting of the board in 1914, directors were to designate those who would serve one-year, two-year and three-year terms. Thereafter, the directors would be selected for a three-year term. This procedure provided for a rotation of directors so that not all would be selected at one time. Thus, the board has some continuity of membership.

By amendment to the Federal Reserve Act in 1977, all directors were to be selected "without regard to race, creed, color, sex, or national origin." Class B and C directors were further to be selected "with due but not exclusive consideration to the interests of agriculture, commerce, industry, services, labor and consumers." Also, the requirement that the chairman be a person of tested banking experience was eliminated. Other amendments in 1918, 1933 and 1966 moved the classification of the banks to the Board of Governors and eliminated the use of number of banks and set classification on capitalization only. Also, provision was made for avoiding multiple nominations and voting by members of a bank holding company. Only one member bank from each holding company is qualified to nominate and vote.

OPEN THE BANKS!

By the end of October all directors and officers of the Reserve banks had been selected, the required amount of capital had been subscribed, the five commercial banks in each district had certified to the organization of their Reserve banks and the necessary documents had been filed with the comptroller of the currency. Some of the banks were still searching for adequate quarters, but most had completed the necessary arrangements so that they could open for business. Not all of the governors of the Reserve banks agreed that they could open, but much of the opposition to opening was uncertainty and to some extent shouting by those who did not want to see the system in the first place. They reasoned that if they could delay the opening long enough, maybe Congress would decide to abandon the idea.

Section 4 of the Federal Reserve Act said in part, "No Federal Reserve bank shall transact any business except such as is incidental and necessary preliminary to its organization until it has been authorized by the Comptroller of the Currency to commence business under the provisions of this Act."

Exercising his judgment and as supervisor of the comptroller of the currency, Secretary of the Treasury McAdoo announced that the first installment of the Reserve banks' capital should be paid November 2, 1914, and the banks would open their doors for business November 14, 1914. He was deluged with protests that it was not possible and unwise, but he held his ground and the banks opened on schedule.

The 12 banks opened with little publicity. Permanent quarters had not been arranged in many cases, and in some areas there was still a question as to how long the Federal Reserve System would last. In some banks a clerk or two oversaw what little business there was. But the Federal Reserve System—less than a year after its creation—was a reality, and it would struggle through many crises as it assumed its rightful place in the business and financial community. (See Appendix for list of directors and officers of each Reserve bank when the banks opened.)

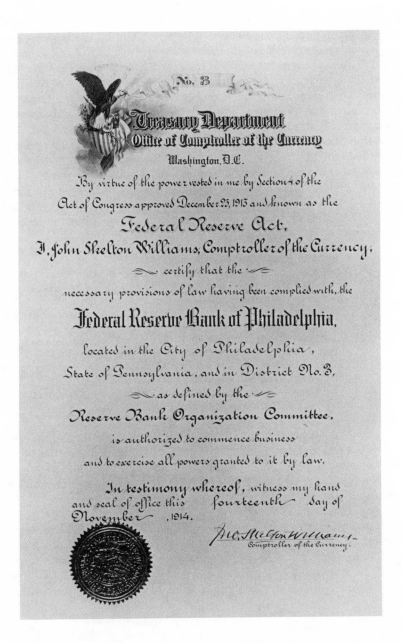

Organization charter issued to the Federal Reserve Bank of Philadelphia, signed by John Skelton Williams, comptroller of the currency, November 14, 1914. Each Federal Reserve bank was issued such a charter. Courtesy Federal Reserve Bank of Philadelphia.

THE "LEAGUE"

Smooth acceptance of the Federal Reserve System by the banking community and leading businesses came as a surprise to many. Work of the National Citizens' League for a Sound Banking System as much as three years before the organization of the Federal Reserve System may well have been an important factor in this acceptance of a new banking system. Organized in Chicago in May 1911, membership in the league included businessmen — not bankers. It was a nonpartisan organization dedicated to assist in the education of the country on some general principles of sound banking. J. Lawrence Laughlin was a prime mover in the organization and held the office of executive director for many years. In his book *The Federal Reserve Act, Its Origin and Problems,* he gives the goals of the league as follows:

1. Cooperation, with dominant centralization, of all banks by an evolution out of our clearing-house experience.
2. Protection of the credit system of the country from domination of any group of financial or political interests.
3. Independence of the individual banks, national or state, and uniform treatment in discounts and rates to all banks large or small.
4. Provision for making liquid the sound commercial paper of all the banks, either in the form of credits or bank notes redeemable in gold or lawful money.
5. Elasticity of currency and credit in time of seasonal demands and stringencies, with full protection against over-expansion.
6. Legislation on acceptances of time bills of exchange, in order to create a discount market at home and abroad.
7. The organization of better banking facilities with other countries, to aid in the extension of our foreign trade.

Laughlin further states, "The education given to all parts of the country by the League served to afford members of Congress the means of supporting a sound banking system when it came up in that body."

No doubt, the activities of the league were helpful in gaining quick acceptance of the Federal Reserve System.

The complexity of the task of installing the Federal Reserve System is illustrated by a statement of Parker Willis in his book *The Federal Reserve System:* "No one could have foreseen the course of events in 1914 even in the dimmest way, but if he could, he might well have questioned the expediency of attempting to install (as one public man put it) an entirely new set of financial machinery in the ship of state while so far from port."

Chapter 3

Open for Business (1914–1919)

November 16, 1914, 9:00 A.M.! The doors of 12 brand-new Federal Reserve banks opened for business!

There is money in the till (capital stock contributed by member banks), rented quarters are adequate, the "Federal Reserve Agent" (a Class C director) is chairman of the board, a "governor" has been appointed to operate the bank and basic regulations have been published by the Federal Reserve Board for the operation of the banks.

Now where are the customers?

A little business would be welcome as the bank is supposed to provide its own funds for operating expenses as well as those of the Federal Reserve Board. In other words, this is supposed to be a self-sufficient operation. No congressional appropriation is available, and commercial banks are the only qualified customers.

(The lack of a congressional appropriation was intentional by Congress, but later that fact was overlooked by many congressmen. Criticizing the board and asking for favors in appointment of employees and officers of the banks and the board, congressmen raised the threat of voting against the board's "appropriation." No leverage here. This would continue to be a sensitive point with some congressmen for the next 75 years. And a point jealously guarded by the system throughout those years.)

How could the Reserve banks make money? Two basic sources of revenue were available: (1) interest earned on paper discounted for member banks and (2) investment in securities. Discounting of paper by member banks was only at the initiative of the member banks. But the Reserve bank could initiate purchase and sale of various credit instruments including securities of the U.S. government. Section 14 of the act gave this power to the Reserve banks.

A central bank, particularly the Federal Reserve System, is a unique creature. Created to give stability to the monetary system of the country, intentionally removed from the federal budget process, charged with the responsibility of acting in "the interests of the country" not in its own profit-making interest and established with a minimum of financial backing, it was truly one of a kind. The capital structure, to be sure, was available and

29

was used, but "invading" capital is not considered prudent action by a sound business.

As might be expected of a new organization, expenses were larger than earnings during the first few months. In fact, during November and December 1914, total earnings of all 12 banks were $63,145, while current expenses were $186,910. Like any good business, conditions improved, and through 1915, earnings totaled $2,173,252 and current expenses were $2,018,282. During 1915, the Richmond and Dallas banks paid a dividend on their stock. The Cleveland, St. Louis, Kansas City and San Francisco banks were still losing money at the end of 1915.

Congress in its eagerness to avoid establishing an institution that would not be dominated by "selfish bankers" nor the "government," succeeded in avoiding those pitfalls but created an institution that would pose many hard questions of policy for its operators. At one point after the system began operating there actually was discussion as to whether the Reserve banks should have as a goal the "making of a profit." Framers of the act were convinced that the system should make decisions on the basis of what was good for the country and not on what would return a profit. Thus, if restraining the volume of discounts would stem inflationary pressures, it should be done even though it would reduce income to the bank. This could be encouraged by raising the discount rate or by "arm twisting" member banks to be more restrained in their borrowing.

WHO'S IN CHARGE?

"Am I responsible to you or are you responsible to me?"

The Federal Reserve Act was very explicit in saying how the directors of the new banks were to be chosen. Several pages of the act are taken up with the details of nominating candidates, voting, and monitoring the election. But the act says nothing about the internal organization of the Reserve bank staff. It does say that one of the three Class C directors appointed by the Federal Reserve Board shall be the "Federal Reserve Agent" and one of the other two as "Deputy Federal Reserve Agent."

The act also directed that the Federal Reserve agent make certain reports to the Federal Reserve Board relating to the operation of the bank. But it was not specific as to who would "run" the bank. The Federal Reserve agent was to be chairman of the board of the Reserve bank, but in the usual organization of commercial banks the chairman often was not the "operating" head of the bank. A statement by Parker Willis, chairman of the committee charged with the task of setting up operating policies for the banks outlines the problem.

> The Federal Reserve Act itself gives no indication on this subject (who will operate the bank) but had intentionally left for later determination the entire question of the internal organization of the Federal Reserve banks. The Board (Federal Reserve Board) therefore, could obtain information

as to the intent of the law only by discussing the situation with those who had been active in furthering it, and from them the members obtained a conviction that what had been sought in framing the Act was to provide oversight and control through government, but to leave to the Federal Reserve banks the actual task of operation, acting through such persons or agencies as they deemed best. On this view of the case the selection of the federal reserve agent was, however, a matter of still greater difficulty. If he was, in fact, not to be the operating head of the bank, it was still a fair question whether he was to be in a sense superior to the operating head — the real chief of the whole situation — or whether he was to be, as some supposed, merely the "agent" of the Board, exercising some clerical or routine functions under the director of the latter.

In this doubt and uncertainty, the first step evidently called for was that of deciding whether or not each bank was to have an operating member independent of the Federal Reserve Agent.... The Board reached an understanding among its members that, in addition to a chairman, or Federal Reserve Agent, there should be chosen an operating head in each of the banks.... It was much more difficult to determine what should be the status of these heads, but after much discussion the Board finally resolved to say to all inquirers that the distinction between the federal reserve agent and the operating head of the bank was to be in a general way the distinction between the maker of policy ... and the factor employed to carry it out.... What to call these heads of the banks on the operating side ... eventually resulted in a decision to assign to each of them the title of "governor."

On top of this uncertain chain of command was the question of salaries. Finally, the banks decided to pay the governor more than the Federal Reserve agent, the difference being from 25 to 100 percent, depending on the bank.

That this uncertainty of the chain of command was well handled by some persons involved is illustrated by the following quote from the first annual report of M.B. Wellborn, Federal Reserve agent at the Atlanta Fed.

The division of work in this bank between the governor and the Federal Reserve Agent is rather evenly balanced, both giving their entire time to the business of the institution. While it is generally understood that the operation of the bank is under the management of the governor, still in practice, this is not exclusively true. The by-laws of the bank provide, ... "to the executive committee is delegated the power in general to conduct the business of the bank, subject to the supervision and control of the board of directors." As chairman of the Board of directors, I am necessarily a regular member of the executive committee and, therefore, called upon to participate in the joint management of the bank. These duties, in addition to the attending to the correspondence with the Federal Reserve Board, and having custody of the Federal Reserve notes and collateral deposited with me to secure the issuance thereof, add largely to the contemplated duties of the Federal Reserve Agent. The duties of the Federal Reserve Agent Atlanta have been further increased by the establishment of the branch bank in New Orleans. Relations existing between the governor and the Federal Reserve Agent are most pleasant and agreeable.

This internal arrangement in the Fed banks was not conducive to efficient management and the degree that it worked satisfactorily depended as much on the personalities involved as any other factor. It continued to be a problem in some banks until the Banking Act of 1935 gave the banks a more realistic organization with the role of the Federal Reserve agent relegated to a nonoperative position. His role in the execution of the processing of note issue and holding of collateral continues today.

A more subtle problem of organization was the fact that the Federal Reserve Board was assigned quarters in the building of the secretary of the treasury. While this seemed on the surface to be generous of the secretary, as the board required more space, the influence of the secretary on the board's activities became a factor. The "landlord-tenant" relationship was not always harmonious. Jealousy began to creep into some thinking, and the subtle struggle for power flared occasionally.

Framers of the act had in mind that the 12 Fed banks would operate independently but assumed there would be cooperation between them. The wide variance between the Fed banks in resources and credit demands made it imperative that they share operating problems and that they be ready to share discounted paper. The supply of capital and the demand for loans varied greatly from the more rural areas to the major cities. In fairly short order, this problem was addressed and resolved amiably.

An interesting and amusing incident illustrates some of the frustration of members of the Federal Reserve Board. As members of the board assumed their duties and became a part of "the government" in Washington, D.C., a question arose as to their "rank" in Washington society. The question was put to Secretary of the Treasury McAdoo, who approached President Wilson for an answer. The president is quoted as saying, "I can do nothing about it. I am not a social arbitrator." To which the secretary replied, "I know that, Mr. President. But they want you to decide." "Decide what?" asked the president. Secretary McAdoo: "Decide their rank in the scale of social precedence." President Wilson replied, "Well, they might come right after the fire department."

CHANGES IN DISTRICT BOUNDARIES

No sooner had the Federal Reserve Board set up shop to do business than it was requested to change the boundaries of districts that had been outlined by the Organization Committee. There was even talk of moving some of the Fed banks to different cities. Advocates of fewer Fed banks again pressed their point. An opinion of the attorney general was requested on the authority of the board to make any of these changes. His opinion issued April 14, 1916, stated in part that "the Federal Reserve Board had no power to change the location of any Federal Reserve bank, and reiterated his previous opinion that the Board could not reduce the number of Federal Reserve Districts or abolish a Federal Reserve bank." He did express the opinion that the board had power to make reasonable adjustments of Federal Reserve districts by changing their boundary lines. A copy of the opinion can be found on page 128 of the Federal Reserve Board's Annual Report for 1916. The following is the summary paragraph of that opinion, which is dated April 14, 1916:

> I sum up my conclusions as follows:
> First, concededly the power to abolish Federal Reserve Districts and Federal Reserve Banks is not conferred upon the Federal Reserve Board in express terms; second, it is a rule of statutory construction that failure to grant in express terms a power of such great consequences raises convincing presumption that Congress did not intend to grant it; third, putting out to view that assumption, there is no provision in the Act from which an intention to confer this power can fairly be implied, but on the contrary there is a provision which shows affirmatively that Congress did not intend to confer it; fourth, the absence of any mention of such a power in the reports of committees and the debates dealing with the legislation shows that the thought of conferring it was not in the mind of Congress. I am of the opinion, therefore, that the Board does not possess the power in question.
> Signed: Very respectfully, T.W. Gregory, Attorney General

Thus ended the question of changing Fed banks to another city or reducing the number. Reasonable changes were made in the districts of New York, Boston, Chicago, Cleveland, Richmond, Dallas, Minneapolis, Kansas City and Atlanta (see Appendix for details).

HOW CAN WE MAKE A PROFIT?

The Federal Reserve System was designed as a central bank whose purpose was to operate in the public interest and not necessarily for profit. Yet, as mentioned, Congress intentionally omitted any source of operating funds for the banks except what they could earn — no appropriation. Funds were provided for the Organization Committee but not for the banks or the Federal Reserve Board. The board was authorized to request funds from the Reserve banks to cover its expenses. So it is not surprising that the question of where to get funds to pay operating expenses became very real during the early days of the system. The following quote from Parker Willis is interesting in this regard:

> The federal reserve system had drawn its staff from commercial institutions, as it had to do. The men whom it thus enlisted were men of mature years whose training had been entirely received in the debilitating atmosphere of banks whose basis of judgement of worth or ability was found very largely in dividend rates and profits. The instinct, therefore, or the desire to make money and to enlarge the success of reserve banks on that

basis was very strong practically from the beginning. So clearly was this obvious to the Board that it took occasion in its various annual reports from time to time to call attention to the fact that the reserve system, like every other central banking system, existed primarily for service and that money-making was only a subordinate element in its nature. In fact, perhaps the Board went to extremes in attempting to impress upon the reserve bankers that they should endeavor to lay aside their money-making instincts and devote themselves primarily to the promotion of sound banking rather than of financial success. Yet, even the members of the Board themselves frequently wearied in well doing and from time to time became affected by the money-making instinct.

The question of profits and the role of the Reserve banks was debated vigorously in the board and among Reserve bank officials. The board was particularly concerned, first, that the banks might never be self-supporting and by the end of the year 1915, that they might make too much money and be too competitive with member banks. It was even suggested that the Reserve banks repay the capital paid in by member banks as the Feds no longer needed it. For the period November 14, 1914, to December 31, 1915, the 12 Reserve banks earned $2,173,252. Expenses during the same period were $2,018,282, including an assessment by the Federal Reserve Board of $302,304. Dividends to member banks were $218,463. By 1917 the banks were paying a franchise tax to the U.S. Treasury. Further details on earnings and expenses are shown in the Appendix.

A WARTIME ATMOSPHERE
Let your imagination run for a moment and pretend you are responsible for making the new Federal Reserve System operate effectively and efficiently. War has just been declared in Europe. Exports of grain and cotton, which have been the main factor giving a favorable balance of trade, have been stopped completely. European nations are demanding payment on Unitd States obligations. Gold is flowing into the country. Currency is inadequate to meet the demands of business and industry. President Wilson has pledged to keep the nation out of war, but that may become a hollow pledge. Your new organization is struggling to pay its rent and doesn't know for sure what it should or can do.

Not an easy place to start a new business. Other authors have written in great detail how these problems were met, and it is a tribute to the men in places of leadership that solutions were found and the system played a major role in facilitating the movement of gold, credit and currency. An English economist is quoted as saying that the Federal Reserve Act was worth to the commerce of America more than two Panama Canals.

GOLD SETTLEMENT FUND
Even before the Reserve banks opened for business, tentative plans were made by the Technical Organization Committee under the leadership of

Parker Willis for the internal operation of the banks. One of the primary devices needed was a way to communicate quickly and transfer balances due to and due from each Reserve bank. Particularly in clearing checks, balances quickly built up, and since each Fed bank was to be "independent," it was necessary that these balances be moved daily. The Gold Settlement Fund was the answer. Each day each Fed bank sent by telegram amounts due to and due from each of the other Fed banks. This information was channeled to the board in Washington, and settlement was made on books maintained at the board; and each Reserve bank notified of its position the following morning. Where necessary, gold was actually transferred between Fed banks. The Gold Settlement Fund proved to be of increasing value as the volume of operations increased at Fed banks. By the time computers and other electronic means of communication became a part of the financial structure of the nation's banking, this settlement fund was the means of moving billions of dollars daily to all points of the nation. The word *gold* was dropped as the metal became unnecessary to complete settlement, but for many years the last action of the day at each Fed office was to send the "gold wire" to the board. As we will see later, the demand of World War I forced the U.S. Treasury to utilize the Gold Settlement Fund to move its money around the country.

A NEW CURRENCY — FEDERAL RESERVE NOTES

A new currency and a new reserve system for the banking industry presented a virtual upheaval to bankers. To a nonbanker, they might seem trivial but not to a person who had spent his or her life with the old system. Although the new Federal Reserve notes would only be an addition to the existing supply of currency, the task of designing them, making engraving plates and printing them was no small job. The new currency was to fulfill one of the major objectives of the Federal Reserve Act — namely, an elastic currency that would respond to the needs of the business community. The Federal Reserve Board started the process before the banks were opened, and under the leadership of Parker Willis procedures were established for their issue and distribution to the Reserve banks. Tight security was essential to avoid loss and to discourage counterfeiting. Section 16 of the act stated: "Federal Reserve notes, to be issued at the discretion of the Federal Reserve Board for the purpose of making advances to Federal Reserve Banks through the Federal Reserve Agents as hereinafter set forth and for no other purposes, are hereby authorized. The said notes shall be obligations of the United States and shall be receivable by all national and member banks and for all taxes, customs, and other public dues. They shall be redeemable in gold on demand at the Treasury Department of the United States, in the city of Washington, District of Columbia, or in gold or lawful money at any Federal Reserve bank." The act also stated that "application [for Federal Reserve notes] shall be accompanied with a tender to the Federal Reserve Agent of collateral in an amount equal to the sum of the

Federal Reserve notes thus applied for.... The collateral security thus offered shall be notes and bills, acceptable for rediscount [by the Federal Reserve bank applying for the notes] under the provisions of section 13 of this Act." (A detailed description of the engraving on the new notes is given in the Appendix.)

The theory of this provision was that as member banks needed more currency, they would take their customers paper (bills and notes) to their Fed bank and rediscount them for cash, and when the notes and bills became due, they would be paid off and the member bank would return the currency. Thus, as the community needed more cash because business was increasing and loans from banks increased, the member banks would need more cash and offer more notes to the Feds. It was the "automatic" procedure envisioned by the framers of the act. However, since the initiative for rediscounting rested with the member banks the Fed's ability to increase resources and earnings through increased note issue was severely limited. Gold and gold certificates could not be used as collateral for Federal Reserve notes.

Where there is a will there is a way, and within a few weeks after the Reserve banks opened, they devised a way around the restriction. When they needed to get more notes, they redeemed the collateral (discounted notes) already pledged with gold and then offered the freed collateral again for more Fed notes. This procedure could go on and on as long as the bank had gold or gold certificates. The procedure was nicknamed "reversing the pump" and was used throughout the system with full knowledge of the board. In 1917, by amendment to the act, Congress authorized the use of gold as collateral for issuing Fed notes, thereby legalizing what was in effect being done. Federal Reserve banks were required by the Act to maintain a 40 percent reserve in gold against notes actually in circulation and a 35 percent reserve, also in gold, against deposits with it. In addition, they were required to keep a reserve with the Treasury of the United States equal to not less than 5 percent of notes outstanding, but this reserve could be counted as part of the 40 percent requirement.

A rather elaborate procedure for actually issuing the Fed notes prevailed until the late 1970s. Here is an example. A Federal Reserve office needs more $20 bills to meet the needs of its member banks. First, it applies to the Federal Reserve agent (who has his office in the bank or to an employee of the bank who has been designated by the agent to represent him in such transactions) and submits the required collateral. The agent or his representative accepts the application and the collateral and pays out the notes from his supply in the vault. If the Fed bank has excess $20 bills, it returns then to the agent and reduces its pledged collateral. As one who has participated in many of these transactions, I can say that the procedure was a bit awkward, time-consuming and redundant. We could look in our vault and see one section which was "bank money" and another area in the same vault accessible only to the agent, which was "unissued" money controlled by the agent. By the late 1970s, this procedure had been streamlined, but collateral was still pledged against the notes.

The Federal Reserve Act also said that any Fed notes received by a Fed bank that had been issued by another Fed must be returned promptly to the issuing bank. Thus, currency received by a Fed had to be sorted as to bank of issue as well as to whether it was in condition to be recirculated or badly worn and should be destroyed and replaced with new notes. This requirement of sorting by bank of issue was eliminated by act of Congress July 19, 1954. After all, they were all Federal Reserve notes, and the Reserve banks were in sufficient financial condition that the question of note liability was not critical to any one bank. At least in practice they were all liabilities of all of the Fed banks.

Other details regarding the issuing, use of and redemption of Fed notes are given in Section 16 of the Federal Reserve Act. Also, this section makes provision for the Fed banks to buy U.S. securities pledged by member banks in support of their national bank notes (currency). It was anticipated that those notes would eventually be replaced by Federal Reserve notes. It did take place, but it was more than 50 years later.

BANK RESERVES

A second problem involving the opening of the Fed banks and their relationship with member banks concerned the shifting of reserve balances from commercial banks to the Fed. The framers of the act anticipated that member bank reserves would be held largely in the vaults of the member bank or in the Federal Reserve office of their district. Section 19 of the act goes into great detail as to the amounts to be held and the time table for shifting from commercial banks to the Fed. But many questions remained as to how much and where the reserves would be held. This was a major change in the reserve system of the nation's banks. Under the National Banking Act, reserve requirements were based on the location of the national bank. Banks located in "central reserve cities" — New York, Chicago and St. Louis — were required to keep in their vaults an amount equal to 25 percent of their deposits. Banks in "reserve cities," of which there were many, including New Orleans, Dallas, Atlanta, Cleveland and Detroit, were also required to keep a 25 percent reserve against their deposits but one-half could be held as a deposit in a central reserve city bank. Country banks, those outside of central reserve and reserve cities, were required to keep a reserve of 15 percent, of which three-fifths could be a deposit in a reserve city bank.

This pyramiding of deposits was a principal cause of money panics prior to the enactment of the Federal Reserve Act. As money accumulated in the larger money centers, it was loaned on a short-term basis, much of it for speculation or investment in the stock and bond market. When demand for funds increased at the country points because of the planting or marketing of crops, country banks would request the return of their deposits. The money center banks would in turn "call" their short-term loans, and the result often was a "money panic." The Federal Reserve Act sought to remedy this situation by placing most of their reserves in Federal Reserve banks. This would give some elasticity to the currency supply. Under the act reserves were to be held largely but not exclusively in Fed banks. Required reserves were reduced to 18 percent at central reserve city banks, 15 percent at reserve city banks and 12 percent at country banks. All banks were required to keep a 5 percent reserve against savings deposits in addition to reserves against demand deposits.

Banks in the central reserve and reserve cities were understandably concerned about losing deposits from country points. Critics of the system predicted that this shift of reserves would shipwreck the banking system. The transfer, nearly 90 percent of which was in gold, was accomplished with hardly a ripple in the banking community. The timing was such that it occurred at a time when loan demand was slow, the stock markets were still closed and business was at a standstill because of the outbreak of war in Europe. The first payment of 1 percent of the required to the Fed banks caused no problem for member banks.

This change in reserve requirements released nearly half a billion dollars to the commercial banks. This eased credit and could have stimulated inflation. However, within two years the demand associated with the war in Europe, and later as the United States joined the Allies in the war, quickly absorbed the excess credit.

SETTING THE DISCOUNT RATE
Before the banks could open for business, it was necessary to fix the rate at which member banks would be charged when discounting paper with the Fed. Section 14(d) of the Federal Reserve Act, in listing the powers of the Fed banks, said: "To establish from time to time, subject to review and determination of the Federal Reserve Board, rates of discount to be charged by the Federal Reserve bank for each class of paper, which shall be fixed with a view of accommodating commerce and business."

Thus, the initiative for establishing a rate rested with the board of directors of the Reserve banks, but it could not be effective until approved by the Federal Reserve Board. Whether or not a uniform rate nationwide was desirable was subject to much discussion. It was of course required that the same rate be charged every member bank in the district for the same class of paper. Also, it was not clear how the Federal Reserve Board might suggest a discount rate for a reserve bank. Early in November 1914, the board sent via telegram to each Fed bank a request for a suggested discount rate. The results were not too helpful. Some banks suggested a high rate to avoid competing with member banks. Others suggested a low rate to accommodate member banks in need of help. The situation was resolved by the board's approving some rates and disapproving others but suggesting another rate. In most cases the Fed bank accepted the suggested change and resubmitted a request for approval of the new rate.

As the Fed banks opened on November 16, 1914, discount rates were 5½ to 6½ percent. Throughout the system's history discount rates have varied from bank to bank but in later years have almost always been the same at each bank. Changes might be delayed a few days while banks assembled their boards of directors, but usually a common rate prevailed. It has not been uncommon for directors of a Fed bank to request a change and not get board approval. Sometimes the Fed bank directors submit a request several times before the board decides it is time to change.

As communications improved and liaison between the board and the banks became closer, a request for a change was frequently made after the president (governor prior to 1935) of the bank had conferred with the board, and it was generally agreed that a change should be made. This was not always the case as boards of directors have not hesitated to request change even though it was known that it probably would not be approved. Directors sometimes felt that they should "make a statement" regarding their appraisal of the economic situation.

A DISCOUNT POLICY

Paramount in the thinking of the framers of the Federal Reserve Act was a belief in the "real bills" doctrine. Briefly, this said that notes eligible for discounting at the central bank must represent transactions that were self-liquidating. Thus, a note covering a loan to produce, market or store real goods would be liquidated when the goods moved to the next step in distribution. The central bank would provide a place to "park" a commercial bank's paper while giving it room to accommodate other customers. It involved no inflation and presented a minimum of collection problems as the goods financed were "real" and not likely to disappear. The thought of discounting notes representing personal loans or capital loans or consumer loan would have been dismissed as "dangerous" and inappropriate. (Of course, consumer loans were unheard of in 1914.)

James Livingston, in his book *Origin of the Federal Reserve System,* relates the problem of currency inflation to the "real bills doctrine." Here is his statement on the subject: "Currency inflation is impossible as long as bank notes are issued only against those bank assets which pertain to actual commodities and verifiable transactions, and therefore, are 'real bills' certain of payment when due."

The wording of the original Act was very specific. Section 13 states in part, "upon endorsement of any of its member banks . . . a Federal Reserve bank may discount . . . notes, drafts and bills of exchange arising out of actual commercial transactions . . . it shall not include notes, drafts or bills covering merely investments or issued or drawn for the purpose of carrying or trading in stocks, bonds, or other securities, except bonds and notes of the United States government."

By contrast, the act as amended by 1989 says in Section 10(a), "Any Federal Reserve bank under rules and regulations prescribed by the Board of Governors [originally the Federal Reserve Board] may make advances to any member bank on its time or demand notes . . . which are secured to *the satisfaction* of such Federal Reserve bank" (emphasis added).

Quite a change in 75 years. The philosophy has changed from one insisting on self-liquidation to one of accommodating the banks (and since 1980 savings and loan associations, credit unions, nonmember banks and savings banks) to meet whatever need is present. This places additional responsibility on the Reserve banks to exercise sound judgment in evaluating the financial condition of borrowing institutions and to provide help in meeting temporary conditions of stress (draught, fire, seasonal demands for credit and unusual loss of deposits) but not to perpetuate unsound management. Events of the 1980s have thrown the Federal Reserve System into the role of "lender of last resort" in a very real sense.

In part because of the huge resources of the Federal Reserve banks and also because of the proven record of sound judgment in administering monetary policy, the system has been called upon to assume responsibility for dealing with more and more financial problems of the nation and the world, a role beyond comprehension by the framers of the Federal Reserve Act in 1913.

CHECK CLEARING

One of the original objectives of the Federal Reserve Act was to reduce or eliminate the circuitous routing of checks. The act was specific in that it gave the Fed banks power to accept checks for collection, but as in many other areas it left the details to the board and the Reserve banks. The following quote from the Federal Reserve Board's annual report for 1916 gives a picture of some of the difficulties incurred in establishing a check collection program.

> The Board found that the introduction of a general and effective clearance and collection system was a highly technical matter, involving legal questions and many complexities of practice. . . . The Board thought best at first, therefore, to leave the actual initiative in the matter largely to the Federal Reserve banks and at their insistence to authorize a voluntary system of clearance and collection in which member banks might or might not participate as they chose. . . . Experience, however, soon showed that the plan was not sufficiently comprehensive, and that many factors were mitigating against its success. . . . For this reason the Board decided in April 1916, to establish a uniform and more comprehensive system and it formulated a plan of clearance and collection which it directed to the Federal Reserve banks to put in effect.
>
> The plan became operative July 15, 1916. Under the new system member banks are free to continue to carry accounts with their present correspondents and with other banks to which they may send items for collection and from which they may receive for similar purposes checks drawn

on themselves or upon other banks. They are, however, required to pay without reduction checks drawn on themselves and presented at their counters. Remittance of such checks by the Federal Reserve bank of their district through the mail is construed as presentation at their own counters and banks must settle with the Federal Reserve bank for checks by acceptable means checks drawn on other banks. Remittance of lawful money or Federal Reserve notes can be made at the expense of the Federal Reserve bank in case they are unable to send in offsetting checks on other banks.

Checks drawn upon a member bank which have been received by the Federal Reserve bank are not charged against its reserve account until sufficient time has elapsed for the checks to have reached the member bank and for returns in due course to have reached the Federal Reserve banks.... A small service charge not exceeding 2 cents per item will be made at stated intervals against such banks as send to the Federal Reserve bank checks on other banks for collection and credit.... It is believed that in numerous instances banks will find it expedient to concentrate their balances and to close many accounts which they now carry with other banks and that a system which will enable them to send all their checks on other banks to the Federal Reserve banks for exchange purposes or as an offset against checks on themselves forwarded by the Federal Reserve banks, will soon be appreciated not only as a convenience but as a necessity.

It still was not a necessity in 1989. In fact, regulations were changed in 1960 to permit a member bank to have checks sent to it paid for by a charge to any other member bank. Thus, a member bank did not have to use its reserve account for paying for checks sent to it by a Federal Reserve bank, nor did it need to use a correspondent in the city in which the Federal Reserve bank was located. The service charge for clearing checks was discontinued in 1918, and these services were free until 1981 (see Chapter 10).

As part of the amendments to the Federal Reserve Act in June 1917, Fed banks were authorized to open clearing accounts for nonmember banks. Remittance for checks sent to such nonmember banks had to be at par and the clearing account had to be sufficient to cover any checks sent to them. Very few nonmember banks took advantage of this provision, and changes made under the 1980 deregulation act made such accounts redundant.

An indication of the success of the check-clearing service in the early years is illustrated by the volume handled by each bank as shown in the table on the next page.

As will be seen later, the development of the check-clearing system may be one of the greatest single contributions to effective banking made by the Fed — exclusive of monetary policy decisions. The struggle to obtain remittance at par for all checks was a critical part of the system. A further word about "par" collection is in order.

PAR CLEARANCE OF CHECKS

If you received a check for $500 in payment for services rendered and then received only $490 when you cashed the check, the $10 being deducted by the drawee bank, you would not be very happy. This "exchange" charge,

Clearings, July 15 to December 31, 1916

Federal Reserve Bank	Total number of items handled	Total amount handled (in thousands)	Cost per item	Service charge per item
Boston	4,847,745	$ 1,002,784	$ .84	$ .90
New York	4,908,674	3,025,978	.72	1.00
Philadelphia	3,506,676	1,837,525	.98	1.50
Cleveland	1,996,122	957,387	1.17	1.50
Richmond	2,020,065	891,078	1.05	1.25
Atlanta	1,602,095	494,368	1.10	1.50
Chicago	2,586,871	1,599,624	1.03	1.50
St. Louis	2,234,060	1,008,757	0.53	1.50
Minneapolis	1,529,407	329,826	1.12	1.50
Kansas City	1,562,860	845,154	0.98	1.50
Dallas	1,495,626	378,491	1.31	1.50
San Francisco	594,475	167,287	4.80	2.0
Total	28,884,676	$12,538,261	$1.01	—

Source: Annual Report, Federal Reserve Board, 1916.

as it was called, was a principal source of income for many banks. It was reimbursement to the bank for the cost of handling the checking account of its customers. Making the recipient of a check bear the cost of the check maker's account was unfair, and framers of the Federal Reserve Act sought to remedy the situation. Section 16 of the act says in part, "Every Federal Reserve Bank shall receive on deposit AT PAR from member banks or other Federal Reserve banks checks and drafts drawn upon any of its depositors etc." (emphasis added). An attempt was made in 1917 to add an amendment to other legislation that would authorize exchange charges. Vigorous opposition by Congressman Glass and President Wilson defeated the amendment.

Several attempts were made by the Fed banks to enforce payment at par, but commercial banks were understandably reluctant to forgo this source of income. The campaign to bring about universal payment of checks at par would continue for nearly 70 years. Not until 1980 would the last bank join the parade. The story of this last convert is amusing. By the end of World War II most banks were remitting at par. But a few still held out. In 1980 a routine correspondence from the Board of Governors stated that only one bank—in Louisiana—still held to the old way of doing business. Upon receipt of this correspondence, an officer of the Dallas Fed called the bank in Louisiana and told them that they would have the honor of being the only bank in the nation on the "nonpar list" when it came out in a few weeks. The officer at the Louisiana bank thanked him for the call and the next morning called the Fed officer and said they did not think they wanted that honor and would begin remitting at par immediately. Thus ended the 66-year-old campaign to end nonpar payment of checks.

Another innovation during this period was the establishment in 1918 of the Fed's own leased-wire network. It no longer had to rely on the facilities of Western Union, and the change greatly expedited the transfer of balances, charges and credits and administrative messages.

WORLD WAR I AND THE FED

Earlier it was pointed out that the outbreak of war in Europe suddenly stopped trade, and goods—especially cotton—piled up at export ports. Business slowed to a snail's pace. Banks were awash in funds and eagerly looked for loans. Germany effectively blocked shipments to Europe, especially Great Britain. However, by late 1916, ships were getting through the blockade and despite many losses of ships, goods began to flow to Europe. The demand for manufactured goods and agricultural products—especially cotton and munitions—skyrocketed. In fact, Great Britain would buy almost anything the United States could provide. America did not anticipate having any American troops fighting on European soil. Furnishing material and food was all that was expected.

Wars are fought with people, and it was soon evident that American troops were desperately needed to fight along with other Allies on the fronts in France. Nearly 2,000,000 men eventually were fighting on foreign soil. The navy escorted hundreds of ships across the Atlantic, some carrying equipment, others carrying troops.

In the years prior to the war the administration through the Treasury had gone to great lengths to avoid selling any bonds and above all not to raise taxes. As a result, the Treasury was ill prepared to finance the war effort. It had balances scattered in national banks and little surplus cash. Fortunately, the Fed banks had gained strength and were in a relatively strong position.

Financing the war in Europe was a concern of the Federal Reserve System leadership almost from the beginning of hostilities in 1914. The financial strain on Great Britain and France, and to a lesser degree on other Allies, soon drained any surplus funds, and soon banks and other investors were drawn into the financing of the war. Merchants in the United States, anxious to take advantage of the very great demand for goods, including munitions, readily accepted a variety of financing methods.

One of the most ingenious and quickly used was the trade or banker's acceptance. The "acceptance" was not a new instrument, having been used in trade in the United States and more particularly in Europe for many years. The Federal Reserve Act made provisions for Reserve banks to discount acceptances and for the instruments to be purchased on the open market. Early in the operations of the system, the board went to great lengths to increase the use of the trade acceptance.

For the nonbanker reader the "acceptance" is a piece of paper that relates to a shipment of goods. It describes the goods and shows the terms of the payment. Since the amount due depends upon what terms the buyer chooses—immediate payment with a discount of 30 or 60 days with

Resources and Liabilities of the 12 Federal Reserve Banks
(as of April 6, 1917)

Resources

Gold coin and certificates in vault	$362,472,000
Gold settlement fund	200,125,000
Gold redemption fund	2,505,000
Legal, tender notes, silver, etc.	19,110,000
Total reserves	$584,212,000

Five percent redemption fund against Federal Reserve bank notes	$ 400,000
Bills discounted — member banks	17,128,000
Bills bought in open market	82,735,000
United States bonds	36,629,000
One year United States Treasury notes	23,042,000
United States Certificates of Indebtedness	50,000,000
Municipal warrants	15,207,000
Federal Reserve notes — net	16,235,000
Due from other Federal Reserve banks — net	3,412,000
Uncollected items	146,422,000
All other resources	4,909,000
Total resources	$396,119,000

Liabilities

Capital paid in	$ 56,100,000
Government deposits	46,461,000
Due to members banks — reserve accounts	758,219,000
Collections items	105,436,000
Federal Reserve notes — net	14,295,000
All other liabilities	620,000
Total liabilities	$981,131,000

Note: The makeup of items in the statement does not coincide exactly with the usual statement of the Federal Reserve banks, but the totals are in line with the official statement as of the end of 1915. See Appendix for more details.

Source: Parker Willis, *The Federal Reserve System.*

interest — the exact dollar amount cannot be shown on the instrument. Usually it is sent by the seller with the goods and when received by the buyer of the goods, he "accepts" it by signing it and returning it to the seller indicating the terms accepted. The seller then has an instrument that can be sold on the market. If a bank also accepts the instrument, it is known as a banker's acceptance. Obviously, a bank's acceptance adds prestige to the instrument. The bank is in effect saying it will stand behind the buyer's agreement to pay. Banking regulations at the time, including those of the Fed, permitted banks to accept these instruments in amounts beyond the ordinary limits on loans. Usually a bank could buy or accept them in an amount equal to its capital and surplus accounts.

In the press to finance the war in Europe, the volume of acceptances skyrocketed. Private bankers who were not under the rules of national, or state-chartered banks could discount the paper if they agreed to file a statement with their Federal Reserve bank. The board even agreed that it could be done and banks became heavily involved in the financing of the war long before the United States entered the conflict.

Also, France and Great Britain sold securities to many U.S. investors, including banks. By late 1916 it was obvious to most persons in knowledgeable positions that it was only a matter of time until the United States would be directly involved in the fighting. In the financial arena France and Great Britain had nearly exhausted their ability to borrow in their own country. Also, an Anglo-French loan of $750,000,000 had been sold in America. Desperate for funds, Great Britain announced that it would offer an indefinite large amount of short-term bills in the U.S. market. The bills would be redeemed by another issue, in other words, rolled over for an indefinite time.

Concerned about the growing involvement of U.S. banks and other investors in foreign obligations, the Federal Reserve Board quickly asked to confer with Secretary of the Treasury McAdoo about this proposed new offering. Learning that he was out of town, they went directly to President Wilson, who agreed investors should not buy the bills and the Fed should not agree to discount them. This announcement was not well received by Great Britain. It is necessary to remember that the United States, although basically sympathetic to the Allied cause, was bending over backwards to remain neutral. This announcement led many to believe that we were siding with Germany.

Shortly afterward, an agreement was finalized for the Federal Reserve System, through the Federal Reserve Bank of New York, to establish a correspondent relationship with the Bank of England. This was confidential, but because of the previous action against Great Britain, it was made public.

During this time the Fed banks had rediscounted or purchased a sizable amount of acceptances, many of which were directly involved in selling war material to the Allies. Restriction of maturities and on the purpose of the underlying transaction were stretched to the limit. Since the opening of the Fed banks, the board had been urging greater use of the two-party acceptances usually with the second party being a bank. The board even approved a differential discount rate in favor of two-party acceptances.

UNITED STATES DECLARES WAR

On April 6, 1917, President Wilson asked the Congress to declare war on Germany. The United States was no longer an observer but an active participant in hostilities. A bill to draft men between ages of 21 to 30 was later changed to 18 to 45. Financing our own war effort now became a number-one priority for the financial community. As mentioned, no preparation had been made to strengthen banks or the Treasury. But Fed banks were in a relatively strong position.

It is helpful to point out that at this time the U.S. Treasury under Secretary McAdoo was not using the Fed banks as fiscal agent for the Treasury. An early version of the Federal Reserve Act said all Federal funds would be deposited with the Fed banks. Strong opposition from the Treasury caused it to be changed to "may be deposited" with the Fed banks. The Treasury had been conducting coin and currency transactions through its "subtreasury" offices for many years. Many transactions were for cash, so the task of the subtreasuries was substantial and an important part of the Treasury with many people employed. Jealous of this role, the Treasury stubbornly resisted any attempt to move this operation to the Fed banks. It was later done by legislation in 1921 when the Congress refused to fund the subtreasuries. They were closed and all federal financial transactions handled by the Feds as fiscal agent for the Treasury.

Lack of coordination in the war effort is illustrated by the fact that on March 31, 1916, the Treasury announced (without contacting the board) the desire to float an issue of certificates of indebtedness in the amount of $50,000,000 at 2 percent—well below the market rate—and expected the Fed to buy them directly. This the Fed could and did do, but only after the rate was raised to 2½ percent and the action vigorously protested.

The idea that the Fed would buy all the securities necessary to fight the war was not good banking, and it was severely criticized. Basically, it would be highly inflationary and would not tap the resources of the nation. Gradually, Secretary of the Treasury McAdoo realized the need to involve the entire nation. And as sales of Treasury securities spread, it became evident that the Fed's settlement fund was an efficient way of storing and moving Treasury funds from remote areas to places where they were needed.

There was much concern as to the ability of the nation to buy the bonds necessary to finance the war. The total amount needed was a subject of a meeting in the spring of 1917 of the Federal Reserve Advisory Council, the Federal Reserve Board and Treasury officials. When asked for estimates of the total need, answers ranged from $500,000,000 to $1,500,000,000. No one dared go beyond that figure although some indicated that in an extreme emergency it might be necessary. Shortly after this meeting Secretary McAdoo announced the First Liberty Loan would be fixed at $2 billion and any oversubscription would be returned to the subscribers. Also, the interest on the securities would be tax exempt. The idea of tax exemption was debated heatedly but because of great apprehension that the issue might not be purchased, Secretary McAdoo went for the tax-exempt status and the rate was fixed at 3½ percent.

While the Fed board did not specifically commit to supporting the issue it was generally assumed that the Fed would see that it was sold. The bonds were an astounding success and were greatly oversubscribed. The Fed

banks were called upon to back the issue to a very small extent. The appeal
of a tax-exempt security was powerful. Prewar profits had been unusually
high, and patriotism was at a high pitch. Probably the bond would have
sold without the tax-exempt feature.

This success greatly encouraged the Treasury and the board. It was apparent that the Fed would back an issue and that the nation was more than
willing and capable of subscribing to a large amount of financing. Before
the war ended on November 11, 1918, the federal government had raised
$21,448,120,300. The last financing was a Victory Loan. These funds were
used not only to finance the U.S. effort but to give aid to several Allied
governments recovering from the war. The Federal debt had jumped from
$1,225,000,000 in June 1916 to $25,834,000,000 by December 1919. Thinking leaders both within and outside of the Federal Reserve System were well
aware of the inflationary pressure this had built. But the Fed had been
powerless to stop it as winning the war was the first objective.

An interesting change in leadership occurred near the end of 1918.
Secretary of the Treasury McAdoo resigned, and Carter Glass was named
as his replacement. This news was welcomed at the Fed as it was expected
that Carter Glass, a major framer of the Federal Reserve Act, would proceed to strengthen the system and encourage its growth. This probably was
his intent, but he assumed a task that was influenced by many factors
beyond his control. The huge debt and the pending issue of the Victory
Loan and the pressure to keep interest rates low to contain costs to the
Treasury could not be pushed aside. Also, Mr. Glass was a loyal party man
and a close friend of Mr. McAdoo's. So there was little change in the policy
of "borrow and spend" that had characterized the war years. The Federal
Reserve banks emerged in a very strong financial position as seen in the
statement of condition of the banks for 1920 shown in the Appendix.

WHAT ROLE FOR GOLD?

In 1913 and well into the 1930s, the prevailing thought was that gold should
be the "discipline" in any program relating to currency and monetary
policy. This thinking is illustrated by a statement written in 1930 by Paul
M. Warburg, member of the Federal Reserve Board from 1914 to 1918 (vice
governor from 1916 to 1918) and member of a Wall Street investment firm.

> For a decade after the conclusion of the War (WWI) we lived in an era
> in which gold had lost its position as the dictator of the policies of central
> banks. In the Old World most countries had cut the hawser that tied them
> to the yellow metal because they had lost the power to command or to hold
> it, while we, in the United States, had accumulated so much more gold
> than we required that it had ceased to exercise any restraining or regulative
> influence. With the gold compass gone, the world began to look about for
> another instrument of direction, and "price levels" became the new star by
> which to guide the policies of central banks. Leaders among European
> economists, as a consequence, became converts to the gospel of "managed

currencies," while here by a combination of fortunate circumstances it had been possible to keep the index of prices fairly level.

We are now entering another era of gold psychology. In one form or another, leading countries in the Old World have once more adopted the gold standard.... It will be a fortunate development for the United States to be forced again to give more head to the effect of gold movements on our own reserve position. For the Reserve System will be less subject to the charges of carrying on arbitrary policies and less exposed to the demands and schemes of dreamers, theorists, and demagogues when once more it is clearly recognized all over the world that the first duty of a central bank is to preserve its country's gold standard.

A GLANCE INTO THE FUTURE

Mr. Warburg would be shocked and would strongly disapprove of today's "managed" currency. To see how the nation has arrived at the position of a managed currency it is necessary to review some facts about the amount of gold in the United States and in the world and the volume of currency needed for the transaction of today's business. More details are shown in the Appendix, but here are some of the vital points.

In 1914 gold holdings of the United States were $1,207,000,000, and currency in circulation was $3,172,000,000 — roughly a 1:3 ratio. In 1920 gold holdings were $2,639,000,000, and currency in circulation was $5,181,000,000 — roughly a 2:1 ratio. Gold holdings reached a peak of $24,563,000,000 in 1949 with currency in circulation at $27,902,859,000 — we were floating in gold. But by 1965 gold holdings dropped to $13,806,000,000, currency in circulation had risen to $39,719,801,000, and Congress was forced to reduce the 40 percent required gold behind our currency to 20 percent.

In 1968 gold holdings were only $10,892,000,000, and currency in circulation surged to $47,640,463,000, forcing Congress to drop the requirement of gold collateral to zero — giving us a "managed" currency with no official gold backing. In the meantime, other nations had also abandoned the gold standard.

GOVERNORS' CONFERENCE

At the meeting in Washington on October 20-21, 1914, of directors and governors of all Fed banks prior to the opening of the Federal Reserve banks, a resolution was passed suggesting the formation of an executive committee composed of the 12 governors with the deputy governors as alternates. The conference was formed immediately and met once in December 1914, four times in 1915, four times in 1916 and once in 1917 before being discontinued for the duration of the war. The purpose of the conference was to discuss and coordinate operations of the Fed banks. The governors were men with banking experience, while members of the Federal Reserve Board were for the most part lacking in practical experience. The ambiguity of the act with respect to the powers of both the board and the banks led to the need for a free and frequent exchange of ideas. But this ambiguity eventually led to a confrontation with the board over its powers. At the January 1916 meeting, W.P.G. Harding, member of the Federal Reserve Board, read a memo to the conference which in effect placed limits on the action of the conference. Basically, it said the conference should meet only at the request of the board and that its action should be limited to giving advisory suggestions to the board. It was stated in firm but cordial terms emphasizing the responsibility of the board under the act and soliciting the counsel of the conference.

This is a good place to bring in the name of Benjamin Strong, governor of the Federal Reserve Bank of New York. This man was to be a dominant force in the system from 1914 till his death in October 1928. He led the Governors' Conference during the early years of the system, and only because of ill health did he reduce his participation in discussions. Even when doctors ordered him to Colorado for rest because of tuberculosis, he continued to write letters and memos expressing ideas and action. More about him later.

REVISIONS OF THE ACT NEEDED

Like any act of Congress or a prototype of a machine, the Federal Reserve Act was not perfect. Hammered out with a variety of ideas and opinions and without a clear vision of what might be required of the system, it was inevitable that some changes would be desirable. By the year 1916 certain weaknesses in the act urgently needed correcting, and the Federal Reserve Board recommended several to Congress. Action also had been vigorously pursued by the Governors' Conference led by Governor Strong. The modification of the definition of eligible paper, the amendment to extend authority of national banks to issue additional currency under the Aldrich-Vreeland Act and the change to permit pledging of gold against Federal Reserve notes have already been mentioned.

A problem that greatly disturbed Governor Strong was the lack of state member banks in the system. All national banks were required to join. But by the end of 1916 only two of the state banks in New York had joined and only 35 out of the 19,231 in the United States. In a speech in May 1915, Governor Strong stated: "No reform of our banking system will be complete and satisfactory to the country until it includes all banks, at least all banks that do commercial banking, in one comprehensive system."

There were many reasons for not belonging. No provision was made in the act for withdrawing if a bank changed its mind. As a member bank, it would lose many of its advantages as a state-chartered bank. For example, most did not clear checks at par, and many states had more liberal loan limits. Fear of stricter examination was also part of the reluctance to join. In addition, there was a fear of "federal" intervention in the bank's operations and a general opposition to the whole idea of a central bank. Congressional action on June 21, 1917, took care of this problem by permitting a state member bank to withdraw from the system after giving six months' notice and allowing state member banks to continue to follow their state's loan requirements.

More than two dozen amendments were made to the act by 1920. Some were minor "housekeeping" changes. Others more clearly defined authority of the banks and the board and expanded the role of the system in financing the war and in serving the public. Here are some of the most significant amendments made during that period.

August 15, 1914: Modified the rules regarding where and when reserves must be held for reserve cities, central reserve cities and state bank and trust companies that chose to be members of the Federal Reserve System. In general, the changes made it easier for member banks to comply with the reserve requirements.

March 3, 1915: Amended Section 13 to increase the authority of the board to increase the amount of acceptances involving imports and exports that could be discounted.

September 7, 1916: Amended Section 11 to permit the board by rule to permit member banks to keep all of their reserves in balances at its Fed bank. Amended Section 13 to remove the limit on the amounts of acceptances that could be discounted by a member bank, made provision for Fed banks to make loans to a member bank for a period not to exceed 15 days on its own promissory note providing it is secured by paper that would be eligible for discount; amended Section 2200 of the National Banking Act to permit national banks in towns whose population does not exceed 5,000 by the latest census to act as agent for fire, life, or other insurance companies; amended Section 14(e) to open accounts for foreign correspondents and agencies; amended Section 24 to limit loans on unencumbered or improved farmland or other real estate by a national bank to an area within a radius of 100 miles of the bank and limited the length of the loan on farmland to five years and on other real estate to one year; amended Section 25 to restrict investments by national banks in branches in foreign countries or dependencies of insular possessions of the United States to 10 percent of the bank's paid in capital and surplus and to place other restrictions on the bank's participation in the foreign branch.

June 21, 1917: Amended Section 3 to expand regulations concerning branches of Federal Reserve banks and set the number of directors at the branches at not more than seven nor fewer than three, with a majority of one to be appointed by the Federal Reserve Bank and the remaining ones by the Federal Reserve Board; amended Section 4 changing the title of the assistant Federal Reserve agent to deputy chairman and authorized the appointment by the Federal Reserve agent, subject to approval by the Federal

Reserve Board, of one or more assistants who shall be persons of tested banking experience; amended Section 9 eliminating reference to the Organization Committee, required state member banks to be subject to examination by the Federal Reserve Board and provided for a state member bank to withdraw voluntarily from membership after six months' notice (discussed earlier); amended Section 13 to broaden the kind of paper that member banks may accept growing out of the shipment or warehousing of goods and providing authority for the board to extend the total amount that a member bank may accept to 100 percent of the bank's capital and surplus; restated Section 16 and included the authority to use gold as collateral to Federal Reserve notes (discussed earlier) and authorized and directed the Treasury to accept such gold and/or gold certificates; amended Section 19 reducing reserve requirements on demand deposits for country banks from 12 to 7 percent, for reserve city banks from 15 to 10 percent, for central reserve city banks from 18 to 13 percent and from 5 to 3 percent on time and savings deposits for all banks; amended Section 22 to clarify that any officer or director of a member bank is entitled to the same rate of interest on his deposits as other depositors and paper bearing his name can be rediscounted on the same terms as other paper.

September 26, 1918: Updated the act to eliminate earlier reference to the organization of the banks and amended the act to make the division of member banks for the purpose of electing Class A and B directors on the basis of capitalization not on number of banks; amended Section 11(k) to give member national banks the same powers in acting as trustees as that given to state-chartered banks; amended Section 16 to include Federal Reserve notes in denomination of $500, $1,000, $5,000 and $10,000; amended Section 19(b) and (c) to give banks in suburban areas of a central reserve city or a reserve city, reserve requirements the same as for the next lowest classification; amended Section 22 to further clarify and stipulate rules for avoiding a conflict of interest between reserve bank directors, officers and examiners and the reserve bank.

March 3, 1919: Amended Section 7 to provide for Federal Reserve banks transferring earnings to a surplus account until such account shall be equal to paid in capital (formerly until it equalled 40 percent); amended Section 10 to eliminate the restriction on members of the board, secretary of the treasury and comptroller of the currency from taking a position with a member bank if such person has completed a full term for which they were appointed.

September 17, 1919: Amended Section 25 to permit, until January 1, 1921, national banks to invest up to an amount equal to 5 percent of their capital and surplus in stock in a United States corporation.

December 24, 1919: Added a new section to Section 25, which authorized the organization by banking corporations of organizations to do foreign banking business, commonly known as Edge Act corporations.

A NEW TASK FOR THE FED

A little noticed development occurred as part of the war effort. The need for a research bureau to assist in determining compliance with the Trading with the Enemy Act, resulted in the establishment, September 1, 1918, of a Division of Analysis and Research with the director and staff located at the Federal Reserve Bank of New York. In the years that followed, this part of the system would grow and become one of the most complete and authoritative sources of banking and business information. Officials of the system would rely on it to provide information on business and economic trends essential to the formation of appropriate monetary policy. Business leaders and government officials would come to depend on this organization for information vital to their own operations. Later named the Division of Research and Statistics and moved to the board in Washington, it would be a vital part of the system's ability to evaluate business and monetary developments.

LEADERSHIP IN THE EARLY YEARS

Congressman Carter Glass of Virginia and Senator Robert Owen of Oklahoma are names that are synonymous with the planning and passages of the Federal Reserve Act. Without the support of President Woodrow Wilson these two men would probably not have been successful in their efforts to complete favorable action by Congress on major banking reform legislation. His support and dedication to achieving a new banking law was critical at several points. Even Secretary of State William Jennings Bryan, of "the cross of gold" speech fame, lent his support at a time when the "liberal" element in Congress threatened passage of the act.

Leadership in the formation of the Federal Reserve banks and the Federal Reserve Board and in the early years of operation centered in men like W.P.G. Harding, John Skelton Williams, William G. McAdoo, H. Parker Willis, Paul Warburg and Benjamin Strong. Many others played important roles in bringing the system into a viable, strong organization. But these men accepted a personal challenge in accepting places of leadership in the system.

W.P.G. Harding was former president of the First National Bank of Birmingham, Georgia, and the only man on the original Federal Reserve Board with practical banking experience. His support for the regional concept of the system and his background from an agricultural area brought approval from persons outside of Wall Street and Washington. He served as governor of the board from August 10, 1916, to August 9, 1922. With the first board split evenly between two factions, one leaning heavily towards strong influence of the Treasury and the other inclined to a more nongovernment posture, Harding held the balance of power. He did not, however, misuse it but pushed for a unified policy that would benefit the system. His term expired August 9, 1922.

William G. McAdoo, secretary of the treasury under Wilson, was active in the fight for passage of the act and together with John Williams, did most of the work on the Organization Committee, selecting the Federal Reserve cities and outlining the districts. He was, under the terms of the act, an *ex officio* member of the board and designated as its chairman when present for a meeting. He was a strong advocate of keeping the influence of the "Wall Street" interests to a minimum. He probably would have supported an effort to make the system a part of the U.S. Treasury. While he was not always in agreement with the board, he worked tirelessly with it to finance the war.

Paul M. Warburg, partner in the Wall Street investment firm of Kuhn, Leob & Company, opposed the Federal Reserve Act prior to its passage. But when it became law, he gave his wholehearted support to making it work. He served on the board from August 10, 1914, to August 9, 1918. At that time he urged President Wilson not to reappoint him because of the feeling in the nation against Germany and persons of German ancestry. His brother served in the German Army, and while Paul was torn between loyalty to his family and his adopted nation, he gave unquestioned support to the United States and its Allies in the war. After leaving the board, he continued to give support to the system and worked for its improvement and influence.

John Skelton Williams, secretary of agriculture under President Wilson, was by law a member of the Organization Committee. He and Secretary McAdoo did virtually all of the work of the committee—a task that most would have refused if possible. Standing firm on his decisions with the committee, he often faced strong criticism.

H. Parker Willis, first secretary of the Federal Reserve Board, came to that position from a broad background of writing and finance. He had been editor of the *New York Journal of Commerce* and professor of banking at Columbia University. He was appointed by Secretary McAdoo to head a group given the responsibility of developing plans for the internal organization of the Federal Reserve Board and the Federal Reserve banks. Even as the Organization Committee under Secretary McAdoo began the task of selecting the reserve cities and the districts, Mr. Parker and his committee of financial experts (the so-called Technical Organization Committee) began to develop procedures and policies for the still-to-be-organized board and banks.

Benjamin Strong, a second generation member of the financial community, accepted the position of governor of the Federal Reserve Bank of New York reluctantly. He had opposed the act, believing that it would not work, in part because of the regional nature of the system. He felt that it would be unwieldy and could not concentrate resources of the nation. He also vigorously opposed the fact that the act stated that Federal Reserve notes were obligations of the U.S. government.

Only after spending a weekend with Strong's close personal friends and associates Henry Davison and Paul Warburg did he agree to accept the position as head of the New York Fed, then only if the board of directors of the bank agreed unanimously with his appointment. This it readily did. The progress in organizing the New York bank into an effective organization is illustrated by his comment in a speech to the bankers of the state of New York on June 24, 1915.

> It may be said that on October 26, 1914, the bank's equipment consisted of little more than a printed copy of the Federal Reserve Act. Whereas, today, it is a fully equipped bank with an organization perfectly capable of meeting any emergency, and is promptly transacting the business entrusted to its care.

A more important contribution to the growth of the system was Strong's leadership in the Governors' Conference and in promoting relations with other central banks, especially the Bank of England. He pursued these responsibilities with a determination and vigor that made a lasting impression on the eventual shape of the system and its internal and worldwide relations. The close relationship that existed between these two great leaders is illustrated by the following letter written to Strong by Norman shortly before Strong's death on October 15, 1928:

> Dear old friend,
>   How hard and how cruel life is. These past few weeks I have often thought and dreamed and spoke of you: I came home expecting most surely to find you on top of the wave. But I sit down in some bitterness to write you such a letter as this....
>   I will not now grumble nor kick against the pricks. I accept the decision that you resign in a few weeks or months. Then the curtain will be run down on *our* stage and then I would like to be on the spot so as to hold your hard hand at the moment of announcement. This about this: It has certain advantages which should appeal to the head as well as to the heart and link the future with the past.
>   But what a stage ours has been over these ten or twelve years! Unique — imaginative — far-sighted. Your dreams set a goal before a world which was then so distracted as to be blind and incredulous. Now the goal has been pretty well reached little by little and your dreams have come true and over these years I have watched the process (as no one else has done) with

Benjamin Strong, governor of the Federal Reserve Bank of New York from 1914 till his death in 1928. He gave strong leadership to the system during his lifetime. Courtesy Federal Reserve Bank of New York.

affection and pride. For the rest of my life that belongs to me as a memory which none can take away.

Whatever is to happen to us — wherever you and I are to live — we cannot now separate or ignore these years. Somehow we must meet and sometimes we must live together. I make a point of this: without knowing any more details of my own than of your future.

I have a feeling that in one way or another you will *still* be useful to those whom you have given service and made sacrifices and they are international and almost world-wide. So I believe the best is yet to be . . . port after stormy seas — life without pressure — counsel without bickering and jealousies — reasonable health without worry — affection. The world and all of us owe you the likes of these. Pray take them and in the taking renew your life and spirit as none other can do so well as you. And remember — when the time comes — let me be near to hold your hand and to watch the coming as well as the going.

God bless you and my love now and ever.

MN [Montague Norman]

DOES THE PUBLIC LIKE THE FED?

Was the Federal Reserve Act a good idea? Did it create confidence in the banking industry? Did the average citizen approve?

Certainly members of the financial community and most members of Congress and other national leaders were well aware of the act and most had a fair idea of what it was all about. But what of the man on the street? It might be safe to assume that if he could continue to do business and rely on his banker for help and his currency was always redeemable, he could care less about the mechanics of the system. The 1916 report of the Federal Reserve Agent of the San Francisco Federal Reserve Bank included the results of a survey of persons seeking licenses as teachers. Two questions were asked: (1) What is the Federal Reserve Act of Wilson's administration? (2) How many banks were formed and how governed?

The answers are amusing and suggest the need for a strong public relations effort. Here is a sample of the answers:

- The Federal Reserve Act was making a park in Colorado very much like the Yellowstone National Park.
- To form national reserve banks to aid in bringing the war in Europe to a close.
- The Federal Reserve Act is one storing money of the country, and anyone who is without money or "broke" can go to those banks and get what money they need.

So much for an informed public. In those early years all of the Reserve banks found it necessary to carry on a program of education as to the nature and purpose of the "new" banks. Some might not have been sure of all of the purposes, but they certainly could explain the organization and why it was created.

Chapter 4
A Struggle for Leadership (1920–1929)

The decade of the 1920s was one of recovery from World War I; a growing national economy; improvement in radios, cars and other machinery; the advent of motion pictures, bootlegging and flappers. It was the era of prohibition, short dresses, the Charleston, speakeasies and the Teapot Dome scandal.

It also was a decade of great expectations. Investments in stocks and bonds rose to staggering heights. With almost no margin required, it was easy to go into debt and gamble on what was assumed to be ever-increasing prices. Agriculture was the exception. Lower farm prices and heavy debt made agriculture unprofitable for many years.

Banking flourished. New banks were organized, and old ones doubled and tripled their assets. Presidents Harding, Coolidge and Hoover were largely content to let the country run by itself as long as it didn't upset the government's apple cart.

WHERE WAS THE FED?
Perhaps it was the mood of the country, but in general the Federal Reserve System joined the crowd and attempted no strong policy. The most energetic and ardent voice with the firmest and well-thought-out ideas was that of Benjamin Strong, governor of the New York Fed. In fairness it should be said that members of the Federal Reserve Board and some other persons in leadership positions watched with concern — perhaps even horror — as the nation went on a faster and higher speculating binge. Knowledgeable persons saw that the boom could not go on forever. When attempts were made to slow the speculation by urging banks to be more restrictive in making speculative loans, nonbank organizations took over, and the party continued until that fateful day in October 1929.

Why didn't the Fed do something? Lack of leadership maybe. Failure to recognize the dangers? No, the record clearly says they were concerned. What then? Lack of a clear policy and inadequate tools to correct what was obviously a wrong attitude, a dangerous journey and improper and unproductive use of credit is the most plausible answer. "It's automatic — the operation of the Federal Reserve System. As the economy needs more money, the Fed banks will discount their notes and as the demand decreases, the loans at the Fed will be paid off." Just like a public utility said some.

It was not that simple. The system was much more complicated and its influence and operation much broader. World War I had left an impact on the system and the financial status of the nation that was not easily handled. Financing the war with borrowed money at low rates brought inflation in prices, and as the Treasury continued to refinance maturing securities, inflationary pressure continued. But the drop in demand for goods as the war came to an end resulted in a short but severe depression in 1921. Agricultural prices were particularly hard hit, and the Fed was accused of bringing on the depression. Commercial banks were not very helpful in this postwar period. As their customers paid off loans taken during the production of war goods, the banks loaned out the funds to customers for other reasons — many for speculative purposes.

So instead of rebuilding reserves, the inflationary binge continued. Pleas from Secretary of the Treasury Carter Glass and others in leadership roles to Reserve banks and commercial banks to be more restrictive were largely ignored: by the Reserve banks because they felt they had no power to demand that their customers — member banks — be more selective in the use of funds obtained by discounting at the Reserve bank, and by member banks and their customers because they were caught up in the apparent opportunity to make a profit. Officers of the Reserve banks felt that they must increase the discount rate to discourage member banks from discounting paper. But little was done, partly because of the reluctance of the Federal Reserve Board to approve higher rates recommended by the Reserve banks.

THE PHELAN ACT

Another solution was offered in the Phelan Act, which authorized Reserve banks to use a progressive discount rate. Under the plan the rates would increase to the member bank as its discounts at the Reserve bank reached certain levels in relation to the member bank's size. Application of the progressive rate was optional and only four Reserve banks — Dallas, Atlanta, Kansas City and St. Louis — opted to use the new rate. The Phelan Act was an excuse to avoid the hard answer to the member banks — denying acceptance of their paper. At this point, however, the power of the Reserve banks was not clear, and they felt an obligation to accept all paper offered. As the Feds attempted to restrain credit, they were accused of wanting a depression.

H. Parker Willis, then secretary of the Federal Reserve Board, sums up the problem facing the Fed in these words:

> Among the peace problems that had to be met by the Federal Reserve System were accordingly those which are always met by any central reserve banking system, and were as follows:

1. Regulation of rates of interest in such a way as to apportion credit along beneficial lines and to prevent undue diversion of capital into channels which might prove injurious rather than helpful.
2. Regulation of the movement of specie into and out of the country.
3. In connection with the specie movement, regulation or supervision of rates of exchange and conditions under which foreign exchange business is carried on.

NO FIRM POLICY

Goals of the system were not firm, and policies were uncertain. Lacking clear direction, confusion was bound to prevail. Ideas once thought to be set in concrete were later reversed, sometimes with little firm basis. Uncertainty and a search for direction were characteristic of the period of the 1920s. For example, Carter Glass, secretary of the treasury in 1920 and a paramount figure in the framing of the Federal Reserve Act, held strong opinions about who could do what. Benjamin Strong, governor of the New York Federal Reserve Bank, also had firm opinions of who could do what and when. These two emotional and strong-minded individuals clashed in the early 1920s as Strong wanted to abandon the preferential discount rates and go to one rate. Glass wanted to continue the preferential rates and said the board had the power to force any Fed bank to accept its position on discount rates. To prove his point, he went to the attorney general for an opinion supporting his position. Partly because he stated his own opinion so strongly, he received confirmation from the attorney general.

The amusing part is that in 1927 when Glass was back in Congress, the Federal Reserve Board forced the Chicago Fed to lower its discount rate, and Senator Glass was furious. The action was, he asserted, unwise and clearly illegal; Congress never intended the board to have such power. Charles Hamlin, an inveterate diarist on the board, reminded Senator Glass of his earlier action to which the Senator replied as follows:

> I very distinctly recall the series of the circumstances which suggested my letter to Governor Harding and subsequently my request for Mr. Elliot's opinion, followed by my written request for the opinion of the Attorney General. Leffingwell had been remonstrating with Ben Strong about the latter's threatened interference with the Treasury loan program, and I think Leffingwell very likely wrote the letter of November 5th for my signature, suggesting that the Federal Reserve Board admonish the Governors of the various regional banks not to expect to control stock and commodity speculation by raising commercial rediscount rates. I am not positive about this; but my recollection is that he prepared the letter after a conference with me on the subject.
>
> Later Governor Strong, then a stranger but since my warm friend, came to Washington and we had a hot altercation of words in my office over his extraordinary contention that the New York Bank had legal right to put into effect a rediscount rate regardless of the judgment and wishes of the Federal Reserve Board. At the moment my idea was to avoid penaliz-

ing commerce by a high bank rate; but, as a preferable alternative, to have the Governors of the various regional banks admonish the individual banks to curtail loans for stock and commodity speculative purposes. Strong, with some show of indignation, aggressively refused to do this and avowed his purpose to proceed in his own way, whereupon I threatened to prevail with the President to remove him.

It was because Governor Strong had long been threatening to take action which we thought would gravely impair the Treasury's operations, and more especially because of the scene in my office in which he challenged the jurisdiction of the Federal Reserve Board, that I asked Elliot's opinion and wrote that opportunist letter to the Attorney General. I had been mad through and through for weeks and desired, more in anger than in reason, to make a case for the Board.

This I seem to have done somewhat to the satisfaction of the Attorney General. However, there is to be noted this exceedingly significant fact, to wit: That however strongly I might have asserted the jurisdiction of the Board, as my individual view, I did not, even in the immediate grave exigency, advise the Board to exercise the power in question nor did the Federal Reserve Board, as such, assert or exercise the power of establishing a rediscount rate for the New York or any other Federal Reserve bank. Here was a case when, if there has ever been justification, the Federal Reserve Board would have been warranted in exercising the right to initiate a rate, if that right in fact existed; but it did not do so. And the Board cannot now justify capricious action in the Chicago case by appealing to the technical opinion of an individual member of the Board given in anger eight years ago in extraordinary circumstances. I am simply amazed that the Board should have deliberately precipitated an issue of this kind, with so little excuse for its action, if any, since it is obliged to involve the bitterest kind of agitation and will inevitably subject the Board and the Federal Reserve System to injurious criticism, if not unwise attempts to radically alter the Act itself.

Adding to the difficulties at the Board were the frequent changes in its membership. From 1918 to 1930 there were nine changes in its membership. The only members of the original Board to continue through the 1920s were Charles S. Hamlin from the Boston district and Adolph C. Miller from San Francisco. Hamlin was reappointed in 1916 and again in 1926, serving until 1936. Miller was reappointed in 1924 and in 1934, and served until 1936. As mentioned, Paul Warburg asked that he not be reappointed because of his German background and the nation's attitude toward Germany during World War I. His successor, Albert Strauss, served less than two years, but his successor, Edmund Platt, served until 1930.

Frederick Delano from the Chicago district resigned in July 1918, and his successor, Henry A. Moehlenpah, completed the unfilled term of Mr. Delano and left the board in August 1920. Mr. Harding's term expired in 1922, and he was not reappointed. Others appointed to the board included David Willis from the Cleveland district, who served less than a year; John R. Mitchell from the Minneapolis district, who served two years; Milo Campbell from the Chicago district, who died eight days after taking office;

and Henry Crissinger from Cleveland, who served four years. This lack of continuity on the board made the establishment of a consistent policy very difficult.

The uncertainties of authority and policy were to continue into the 1930s, but now that we have seen ample evidence of this weakness, let's look at some data that show what the Fed did during this period.

SOME POSITIVE FACTS

One fact that should not be overlooked is the continuing dialogue between Governor Strong and Montagu Norman, governor of the Bank of England. This relationship was to build strong ties not only with the Bank of England but eventually with other European central banks. The value of the relationship was to grow in importance as the role of the United States in world affairs expanded and eventually the nation became the leader in world finance. Strong was often criticized for his action, but he as well as Norman believed it was to the benefit of both countries. Governor Strong encouraged other Fed banks to participate but believed the New York bank should be the major player in dealing with other central banks.

All war is destructive, creates maladjustments in the economy and makes all men losers in the long run. But World War I created a situation that forced the relatively new Federal Reserve banks into action that led to the strengthening of their financial position. Although the general price index had doubled from 1914 to 1920, the strength of the Reserve banks quadrupled. The following table is a summary of the bank's position for selected dates.

Condition of Federal Reserve Banks as of Given Dates
(in millions of dollars)

Item	Apr. 6–7 1917	Dec. 27 1918	Jan. 4 1920
Total cash	$ 962.70	$2,146.20	$2,121.20
Net deposits & note liability	1,136.80	4,238.10	4,849.00
Required reserves	416.70	1,619.60	1,847.00
Reserve percentage	84.70	50.60	43.70
Earning assets	225.60	2,318.20	3,181.80
Reserve notes	400.70	2,855.60	2,998.90

Source: Parker Willis, *The Federal Reserve System.*

This strength was needed. By early 1920, world prices for many commodities fell sharply, and in a few months all economies were in recession. Farm prices were hit the hardest. The index of prices for farm products dropped from 92.2 in 1920 to 54.1 in 1921 and was only 57.4 in 1922. During the same period the price of wheat tumbled from $2.45 to $1.21 per bushel. The price of cotton fell from 11.5 to 7.03 cents per pound.

ıf falling prices after years of increasing prices shook the
prices fed upon themselves, so they fell lower. Banks
the Feds did their best to take care of their customers,
ₕₑₗpless to force any liquidation. In fact, the theory of the
ₜₒ let the market take its course and make the necessary correc-
ₜᵢₒns. Remember, the basis of the Federal Reserve System was to be
available to finance transactions that were self-liquidating – the "real bills"
theory. The idea of supporting the economy would not be a part of the Fed
policy for another generation. Financial leaders and economists were
quoted as saying, "We must go through a deflation to cure our ills." Benjamin Strong defended the Fed's position, saying (1) the Reserve banks
stood ready throughout the period to lend for legitimate purposes, and
(2) the Federal Reserve had prevented disorderly and panicky liquidation
and financial crisis.

Professor H. Parker Willis wrote on Armistice Day, 1918, "It is ...
desirable, not to say urgently necessary, to eliminate the inflationary element from our circulating medium." Professor E.W. Kemmerer, of Princeton University, agreed as he told a meeting of Robert Morris Associates in
June 1920, "We must have contraction; we must get it cautiously and
carefully. We can't go ahead with our business and make much progress,
however, until we get substantial contraction. If I were to summarize the
rest I have to say in three words, I would say, 'work, save, and pay up.'"
John Shaforth, of Colorado and the Senate Banking and Currency Committee, warned that attempts to reduce prices to their prewar level would
be too drastic, but he recommended that the Federal Reserve lower
wholesale prices about 25 percent below their peak in September 1918.

SPECULATION ON THE RISE

The story of the economy of the United States and the world following
World War I is a familiar scenario. The war had stimulated an urgent increase in the production of goods – almost all goods, including agricultural
products. With the Armistice came a drastic drop in the demand for goods.
But it is not possible to slow down the production machinery by a wave of
the hand or the signing of an armistice. Moreover, the psychology of rising
prices favored excess orders to buy before prices increased further and to
insure a supply of raw materials. This increase in orders gave a false impression of a growing demand and encouraged lenders to finance anyone with
a reputation for producing goods. Stocks of commodities were financed
even if they were stored in warehouses. When the lower demand backed up
the supply and slowed liquidation, loans were extended.

Sooner or later the facts of life became apparent, orders were canceled
and prices fell. This happened in late 1919 and early 1920. When it happened, the Fed was accused of causing the drop because it didn't discount
enough paper – especially in agricultural regions. Discounting of agricultural paper did not drop off as suggested. Rather Fed banks in agricultural

areas increased their discounting of agricultural paper. A study prepared for the Congress by the Joint Congressional Commission of Agricultural Inquiry found that from June 30, 1920, to June 30, 1921, borrowings from the Fed by member banks in rural areas increased 56 percent. During the same period borrowings from Fed banks nationwide declined 19.5 percent. The discount rate was lowered six times during the period, but that was not enough to quiet the criticism. The committee's report to Congress was unexpectedly favorable to the board and thus did not please those who wanted to find a reason for drastic action against the board.

INTERNAL PROBLEMS AT THE FED
Struggling to find their way in the world of finance, several Reserve banks found their reserves of gold dropping below the required 40 percent. Reserve ratios on October 20, 1920, ranged from 80 percent at the Cleveland Fed to 16 percent at the Atlanta Fed.

Discussion during the framing of the act questioned the ability of the 12 banks to stand entirely on their own. The wide variation in resources and the differential in economic development of the 12 regions made it impossible for areas such as Dallas, Kansas City, Minneapolis and Atlanta to meet the needs of their member banks and still maintain their required collateral in gold. Banks in New York, Cleveland, Boston and Philadelphia were able to provide assistance to other Fed banks which needed to improve their reserve position.

To illustrate the difference in size of the Fed banks, at the end of 1920 the New York Fed had total resources of $1,842,478,000, while the Atlanta, Dallas, and San Francisco banks had total resources of $275,193,000, $173,998,000 and $461,574,000, respectively. Rediscounting between Fed banks during the first seven months of 1921 is shown in the following table.

Rediscounts and Sales of Paper Between Federal Reserve Banks
First seven months of 1921
(in thousands of dollars)

Federal Reserve Bank	Amount received		Amount furnished	
	Rediscounted	Sold	Discounted	Purchased
Boston	$	$	$ 84,550	$10,671
New York		57,646	267,500	340
Philadelphia			5,000	6,823
Cleveland			172,415	25,094
Richmond	220,000			
Atlanta	27,957			
Chicago		1,315		
St. Louis				1,000
Minneapolis	69,000			
Kansas City	9,008			
Dallas	203,500			
San Francisco		25		15,058

Source: J. Parker Willis, *The Federal Reserve System.*

By the end of 1922 all Fed banks were out of debt to other Fed banks. But the ability to make these interdistrict movements of credit enabled the banks to act more as a unit in meeting the credit needs of the entire nation. As the nation developed economically and financial resources were more equally distributed, the need for interdistrict movement declined and was not used again.

POLITICS ERUPTS

President Warren Harding was looking for opportunities to change the makeup of the board so it would be more favorable to Republicans. Board member W.P.G. Harding's (no relation) term expired August 6, 1922, and President Harding was not inclined to renominate him. However, not to do so would have subjected him to criticism of playing politics with the board. This did not deter the president, and he selected Daniel R. Crissinger, then comptroller of the currency and an *ex officio* member of the board, as a nominee to fill Governor Harding's spot. Harding went to the Boston Fed as governor.

In the meantime, Congress had amended Section 10 of the Federal Reserve Act, increasing the number of appointed members of the board from five to six. Also, it changed the wording of the directive to the president in selecting nominees to the board from "due regard to the fair representation of different commercial, industrial and geographical divisions of the country" to "due regard to fair representation of financial, agricultural, industrial and commercial interests, and geographical sections of the nation." The addition of "agricultural" went with a message to the president — "one must be from agriculture."

President Harding nominated and the Senate confirmed Milo D. Campbell, head of the Michigan Milk Producers Association, as the "farmer" member of the board. Unfortunately, he died after eight days in office. The position was then filled by George S. James from the St. Louis Federal Reserve District. The board continued with six appointive members until the Banking Act of 1935 eliminated the *ex officio* members and set the number of active members at seven, all appointed by the president and confirmed by the Senate.

A CHANGE IN MOOD

The system was gradually moving from the real bills theory of "the market would take care of itself" to a more positive position of assisting the market in making adjustments. The board and the Reserve banks still lacked experience in the use of the tools available to direct the use of credit. But officials had come to realize the need for positive action to prevent crises rather than wait for them to happen. In all of this discussion and debate on policy, Governor Strong and Board member Harding were leaders in forming policy.

A PROBLEM WITH GOLD

In 1924 a heavy inflow of gold threatened to upset the balance of the financial community and was a special threat to European economies as gold flowed to the United States for higher returns. This inflow of gold enabled the commercial banks to liquidate debt and increase loans without recourse to the Fed. A drop in the discount rate and easing of funds by selling securities slowed the inflow of gold and stabilized the situation. However, by 1927 one-half of the world stock of monetary gold was in the United States.

STORAGE OF GOLD

A word is in order about the holdings of gold. For decades, even centuries, when payment was made by gold, the actual bars or bullion or coins were physically transported to the new owner. Considering the weight of gold, this transfer was often expensive, and the price of the metal was set accordingly. As facilities for the storage of gold became available and trust in the custodian increased, it became more practical to simply "earmark" the required bars or bullion with the new owner's name. Thus, a transfer usually simply means moving the gold from one area of the vault to another or just changing the name of the owner on the bar. The Federal Reserve Bank of New York, because of its location in the money center and adjacent to a major port, soon became the favored place to store gold. Thus, the value of gold stored at the New York Fed at any given point in time usually exceeded by a substantial amount the bullion owned by the United States.

BEGINNING OF OPEN MARKET OPERATIONS

The decade of the 1920s saw the evolution of the use of the purchase and sale of government securities as means of influencing the availability of credit. The original Federal Reserve Act gave the Reserve banks the power to buy and sell securities, but not until the 1920s did it occur to the men of the Fed that this was an effective tool of monetary policy. Writing to Professor O.M.W. Sprague of Harvard University in 1922, Governor Strong of the New York Fed reflected this change in thinking as he wrote about the change that must be made as the discipline of gold no longer restrained speculative activities. The enormous stock of gold precluded this as a limiting factor in the expansion of credit.

In his letter to Professor Sprague, Governor Strong pointed out:

> Since the Federal Reserve System has found its position as a large lender it becomes one of the most important factors in the economic machine because it must, whether it wishes to or not, exercise control over the volume of credit, which in turn has such a far reaching effect upon prices, wages, etc. Prior to the war (WWI) the development of speculation and extravagance in a period of expansion would normally have been checked — so to speak — by advancing prices, adverse trade balance, and loss of gold. With the world no longer shipping gold, and the American

exchanges at such a premium, and with such enormous gold reserve in our hands — as we now have — no such check upon speculation and advancing prices can be expected to operate — at least not until such a development has reached an extreme stage.

Therefore, the Federal Reserve System, as the central factor in the control of credit, must rely upon the application of wisdom and intelligence of the first order. There are no automatic penalties which would apply as in ordinary times. In view of that, students of the System should watch it, criticize its affairs, protect it against the invasion from political or other sources, as the protection of the System hereafter will depend upon the interest of the member banks in insuring that it has good management, and a sound public opinion to protect it against misuse.

In late 1923, the country experienced a drop in business activity with the textile mills hit especially hard. Under Strong's leadership the system took aggressive action to stem the recession and to halt the loss of gold to Europe. A purchase of $500 million of government securities turned the tide, and stability was achieved in the economy and a money panic avoided. Referring to the result of this positive action by the Fed, Governor Strong proclaimed "a greater feeling of tranquility and contentment throughout the country than we have experienced at any time since the war."

As nations — especially those in Europe — recovered from the impact of World War I, they began to look for a return to financial policies of the prewar days. In April 1925, England returned to the gold standard, and by 1927 almost all countries had adopted the metal as the standard for their currency. The system agreed to assist Poland and Italy as they made the change, but such help was not needed. Gold stocks in the United States continued to grow throughout the decade, and by 1930, at more than $4 billion, were nearly three times the amount held in 1914.

MARKETS FALL APART

Stock prices crashed. Suicides increased. Banks failed. Foreigners lost millions in the stock market. The stock market crash on Monday, October 24, 1929, has to be the dominant event of the decade of the 1920s! Fortunes were lost. Confidence in the financial markets and the economy plummeted. A worldwide depression was in the making. Recovery took nearly a decade as unemployment skyrocketed, businesses failed and fortunes were lost in every aspect of the economy.

What caused this catastrophe? Was the Federal Reserve System at fault? Could it have been stopped? Who was to blame?

These questions and many related ones have been debated for decades, and it would be difficult to achieve total agreement on answers even in the 1990s. Part of the differences of opinion stems from the uncertainty of the cause and effect of various factors and part from the lack of complete data to reflect changes in the financial and business picture at the time. There are, however, sufficient data to point to some obvious problems that might have been corrected if knowledge of the cause and effect of economic factors and financial positions had been available. The break in the stock market was the result of events that had been developing for several years. Credit was easy. Rates were low, and the mood of the country was that prosperity would go on forever. Here are some basic facts concerning the financial situation as it developed from 1921 to 1928.

- total loans at all commercial banks increased 35 percent;
- total deposits increased 60 percent;
- investments in securities, other than U.S. government securities, increased 96 percent;
- borrowing by member banks at Federal Reserve banks increased 96 percent;
- the discount rate at Federal Reserve banks remained relatively low ranging from 3½ to 5 percent until August 1929 when it was raised to 6 percent;
- total Reserve bank credit outstanding remained nearly constant and was never tight;
- broker's loans jumped from $1,190 million to $6,440 million—an increase of 441 percent, $1 billion during the four months prior to the crash;
- Federal Reserve Bank holdings of U.S. government securities rose from $234 million to $617 million at the end of 1927 but dropped to $228 million by the end of 1928.

Speculation fever gripped the nation. With easy credit and booming industry it was assumed the nation was in a state of perpetual prosperity. Fortunes were being made in the stock market as prices skyrocketed. Standard and Poor's index of common stocks rose from 6.86 in 1921 to 26.02 in 1929. Volume of transactions rose from 173 million shares to 1,125 million. There were no margin requirements except those that a broker might impose on selected customers.

A TIME FOR ACTION

What was the Fed doing all this time? Couldn't they see that the nation was heading for a fall? Governor Strong's statement quoted earlier is typical of the thinking of many leaders in the financial world. It was obvious to many that the accelerating use of credit, especially in the stock market, was not prudent. But the mechanics to change it were not adequate. The Federal Reserve Board did issue a statement on February 7, 1929, strongly urging all member banks to refrain from making speculative loans. For a few weeks some restraint was exercised, but it didn't last. The boom atmosphere and the fact that paper profits were huge made it impossible for banks and other lenders to say no to customers.

Timing of action by a central bank has frequently been criticized as being too little too late or too much too soon. The inability to know the degree and timing of the impact of Fed's action makes it most difficult to do the right thing. The very action of the Fed may change the impact that was desired. Sometimes action is not reflected for months, sometimes the next day. If restraint is imposed too soon, a rise in business activity may be stopped too soon. If action is delayed, it may be too late to correct the situation.

It is to the credit of the leaders of the Fed that they did see a dangerous situation developing and did take some steps to correct it. For example, during 1928 government securities were sold beginning in February, and during the next 19 months $275 million were sold in an attempt to soak up some of the liquidity in the market. Unfortunately, during the same period, bills discounted increased $507 million so that total Reserve Bank credit increased. The "real bills" theory and the philosophy that the Fed should not dictate when or how much member banks should discount with them in effect erased any power of the Fed to control the volume of credit.

In later years, this would change drastically. In the author's experience, he had occasion during the 1960s and 1970s to "jawbone" member bank officers to reduce discounting paper or borrowing from the Fed during a period when attempts were being made to tighten credit. In fact, member banks were told not to increase loans when they were borrowing except for reserve position adjustments.

The experience of the late 1920s illustrates the power of speculative fever. When the banks finally attempted to slow credit expansion, nonbank lenders came into the picture and provided the credit demanded by speculators. The Fed struggled to find its role in the economy. Action was taken immediately following the market crash. The system bought $150 million of government securities the first week. The discount rate was dropped from 6 percent to 5 percent on November 1 and to 4½ percent on November 15. The commercial banks in New York City absorbed $1.4 billion of loans that had been made by nonbank lenders.

The action of the Fed and of commercial banks was not adequate to stem the tide of discouragement, and the country quickly assumed an atmosphere of despair. True, stock prices rallied briefly, but even at the end of 1929, they were 35 percent below their peak in September. A slowdown in the pace of industrial activity and lower corporate profits in the second quarter of 1929 foretold a less robust economy. The wild speculative fever of the 1920s was over, and the nation would not fully recover for a decade. In fact, the economy would not reach bottom until 1933 when a banking crisis resulted in the banking holiday and a major revision of banking law.

It is helpful to remember in evaluating the action or inaction of the Fed that the Federal Reserve Act gave little direction for specific action. Originally, the act was a solution to banking and currency problems largely involving the issuing of currency, maintaining of bank reserves and effecting an elastic currency. The working of the system was expected to be quite automatic. The real bills theory maintained that as the economy expanded the discounting of paper with the Fed would provide room for expansion, and as the transactions of business were completed, the bills would be paid off and the retrenching of currency would occur. Little thought was given to the possibility of the system being a causal factor in the business cycle. In fact, if this thought had occurred to many in the Congress, it would have been quickly dismissed as "meddling" and would have been prohibited.

The feeling of inadequacy to deal with the problem of the late 1920s is illustrated by the following statement in the Board's Annual Report for 1929:

> The measures taken by the Federal Reserve banks in the year 1928 to firm-money conditions by sales of open-market investments and by successive increases of discount rates from 3½ percent at the opening of the year to 5 percent by midyear had not proved adequate. The second half of the year 1928 witnessed an aggravation of the conditions that had called forth the firm-money policy of the Federal Reserve banks in the first half of the year.
>
> The credit situation confronting the Federal Reserve System at the opening of the year 1929, therefore, still stood in need of correction. The problem was to find suitable means by which the growing volume of security credit could be brought under orderly restraint without occasioning avoidable pressure on commercial credit and business. With the System's portfolio of Government securities practically exhausted by the sales made in the first half of 1928 the main reliance in a further firming of money conditions must have been further marking up of Federal Reserve discount rates, unless some other expedient could be brought to bear on the situation.
>
> The Board was not disposed to regard further increases of the discount rate as the appropriate method of dealing with the situation presented, . . . the Board therefore, did not approve the discount rate advances voted by some of the Federal Reserve banks. It set forth its views of how the Federal Reserve banks would best proceed in the circumstances in a letter to them . . . reading as follows:
>
> . . . The resources of the Federal Reserve System are ample for meeting the growth of the country's commercial needs for credit, provided they are competently administered and protected against seepage into uses not contemplated by the Federal Reserve Act. The Federal Reserve Act does not, in the opinion of the Board, contemplate the use of the resources of the Federal Reserve banks for the creation or the extension of speculative credit. A member bank is not within its reasonable claim for rediscount facilities at its Federal Reserve bank when it borrows either for the purpose of making speculative loans or for the purpose of maintaining speculative loans. The Board has no disposition to interfere with the loan practices of a member bank so long as they do not involve the Federal Reserve banks. It has, however, a grave responsibility whenever there is evidence that member banks are maintaining speculative security loans with the aid of Federal Reserve credit. When such is the case the Federal Reserve bank becomes either a contributing or sustaining factor in the current volume of speculative security credit. This is not in harmony with the intent of the Federal Reserve Act nor is it conducive to the wholesome operation of the banking and credit system of the country.

This letter failed to stem the speculative boom, and the Fed seemed helpless to take more effective action.

What are the "tools" available to the Fed? Let's take a closer look at them.

"TOOLS" OF THE FED

We mentioned earlier that perhaps by accident, during World War I and the churning of the economy immediately thereafter, some officials of the Fed and especially Benjamin Strong, governor of the New York Fed, saw that the buying and selling of government securities in the open market, authorized by Section 14 of the act, could influence the course of business and impact on the availability and cost of credit. Later, in the mid-1920s, action in this area again demonstrated the potential of this "tool." Thus, in addition to the power to increase rates through the discount rate and the authority to increase or decrease reserve requirements (within limits), the Fed banks had at their disposal a powerful tool to influence the supply and cost of credit.

The use of the discount rate to impact the cost of credit is quite easily understood. If the interest rate charged by the Fed when its member banks borrow from it goes up, the rate charged member bank customers will also increase—a fairly direct connection. Likewise, the changes in reserve requirements is no mystery. If member banks must keep more of their reserves with the Fed, it leaves less for them to loan out to customers or to invest—a technique not unlike the use of minimum balances banks may require of their customers.

Open market operations—the buying and selling of securities by the Fed—is unlike any relationship a commercial bank has with its customers. Perhaps an example will best illustrate the use of this "tool."

Assume that the Fed banks sell on the open market $100 million of U.S. Treasury notes. Further assume that they sell them to a broker in New York City. In payment for these securities the broker gives the Fed a check drawn on its bank in New York. The Fed will send the check to the bank for collection. The bank will either send money to the Fed or more likely ask it to charge its reserve account at the Fed. However, the member bank must keep a minimum amount in that reserve account, so if the charge reduces it below the minimum, it must find other funds to replace the charge. This may mean selling an asset or calling a loan. The net effect is to "tighten" the supply of funds available to the member bank.

A purchase of securities by the Fed simply works in reverse. The member bank winds up with an increase in funds, so it can look for another investment or make additional loans. Because banks buy and sell funds among themselves, any surplus is quickly dispersed in the banking system; conversely, any tightening is felt throughout the money market. (See Chapter 7 for a more detailed discussion of the way purchases and sales of government securities are originated and completed.)

In the early years of the system, the volume of U.S. government securities available in the market was limited. The national debt was only $1.2 billion in 1916. But with the cost of World War I this figure quickly increased to $25.5 billion by June of 1919. As the market for these securities grew in volume, the opportunity for use of open market operations by the Fed expanded greatly.

During the decade of the 1920s leadership in the Fed was still cautious about taking direct action to influence the economy. Lacking a clear direction from Congress through the act, there was reluctance to move into areas that were unsure. The system was subject to enough criticism without adding opportunities for enemies to cry "foul."

In the early years of the system each Fed bank executed its own buy and sell transaction in the securities market. As pointed out earlier, this was a major source of income as the volume of discounted paper from member banks sometimes did not provide sufficient income to cover expenses. Purchases and sales were made basically on the basis of what was profitable. This uncoordinated action by 12 banks was sometimes disruptive in the market and also caused the Treasury problems in handling its debt. Also, the Treasury was under pressure to keep rates low in order to reduce its cost, and the Fed banks were inclined at times to wish for higher rates.

As a partial solution to the problem and as mentioned earlier, the Federal Reserve Board in 1923 disbanded the old open market committee composed of the governors of the Fed banks, which had the awkward title of Committee of Governors on Centralized Execution of Purchase and Sale of Government Securities by Federal Reserve Banks, and reconstituted it with the same membership under the name Open Market Investment Committee. Not much help but at least a change in name. Later developments in the operation of the Fed were to find open market operations one of the most important keys to monetary policy and action that would be watched hour by hour by those in the financial world.

LEADERSHIP AT THE FED

Strong leadership is needed in every organization, and the Federal Reserve System during the decade of the 1920s lacked that essential ingredient. Several factors contributed to this deficit. First, it was not a recognized role of importance either in government or in the financial community. As President Wilson found out when he searched for the first members of the Federal Reserve Board, some men simply didn't want the job. The role of the system was not clearly defined, and many in politics and in business were not sure it was here to stay.

Second, the pay was not an enticement. Rated along with cabinet members in salary, it was far below what strong leaders could earn in business or industry. To accept a job on the board meant personal sacrifice, and many were not ready to give that to an uncertain future. Governors of the Fed banks were not so limited in salary, and for the most part they were paid salaries competitive with others in the financial field. In fairness, it should be said that the original members of the Federal Reserve Board were dedicated men who believed in the system. As vacancies occurred, the fear of politics expressed by debators on the bill to create the system were partially justified. When W.P.G. Harding stepped down as chairman of the board, President Harding appointed Daniel R. Crissinger, a boyhood chum, to the board. Crissinger was from Ohio and had been brought to Washington by President Harding as comptroller of the currency. Crissinger soon found that he had little power, and he resigned soon after the "Chicago" incident where the board's attempt to force a Reserve bank to change its discount rate failed. President Coolidge then appointed Roy A. Young, for ten years governor of the Federal Reserve Bank of Minneapolis. Mr. Young did not give strong leadership, and it remained for the Great Depression to bring out new leadership.

Throughout the first 14 years of the system — from 1914 to his death on October 15, 1928 — Benjamin Strong, governor of the Federal Reserve Bank of New York, was the strong hand of the system. His background in finance and his position as leader of the largest Fed bank gave him a base from which he gave strong leadership to the system. He was criticized for being too strong-handed and trying to dominate the system and of spending too much time abroad with Norman Montagu, governor of the Bank of England. But without his insight into the working of financial institutions and his ability to lead, the system would have floundered and might not have survived. Ill health kept him from being present personally at many meetings, but his voluminous memos and letters kept his thinking and his influence in the forefront. His insistence on developing relations with the central banks of Europe proved to be crucial in later years.

DAY-TO-DAY OPERATIONS AT THE FED BANKS

Much has been written about the organization and legal responsibilities of Federal Reserve banks. This is appropriate. Their major role in the nation's economy is in the area of monetary policy and the maintaining of a stable currency. However, in the day-to-day operations of a Federal Reserve bank, most of the employees are involved not in monetary policy but in the clearing of checks, paying out and receiving currency and coin and performing duties as fiscal agent for the Treasury.

The work of each bank differs in that some have more responsibilities in the development and execution of monetary policy. For example, the large research force, a staff for handling international transactions for the system and execution of the open market operations conducted at the Federal Reserve Bank of New York necessitates a large proportion of its employees working in these areas. All of the Fed banks now have research staffs plus examiners, but at a branch of a Fed bank more than 90 percent of its budget will be for expenses involved in check collection, paying and receiving currency and coin and carrying out operations as fiscal agent of the Treasury.

Section 13 of the act specifically authorized Federal Reserve banks to accept checks and other cash items for collection. In fact, one of the purposes of the banks was to improve the check collection system of the nation. As the source of a stable currency and an issuer of Federal Reserve notes, Fed banks became the place for member banks to order additional currency and to deposit surplus currency for credit. As a part of the Appropriation Act of 1920, all functions of the subtreasuries were transferred to the Fed banks. This involved such activities as paying out and receiving coins, acceptance of gold and silver certificates for redemption and cancellation of currency unfit for further circulation. Most of the expense of performing operations as fiscal agent of the Treasury were reimbursed by the Treasury.

Personnel required to process paper offered to the Fed banks for discount varied with the volume offered. In some periods one or two persons could easily do the job. At other times it might require a dozen or more to examine the notes and perform the paperwork. The fluctuations in the volume of paper offered for discount are illustrated by the fact that in the year 1920, 1,190,000 bills were discounted at all 12 Feds. But in 1930, only 415,000 were handled. Except for 1920, the total for any one year during the decade did not exceed 850,000. Accounting, auditing and the usual housekeeping duties required a substantial staff. Security at the banks was a must, and guards were a part of each bank's staff.

WHAT ABOUT PAR BANKS?

Remember the big push to force all banks to remit for checks drawn on them at par? No discounting to the payee. Sorry to say, not much progress was made during the 1920s. In 1920 there were 1,755 nonpar banks in the United States, and by 1930 there were 3,437. However, the percentage of all banks parring checks remained at 94 percent. A jump of 6,000 in the number of banks accounted for the change in number of nonpar banks. The number of banks peaked in 1921 at 30,419.

An interesting incident during the 1920s relating to par banks was told to the author by an officer of the Federal Reserve Bank of Dallas who was assigned the job of presenting checks over the counter to nonpar banks in an effort to force them to remit at par. Checks presented in person over the counter of the drawee bank, by law, had to be paid at par. As my friend walked into a bank early in the morning, he presented the bundle of checks drawn on the bank and asked for payment. Each bank was entitled to examine each check and ascertain that funds were available to pay for it. Payment had to be made that day but not immediately. The teller of the bank said, "This will take a while. Have a seat in the lobby." A few minutes later, the teller tossed a one-dollar bill tied in a knot over the teller's cage to my friend with the comment "Here's one of them." This procedure continued throughout the day, and needless to say, the Fed looked for other techniques to accomplish its purpose.

OPERATIONS DURING THE DECADE OF THE 1920S

Check clearing operations at the Fed banks showed a steady growth throughout the decade. In 1920 the 12 banks processed 504,198,000 checks, and by 1930 the volume had grown to 904,975,000. During the same period the number of bills offered for discount by member banks dropped from 1,190,000 to 996,000. The number of pieces of currency handled more than doubled from 1,085,459,000 to 2,441,989,000. The volume of coin handled also nearly doubled. Despite this growth in volume of several operations, the number of employees dropped from more than 12,000 to just under 10,000. All of the Fed banks were able to show a profit — or more appropriately, net earnings — during the decade, but by 1930 the Kansas City and San Francisco banks dropped to a negative position. Total earnings for the 12 banks were $150 million in 1920 and $8 million in 1930. A sharp drop in bills discounted and lower earnings on investments contributed to the decline in earnings.

LEGISLATION

Numerous modifications were made to the Federal Reserve Act during the 1920s. Some were minor such as prohibiting the use of the words "federal," "reserve" and "United States" in the title of corporations. More significant ones included

- changing the number of appointive members of the Federal Reserve Board from five to six;
- eliminating the requirement that two members of the board have banking experience;
- making paper from the Federal Intermediate Credit Banks eligible for discount;
- limiting the expenditure for a Federal Reserve Bank branch building to $250,000.

The McFadden Act, passed February 25, 1927, amended Section 4 of the Federal Reserve Act, giving the Federal Reserve Board authority to order the closing of any branch of a Federal Reserve bank, and extended the charter of Federal Reserve banks from 20 years to "indeterminate." Thus, they could be terminated only by an act of Congress.

Not involving the act but important to the system was the upholding of the legal right of the Fed banks to demand payment of checks at par. Several states passed legislation making nonpar payment legal, but the courts refused to uphold the law and referred to the Federal Reserve Act as prevailing.

Chapter 5
A Decade of Change (1930–1939)

Breadlines, bankruptcies, unemployment, labor unrest, broken dreams and the fruition of the seeds of war were all a part of the decade of the 1930s. Hitler and Mussolini came to power in Europe. The military capability of the United States and Britain was at its lowest point in years. Britain's prime minister, Neville Chamberlain, returning from a visit to Munich, proclaimed "peace in our time," a hope that was shattered within months by Hitler's march into Czechoslovakia.

Financial markets were in shambles. More than 9,000 banks failed during the years 1930 to 1933. Prices fell like rocks rolling down a mountain. The price of wheat dropped to $.50 a bushel, cotton to $.06 a pound; break was 7 cents a loaf, oranges 30 cents a dozen and a farm laborer could be hired for $1.15 a day. The author in his first year of college in 1935 bought dinner—meat, two vegetables, salad, drink and dessert—for $.25. A man with a master's degree in education accepted the job of teaching a small country school (grades 1 through 8) for $60 a month—and was glad to get it.

Unemployment hit 25 percent. Men walked the streets looking for any kind of a job. The United Auto Workers union showed their muscle and shut down many auto plants demanding more pay. It was the day of the NRA, the WPA, the CCC and a host of other alphabet programs. With the election of Franklin Roosevelt as president in 1932, the "New Deal" was born. It was the decade of the big bands and Bing Crosby. Fred Astaire and Ginger Rogers danced their way into the hearts of America through wonderful movies.

The decade culminated in the declaration of war in Europe and the unofficial support of the Allies by the United States. It was inevitable that the United States would become involved in the war, but until the attack on Pearl Harbor in December 1941, the American people were only lukewarm toward involvement in "other people's" war. Except for the early years of our republic and the decade of the 1860s, the decade of the 1930s saw more changes in government, in banking, in economic theories and in the attitudes of people than in any other period of our history.

WHERE WAS THE FED?

Much criticism has been heaped on the Fed for not taking action during the period from 1928 to 1939. Some of the criticism is warranted, but it should be pointed out that influencing the business cycle was not one of the original purposes of the Fed. Rather it was supposed to stabilize the currency and provide a source of credit to facilitate the marketing of goods. There had been limited experience during the 1920s in using open market transactions to modify shifts in gold and swings in interest rates, but the idea of using the Fed to reduce swings in the business cycle was an idea yet to be accepted as a role for the Fed.

Second, opinions varied as to the impact of various actions that might have been taken. The ratio of the Fed's holding of securities to the nation's GNP was less than 1 percent in 1930 and just over 2 percent in 1940. By contrast, the ratio in 1980 was nearly 5 percent (further details in the Appendix). Whether or not this is a significant difference, it does suggest that the Fed's action in the open market of securities would have had a smaller impact on the economy. To the Fed's credit the discount rate was reduced — quite sharply percentagewise — as the economy faltered.

Perhaps another factor is more important. As the Depression deepened, no one wanted to borrow money. All during the period member banks held excess reserves, and to quote an expression that became popular later, making more credit available when no one wanted it was like "pushing on a string."

LOOKING BACK

A review of the 1930s must of necessity begin with the stock market crash of October 28-29, 1929. This cataclysmic event was like a boulder roaring down the mountainside of our economic and business workplace. Samuel Eliot Morrison, in his book *The Oxford History of the American People,* points out how greatly the importance of developing trends was underestimated.

> No nation ever faced a business decline more optimistically than America did this one. Nobody highly placed in government or finance admitted the existence of a depression for six months or more after the crash. Everyone wanted to stop the decline, but nobody knew how. Incantation was the favorite method for the first six months.... [But] more than talk was needed to swell the shrunken gourd and plump the shriveled shell.

It is small wonder that the men at the Fed were hesitant to take strong action. After all, they were not even sure they should do anything. The governor of the Federal Reserve Bank of Philadelphia, George W. Norris, stated in 1930, "Unemployment and the decline in prices have just about run their course and the foundations for business revival have already been laid." Many Fed officials saw the Depression as the inevitable result of the excesses of the 1920s. With the death of Benjamin Strong in 1928, the

Federal Reserve System drifted with the "stream" lacking any strong leadership.

The structure of the nation's banking industry was virtually falling apart. The acceleration in bank failures has been mentioned. In addition, loans dropped from $36.1 billion in 1930 to $15.7 billion in 1934. Deposits shrank from $49.4 billion to $36.8 billion. Runs on banks created panic in many communities as depositors rushed to get cash.

HOW TO HANDLE A RUN ON YOUR BANK

A "run" on a bank is a terrible thing to behold. In the days of no deposit insurance, if there was a question about the solvency of a bank, depositors ran to the bank to withdraw their money. No bank ever carries enough cash in its vault to pay off all depositors at the same time. The depositors' money is loaned out or invested. Sometimes a bank might have an amount of cash equal to 20 or 25 percent of the depositors' money, but often it is less as the bank endeavors to make maximum use of its resources (largely the depositors' money).

So if you are a depositor and you hear a rumor that your bank is weak and might close its doors, you "run" to the bank to get your money before the other depositors get theirs, and the bank runs out of money. If enough of your fellow depositors have the same idea, the bank will soon run out of cash and will not be able to pay its depositors. In effect, it will have to close its doors even though it might have good loans and sound investments. The fact that they cannot be quickly liquidated and turned into cash may force the bank to close. It does not take a lot of imagination to see how a rumor can get started and a "run" on a bank accelerate. Also, if one bank in a community fails, depositors are likely to assume that other banks in the town are weak, and a run will be started on all banks.

Obviously, confidence in a bank is the key to stopping a run. Once depositors see that they can get their money, they are likely to leave it in the bank. Of course, the bank must have the resources to project that confidence, and the best way is to pay off the first few depositors that ask for their money. An interesting case involved the Frost National Bank in San Antonio, Texas, during the upheaval in the industry during the 1930s. The Frost Bank was a sound bank and in no danger of closing, but another bank in the city experienced a run and was forced to close. Many banks in the nation had closed, and depositors were understandably jittery about their deposits. This was enough to start a run on the Frost Bank. Many stories about how it was handled have persisted in the years that followed.

Here is the true story as told to the author by Tom Frost, chairman of the board of the bank in 1989. As soon as the run started, all tellers were told to pay out any requested deposits *without comment*. Arrangements were quickly made with the local Fed to obtain more currency if needed. As the line of waiting depositors stretched around the block and the time of regular closing hours approached, Mr. Frost (Tom's great uncle) announced to those standing in line that the bank would remain open until all had been waited on. This act of confidence and the fact that those who had requested their deposits were getting them broke the run, and depositors gradually changed their minds and left their deposits with the bank.

One additional point: The tellers were asked to stack their currency in plain view of the customers as they came for their deposits. Cooperation among the community's banks worked out that evening prevented further runs on the banks in San Antonio, at least for the time. The key? Establish confidence among depositors.

WHAT ACTION SHOULD THE FED HAVE TAKEN?

Hindsight is always 20-20, and viewed from the 1990s it seems incomprehensible that the Fed did not take some aggressive action to stimulate the economy. But as pointed out, there was lack of leadership and lack of knowledge as to the appropriate action. In 1930 Roy Young, chairman of the Federal Reserve Board, resigned, and President Hoover appointed Eugene Meyer, a New York banker, to replace him. Lacking any other program that the board felt was within their authority, they reverted to the "real bills" theory. This meant that if member banks did not discount paper, nothing happened. And member banks were not in any frame of mind to discount paper. They already held excess reserves, and loan demand was almost nonexistent.

President Hoover was convinced that positive action was imperative. But his urging had little effect on the board. Board member Adolph Miller was the lone dissenter, and he urged the board to help get the economy moving. Addressing the Open Market Committee, he said, "Money is sleeping, and it is conceivable that a part of a constructive program is to wake it up and make it do something." Lacking accurate indicators of the state of the economy and short of leadership, the board did nothing. A New Jersey banker telegraphed President Hoover, urging him to convince the Fed to take strong action. Hoover replied, "I am afraid that I cannot run the Federal Reserve banks as much as you and I might like to have it that way." Hoover did write Chairman Meyer concerning the board's apparent concern over the condition of foreign central banks, especially the Bank of England, and little regard for problems at home. Meyer replied that the Fed was "working on the problem."

In 1931 the Fed purchased $88 million of U.S. government securities and dropped the discount rate another ½ point to 2 percent. But in early 1932 it sold nearly that much in securities and raised the discount rate 1½ points. In April of 1932 purchases of government securities were resumed, adding a billion by the end of the year. However, the discount rate was kept at 3½ until June of 1933 when it was dropped half a point. It was not until 1934 that it was moved to 2 percent, a level that was maintained until late 1937 when it was lowered another half point. Then in September 1939 it was lowered further to 1 percent (see Appendix for discount rates, 1914-1989).

Whether more aggressive action by the Fed to stimulate the economy would have been helpful is open to debate. If it had occurred earlier, it would have sent a message to the nation that it was trying to help ease the cost of credit. But by 1931 the nation's economy as well as that of most foreign nations was in a precipitous downturn. By 1930 the Fed's index of manufacturing had dropped 17 percent from its peak in 1929. It fell another 21 percent by 1931. The index of wholesale prices was 25 percent below its peak in 1928 and dropping steadily. It is reported that Henry Ford said, "These are the best of times" and denied that there was depression at all. But few industrialists or bankers would have agreed.

Lacking the necessary tools and saddled with timid leadership, the Fed simply staggered along until major changes were made in the statutes and in the directed role of this uncoordinated organization.

ROOSEVELT ELECTED PRESIDENT

Franklin Delano Roosevelt, campaigning on, among other issues, "a balanced budget," swept into office in the November 1932 presidential election. Between the November election and inauguration day, March 4, 1933, even with urgent requests from lame-duck President Hoover, the Fed did nothing. Aware of the fragile nature of the nation's banking structure, Hoover repeatedly requested the Fed board to "do something." On February 22, 1933, Hoover told the board, "I wish to leave no stone unturned for constructive action." All of the board members joined in this reply: "At the moment the Board does not desire to make any specific proposals for additional measures or authority, but will continue to give all aspects of the situation its most careful consideration." Just two days before the inauguration, Hoover proposed involving the Trading with the Enemy Act and declaring a bank holiday and a guarantee of bank deposits. President-elect Roosevelt is reported to have said it was OK with him, but he did not lend his support and neither did the Federal Reserve Board.

Thus, it remained for the new president to take positive action, and on Monday, March 6, 1933, acting under the power of the Trading with the Enemy Act of October 6, 1917, amended September 24, 1918, he issued a proclamation closing all the banks in the nation.

THE CRISIS HAD BEEN BUILDING

Closing of the banks came as no surprise to the financial community. Conditions had been going from bad to worse for some time. The table on the next page illustrates this catastrophic trend.

The significance and the timing of events during this hectic period are best shown by an excerpt from the Board's Annual Report for 1933. It is quite detailed but because of its importance is quoted in some length.

The development of the banking crisis was accompanied by a sharp increase in money rates. In the New York money market, rates on bankers'

Number of Banks and Total Assets for Selected Years

Year	Member Banks of Federal Reserve System				Nonmember Banks	
	National Banks		State Member Banks			
	Number	Assets (mil. $)	Number	Assets (mil. $)	Number	Assets (mil. $)
1915	7,597	$11,790	17	$ 97	19,776	$12,219
1920	8,024	23,267	1,374	10,351	20,893	13,891
1929	7,530	27,260	1,177	18,194	16,263	16,198
1930	7,247	28,828	1,068	18,521	15,364	16,776
1931	6,800	27,430	982	17,406	13,872	14,181
1932	6,145	22,318	835	13,538	11,754	10,448
1933	4,897	20,813	709	12,226	8,601	7,472
1934	5,417	23,854	958	13,529	8,973	7,595
1935	5,425	26,009	985	14,710	9,078	8,186
1940	5,164	36,816	1,234	21,030	8,136	9,958

Source: U.S. Department of Commerce, Historical Statistics of the United States, Colonial Times to 1970.

acceptances, which were sold in large quantities by banks and dealers, rose from the low level of one-fourth of one percent early in February (1933) to as high as 3 and three-eighths percent in the week ending March 4. The official rate for new call loans on stock-market collateral rose from a nominal level of 1 to 4 percent, with outside bids as high as 5 and 6 percent on March 3. Commercial paper rates also advanced. In line with the general rise in money rates and in order to combat both domestic and foreign withdrawals of funds from the banks, the Federal Reserve Bank of New York on March 3 raised its rediscount rate from 2 and one-half to 3 and one-half percent and effective March 4 the Federal Reserve Bank of Chicago made a similar change in its rate.

Banking authorities in different states had been obliged to adopt emergency measures from the beginning of February. On February 4 a 1-day holiday was declared in Louisiana to permit the New Orleans banks to raise funds to make adjustments necessary to enable them to continue to meet their obligations. On February 4 a 4-day banking holiday was declared in Michigan to enable the banks in Detroit to make similar arrangements and to protect in the interim, as stated in the Governor's proclamation, "for equal safeguarding without preference of the rights of all depositors." Satisfactory settlement of the difficulties was not reached, however, and the holiday was extended.

While the Michigan holiday arrested withdrawals of deposits from banks in that state, outside Michigan there was an increase in the movement of funds from weaker to stronger banks and in currency withdrawals. Funds were withdrawn from banks in other states to send to Michigan or to meet payments that would otherwise have been met from deposits in Michigan banks. Developments of this nature were partly responsible for the rapid spread of the bank holiday movement among other states. On February 25, the Governor of Maryland declared a bank holiday, chiefly on account of conditions in Baltimore, and at about the same time restrictions were authorized on withdrawals of bank deposits in Indiana, Arkansas and

Ohio. In a number of states new laws were passed to provide for safe-guarding bank deposits or for readjusting the liabilities of banks without establishing receivership. With a view to enabling the banking situation in any particular state to be handled as a whole, a joint resolution was adopted on February 25 by the Congress of the United States authorizing the Comptroller of the Currency to exercise with respect to national banks such powers as state officials might have with respect to state banks.

On March 1 Alabama, Kentucky, Tennessee and Nevada declared bank holidays, and similar action was taken by 6 other states on March 2 and 7 [and] others on March 3. On the morning of March 4, the Governor of the state of New York issued a proclamation declaring that day, which was a Saturday, and the following Monday to be bank holidays. Similar action was taken in Illinois, Massachusetts, New Jersey, Pennsylvania and else-where.

The Bank Holiday, March 4–12 — Declaration of holidays in the various states had by March 4 closed or placed under restrictions practically all banks in the country. Federal Reserve banks also observed state holidays and closed on March 4. All leading exchanges ceased operation and business generally was at a standstill. On March 6 the President issued a proclamation declaring a nation-wide bank holiday to continue through the 4 days ending March 9. An important purpose of the action was to attack the problem of bank failures comprehensively by reviewing at one time the condition of all banks and reopening only such banks as could meet all the demands upon them. This procedure was intended both to assure more equitable treatment between depositors and those who were not, and to restore confidence in the banking situation as a whole.

The President's proclamation ... declared that there had been heavy and unwarranted withdrawals of gold and currency and extensive specu-lative activity in foreign exchanges, which had created a national emer-gency, and the bank holiday was ordered to prevent a continuation of such hoarding and speculation and to permit the application of appropriate measures for protecting the interest of all bank depositors, and other per-sons dependent on the banks. During the holiday banks were not to pay out any coin, bullion, or currency or to transact any other banking business whatsoever, except as might be permitted by the Secretary of the Treasury. The Secretary of the Treasury was authorized to permit banks to perform any or all functions, to require or permit the issuance of clear-ing house certificates, and to authorize special trust accounts for receipt of new deposits.

At the same time the President called a special session of Congress to meet on March 9 to enact such legislation as might be needed for the reopening of banks. In the interim, attention was devoted not only to devising measures for reopening banks but also to effecting arrangements for meeting during the holiday certain essential payments. The Secretary of the Treasury distributed through the Federal Reserve Banks a series of regulations permitting specified types of transactions, and a number of statements interpreting these regulations.

Some of the more important Treasury regulations were as follows: banks were permitted to perform in a limited manner specified banking functions, such as to make change, complete settlements not involving payment of currency, allow access to safety-deposit boxes, deliver documents for safekeeping, and transact certain fiduciary business. They were also given permission to perform functions essential to provide the community with food, medicine, and other necessities of life, for relief of distress, for payment of usual salaries and wages, and for similar purposes.... These regulations contained provisions that in the exercise of these powers no bank should pay out any gold or gold certificates, and that banks should not permit withdrawals of currency for purposes of hoarding.

On March 7, Federal Reserve Banks were authorized to supply currency, extend credit, and make transfers required by member banks in exercising the powers granted to them, provided that the member banks should inform the Federal Reserve Banks of the amounts of currency held and the circumstances giving rise to need for more currency and should deliver to the Reserve bank all gold and gold certificates held.

The Emergency Banking Act — On March 9, 1933, Congress assembled in special session and received a message from the President asking for legislation giving to the executive branch of the Government control over banks for the protection of depositors; authority to open such banks as have already been ascertained to be in a sound condition and other such banks as rapidly as possible; and authority to reorganize and reopen such banks as may be found to require reorganization to put them on a sound basis.

On the same day the legislation requested was passed by Congress and signed by the President.

The *Congressional Record* for that day makes interesting reading. There was little question but that the requested legislation would be passed. But the comments by members of Congress — especially Senators — gave further evidence of the seriousness of the emergency. Senator Huey P. Long (D–LA) wanted to amend the bill to be sure that state banks would be given proper attention. It was even suggested that all state banks automatically be made members of the Federal Reserve System. The proposed amendment was changed to say "with their permission," but the amendment was defeated.

Perhaps the most significant comments came from several senators including Carter Glass (D–VA) and Senator Arthur H. Vandenburg (R–MI) to the effect that if it were not for the seriousness of the situation, they would not vote for the bill. It was moving too fast. Several senators had not even read the bill. The Senate Banking Committee met to consider the bill and reported back to the Senate within an hour. Several senators raised questions about the meaning of various sections but added that they would support the bill because of the urgent need to act. The president's proclamation closing the banks expired at midnight, and if Congress did not make a positive move, it was likely that chaos would break out as the nation floundered in an effort to break the psychology of despair. At 7:20 P.M., Thursday, March 9, 1933, the Senate voted on the proposed bill without amendments with 73 yeas, 7 nays and 15 not voting. The House had already passed the identical bill with a minimum of discussion. The Senate went into recess for 30 minutes so the presiding officer could sign the bill and forward it to the president. The Senate adjourned at 7:50 P.M. and went home to get some rest. It had given the president broad powers, and every senator prayed he would use it wisely.

Now back to the Board's Annual Report:

> **Program for reopening banks**—After the passage of the Emergency Banking Act on March 9, the President issued a proclamation indefinitely extending the bank holiday and on March 10 by executive order he conferred upon the Secretary of the Treasury power to license members of the Federal Reserve System found to be in satisfactory condition to conduct a usual banking business with exception as to the paying out of gold and the furnishing of currency for hoarding. A like power was granted to the banking authorities of the various states with respect to banks outside of the Federal Reserve System. The Federal Reserve banks were designated in the executive order to act as agents of the Secretary of the Treasury for the receiving of applications and the issuance of licenses in his behalf and upon his instructions.
>
> On Saturday, March 11, the Reserve banks were authorized by the Treasury to reopen on the following Monday for the performance of all usual banking functions, except as to the paying out of gold and the furnishing of currency for hoarding. On the same date it was announced that on March 13 banks in the 12 Federal Reserve cities would be reopened, on March 14 banks in approximately 250 other cities having reorganized clearing houses, and on March 15 banks in other places. On Sunday evening, March 12, the President made a statement by radio in which he gave an account of what had been done during the crisis, outlined the program on which banks were to be reopened, gave assurance that banks reopened would take care of all needs and indicated that the success of the whole program was dependent upon the cooperation of the public.

Also included in the Emergency Act was a provision permitting banks to issue new stock, and such stock would not be subject to double liability as all previous bank stock had been for years. (A stockholder was liable for an amount equal to twice the value of the stock he held.) The elimination of double liability was made permanent May 25, 1938, by an amendment to Section 13(b) of the Federal Reserve Act, a section that was repealed effective August 21, 1959, but the elimination of double liability remains permanent.

A lot of detail. But those were "scary" times. Some historians have speculated that the country was near anarchy. But quick, definite and positive action and the quiet, confident voice of the new president as he said to the nation via radio, "We have nothing to fear but fear itself," began the steps back to a confident frame of mind. His actions can be debated and the results questioned, but without a doubt, he gave a spark that shifted the nation from despair to "we may make it."

With this traumatic event that shook the very foundations of the nation's economy, a new era for the Fed was born, and during the next eventful years, legislation would change the face and the stated purpose of the Federal Reserve System.

A NEW FACE AT THE FED

Even before Roosevelt was inaugurated, his proposed staff, often referred to as the brain trust, was making plans and contacting persons to be a part of the new administration. Out in Utah was a banker who was ahead of his time. Marriner Eccles had never heard of the English economist Lord Maynard Keynes, but his philosophy could have been taken right out of Keynes's book. Eccles said the depression was the result of inept leadership, both political and financial. He argued that the problem was not excessive federal spending but too little government spending to stimulate the economy. Eccles did not, however, suggest a perpetual deficit but said that in times of prosperity, the deficit should be reduced (a thought with which Keynes would have agreed).

Eugene Meyer resigned from the board shortly after Roosevelt took office. Eugene R. Black, governor of the Atlanta Fed was chosen by Roosevelt as his replacement. However, Black accepted the position on a temporary basis for three months. Three months grew into 15 as he attempted to help bring order out of chaos in the banking community. In the meantime, Marriner Eccles had agreed to come to Washington as special assistant to Secretary of the Treasury Henry Morgenthau, Jr. When Governor Black returned to his post as governor of the Atlanta Fed, which he said was the "best job in the world," Morgenthau recommended Eccles for the job. Impressed by Eccles's ideas for improving the Fed and for getting the country back on its economic feet, Roosevelt quickly agreed. However, Eccles said he would like the job only if fundamental changes were made in the system.

Eccles had some very definite ideas about what the Fed should do. Most importantly he believed that control and power to initiate and to execute monetary policy must be centered in a strong Federal Reserve Board. He presented these ideas to President Roosevelt in a three-page memo and a two-hour discussion as he was being considered for the post of chairman of the Federal Reserve Board.

President Roosevelt agreed to support Eccles in his effort to bring about changes in the system. During the next 10 months Governor Eccles learned a great deal about the politics of Washington. Firm in his conviction as to what needed to be done, he moved quickly — and not too diplomatically — to push his ideas through the halls of Congress. One of his first "mistakes" was to offend Senator Carter Glass (D–VA). Senator Glass was a prime mover in writing the original Federal Reserve Act and seeing it successfully pushed through Congress. It was his "baby," and he did not like the idea of centralizing control in the board. More importantly he wanted to be consulted about any proposed changes in the system. All the old fears that surrounded the original act came to light. Control should not be given to bankers, and it should never be centered in Washington. If it is tied too closely to the president, it will be a political football.

Eccles countered this argument by saying, "The Fed is not to act as the

Marriner C. Eccles, chairman of the Board of Governors, Federal Reserve System, November 15, 1934–January 31, 1948. A major player in reorganizing the system under the Banking Act of 1935. Courtesy Board of Governors of Federal Reserve System.

captive of any administration but in the public interest." It must be "publicly controlled" — by Congress's oversight and its own sense of the general public's needs — "rather than governmentally controlled" by the president's presumably more narrow interests.

Another source of opposition to a strong centrally controlled system was the emerging "monetarist" theory. This theory said the only safe way for the system to operate was by fixed formulas that left no room for discretion or judgment, a theory that would persist for at least another 50 years. It would be argued vehemently in the press, in the halls and classrooms of universities and in Congress. Eccles's principal reply was: "The fatal objection to automatic controls is that the combination of factors that bring about a business situation is never the same. Each new business situation with which we are confronted is in a large and significant measure a situation we have never confronted and will never confront again."

Eventually, Eccles achieved most of what he wanted. The Banking Act of 1933 was passed May 12, 1933, and the Banking Act of 1935, passed August 23, 1935, materially changed the Federal Reserve System. A whole array of duties were given to the Fed, and its internal organization would hardly be recognized by the original framers of the Federal Reserve Act. Here is a list of the major bills impacting on the Fed. Some will be discussed in more detail because of their importance.

- Creation of the Reconstruction Finance Corporation, January 22, 1932: The Corporation was authorized to make loans to corporations having difficulty. It was quite helpful for most of the 1930s. It could have been more helpful in 1932 and 1933 if Congress had not required it to publish the names of banks needing aid. No bank wanted to be on the list.
- Glass-Steagall Act of February 27, 1932: gave Fed banks authority to use their own securities as collateral against Federal Reserve notes until March 3, 1933. Also added sections 10(a) and 10(b) to Federal Reserve Act which authorized Fed banks to make loans to member banks on any collateral satisfactory to the Reserve bank.
- Emergency Relief and Construction Act of July 21, 1932: amended Section 13 of Federal Reserve Act authorizing Fed banks to make loans to individuals, partnerships and corporations if they could not obtain credit elsewhere. The first loan was made on August 4, 1932.
- Banking Act of 1933 enacted June 16, 1933: a very broad act, and its provisions will be discussed later.
- The Emergency Banking Act of March 9, 1933 (mentioned earlier): gave to the executive branch of the government control over banks for the protection of depositors; authority to forthwith open such banks as have already been ascertained to be in sound condition and other such banks as rapidly as possible; and authority to reorganize and reopen such banks as may be found to require reorganization to put them on a sound basis. The act also authorized banks to issue preferred stock and such stock to be without double liability. (Nationwide elimination of this feature of bank stock was finally achieved through an amendment to Section 13(b) of the Federal Reserve Act, which permitted FDIC to waive any claim which it might have for double liability against stockholders of a failed bank. This was necessary because the constitution of some states required double liability and it would take several years before all states could change their constitutions.)
- Securities and Exchange Act of June 6, 1934: gave the board control over margin requirements on security transactions.

- Gold Reserve Act of June 30, 1934: gave title to all gold held by Reserve banks to the U.S. Treasury, and transfer was made at a value of $20.67 per ounce. On January 31, 1934, by executive order, the president raised the price to $35 per ounce. This reduced the gold content of the dollar from 25.8 grains of nine-tenths fine to 15 and five twenty-firsts fine.
- Silver Purchase Act of 1934: while not directly impacting on the Federal Reserve System, it was an important part of the coinage program. It declared that it was the policy of the United States that the proportion of silver to gold in metallic monetary stock be increased to one-fourth silver.
- Banking Act of 1935 approved August 23, 1935: a major legislation affecting the Federal Reserve System.

Two acts, the Banking Act of 1933 and the Banking Act of 1935, are the heart of changes made in the banking structure during the 1930s. Let's look at each one.

THE BANKING ACT OF 1933

This act in one sense followed up on the Emergency Banking Act passed by the Congress on March 9, 1933. The act did the following:

- Gave the Federal Reserve Board authority to regulate the volume of loans made by member banks on securities. The purpose was to limit speculation in securities.
- Required the board to supervise foreign relations of Federal Reserve Banks.
- Liberalized the rules for member banks to establish branches, primarily eliminating or reducing the geographic limits previously imposed.
- Forbade member banks from dealing in securities and required them to divorce themselves from affiliates dealing in securities.
- Forbade member banks' paying interest on demand deposits. Many analysts believed that competition for deposits, including the paying of interest on them, was a major cause of bank failures. In later years, this theory would be debated and largely dismissed as inaccurate. In fact, the Financial Institutions Deregulation and Monetary Control Act of 1980 gave banks authority to pay interest on demand deposits under certain restrictions.
- Gave the board authority to regulate the interest paid on time and saving deposits in member banks.
- Provided insurance of bank deposits up to $2,500 on a temporary basis. Member banks were required to participate, and nonmember banks could by meeting certain requirements.
- Required the Federal Reserve Banks to provide capital for the Federal Deposit Insurance Corporation in the amount of half their (the Reserve banks') surplus.

- Holding company affiliates which owned bank stock were required to get board approval before voting such stock.
- Broadened the scope of the Clayton Act, requiring approval of the board for any interlocking directorships.

RESERVES FOR FEDS SUSPENDED

As the demand for currency and hoarding of gold continued, the Reserve banks found their reserve dropping to near the 40 percent requirement. On March 3, 1933, as an emergency measure and under authority of Section 11(c) of the Federal Reserve Act, the Federal Reserve Board suspended the reserve requirement for 30 days. A return flow of gold and other events reversed the situation, and the suspension was allowed to expire without ever being utilized.

THE BANKING ACT OF 1935

This was a "biggie"! This act made more changes in the Federal Reserve system than had been made in the previous 20 years or would be made in the next 55. The Depository Institutions Deregulations and Monetary Control Act of 1980 came close, but the 1935 act, approved August 20, 1935, completely changed the basic organization, the power structure and the stated purpose of the system. Here are the most important provisions.

- Amended Section 10 of the Federal Reserve Act, changing the name of the Federal Reserve Board to the Board of Governors of the Federal Reserve System; changing the title of Governor to Chairman; the title of Vice Governor to Vice Chairman and set the term of the chairman at four years.
- The number of governors was set at seven, and all were to be appointed by the president with the advice and consent of the Senate. The comptroller of the currency and the secretary of treasury were dropped completely from the board. The term of office of a governor was set at 14 years, and they could not be reappointed after completing a full term.
- Amended Section 4 of the Federal Reserve Act, eliminating the title Governor and naming the head of each Federal Reserve bank as President. Each president and first vice president would be elected by the board of directors of the Fed Bank but with the approval of the Board of Governors. The president's term would be five years. This in effect centered power in the Board of Governors. The president of the Fed Bank would be the chief operating officer, and the position of Federal Reserve agent at the Fed banks would become a nonsalaried position with the chairman of the board of directors carrying out those duties mostly through designated employees of the bank.
- Further power was centered in the board by constituting the committee to make open market purchases and sales as the Federal

Open Market Committee, composed of the seven governors and five presidents of the Reserve banks. The Reserve bank presidents were to serve on a rotating basis. All open market transactions were to be made through this committee, which soon became known by the initials FOMC. All Reserve banks were required to participate in the transactions of the FOMC.

- Gave the board authority to change member bank reserve requirements to twice the current rate but not lower than the rate on the day of this act.
- Removed from the Federal Reserve Act definitions of "time" and "demand" deposits, and gave authority to the board to make such definitions.
- Made the insurance of deposits by FDIC permanent with the amount of $5,000 per depositor.
- Required nonmember insured banks to follow the same restrictions on payment of interest on demand deposits and regulation of rates on time and saving deposits as was required of member banks, definitions of terms to be the same as for member banks.

Other changes involved modification of restrictions on loans by member banks on real estate.

Struggling to recover, the nation's economy fought to find its way in an environment that was strange and bewildering. Confidence had returned, and few doubted that we were on our way to something better. Just which road to travel and how fast to go were questions yet to be answered. Bank failures were behind us, at least for the time being. Deposit insurance added to the confidence in reopened or reorganized banks. Banks were drowning in liquidity. Excess member bank reserve balances leaped from $35 million in January 1932 to $363 million by June 1933 and to $3 billion in January 1936. At the end of the decade they were over $6.6 billion dollars.

The newly constituted Board of Governors of the Federal Reserve System attempted to sop up excess reserves and boosted reserve requirements three times.

Even though commercial borrowers could borrow at an interest rate of 2 to 3 percent, many were reluctant to incur debt with the vivid memory of the past few years still fresh in their minds. Also, lenders were overly cautious for the same reason.

The business climate had improved, yet the economy struggled to move forward. Unemployment remained in double-digit figures until 1941 when it dropped to 9.9 percent. The index of manufacturing rose from the bottom of 12 in 1932 quickly to 18 in 1935, but struggled to gain a few more points in the next five years. Average hourly earnings in manufacturing remained near the 1929 level throughout the decade. They dropped from $.58 to $.49 but quickly recovered and by 1939 were at $.72. It remained for World War II to bring the economy up to full speed. When it did, it was fantastic. Production of war materiel was at an unbelievable rate.

Member Bank Reserve Requirements
June 21, 1917–December 31, 1941
(percent of deposits)

Class of deposit and bank location	June 21 1917 to Aug. 15 1936	Aug. 16 1936 to Feb. 28 1937	Mar. 1 1937 to Apr. 30 1937	May 1 1937 to Apr. 15 1938	Apr. 16 1938 to Oct. 31 1941	Nov. 1 1941 to Dec. 31 1941
On net demand deposits:						
Central Res. City	13	19½	22¾	26	22¾	26
Reserve city	10	15	17½	20	17½	20
Country	7	10½	12¼	14	12	14
Time deposits (all)	3	4½	5¼	6	5	6

WHAT FED POLICY NOW?

During the period after the passage of the Banking Act of 1935 till into the 1950s the major policy question at the Fed was "How do we let interest rates rise and prevent a repeat of the inflation of the 1920s?" The Treasury was adamant that rates stay low to keep the cost of the war as low as possible. The Fed had no choice but to agree that rates would stay low during the war. After the war was another story that we will discuss later.

Eccles continued to build his power structure both within the system and within the administration. President Roosevelt was a confident and a strong supporter although he sided with the Treasury on interest rates. Eccles and the president, as a team, made rapid progress in promoting a stimulative policy at the Fed and in the administration. The president was anxious to get the economy back on its feet and subscribed to the theory of strong government involvement, heavy deficit spending and any activity that would increase business activity and incomes. Eccles agreed. Eccles later was to argue for reducing the deficit when the economy was strong.

By 1936 the Fed, including Eccles, sensed that the large government spending was going to result in another inflationary period. Eccles pushed hard for raising interest rates. Secretary of the Treasury Henry Morgenthau, Jr., was adamant that the cost of financing the government must be kept low. When the Fed raised reserve requirements, Morgenthau countered with his own plan called the Treasury Stabilization Fund, which sold short-term bills and used the money to buy gold. This in effect kept foreign gold out of the banking system, thus keeping interest rates low. His plan worked for several months, and only after the president sided with Morgenthau did Eccles capitulate and agree that the Fed would keep "an orderly market" (for the Treasury this meant low interest rates) for Treasury securities. The battle on interest rates went on until war broke out, and then it was a question of national defense, and the Fed agreed to "peg" the price of Treasury issues, thus effectively freezing rates very low.

President Franklin D. Roosevelt (center) at the dedication of the new building for the Board of Governors of the Federal Reserve System, October 20, 1937. Others in picture not identified. Courtesy Board of Governors of Federal Reserve System.

Eccles and Morgenthau disagreed on another point—the supervision of commercial banks. Eccles did not like the divided examination structure—the comptroller of the currency examined national banks, the Federal Deposit Insurance Corporation (FDIC) examined insured nonmember banks and the Fed examined state member insured banks. Eccles called it a "crazy quilt that made for inefficiency, waste and above all, bad banking." Morgenthau saw this as an attempt to grab power, and he fought against any change. This question would be debated and argued for the next 50 years with no solution. Better coordination was achieved, but the three agencies still are involved in the examination of banks.

FED GETS A NEW HOME

A milestone in the history of the Fed occurred in 1937 when the Board of Governors moved out of the Treasury Building into new quarters constructed specifically for the system. In dedicating the building, President Roosevelt pointed out that if changes in banking laws had been made in the 1920s, the Fed would have been in a far better position to moderate the forces that brought about the Great Depression. He stated that the act has concentrated the Fed's power to a greater degree than before in a single body, so that it can be used properly and effectively in accordance with the changing needs of the country.

Separate quarters for the board finally reduced its dependence on the Treasury. As long as it was a "tenant" in the Treasury's building, it was difficult to exercise adequate independence. The physical separation did, however, raise another problem — that of communications. Instead of "going down the hall" to confer, it was necessary to set up "appointments." The problem was soon resolved, at least in part, by arranging weekly luncheon meetings between Eccles and Morgenthau. Later, Roosevelt established a presidential advisory council composed of the chairman of the Advisory Council on Natural Resources, the Fed chairman and the secretary of the treasury. The council ceased to function after war broke out, but it was a forerunner of similar arrangements that came into being later. With the United States' entry into the war, all hands devoted their entire energy to winning the war. The Fed vowed to make available whatever funds were needed and to keep interest rates low.

MEANWHILE IN THE BACK ROOMS OF THE FEDS

Monetary policy and a struggle with interest rates and the politics of Washington occupied the time and effort of Fed personnel in Washington and the senior officers of the Fed banks. But in the "work areas" of the 12 Fed banks it was check clearing, paying out and receiving coins and currency, sorting currency and performing operations as fiscal agent of the U.S. Treasury.

From 1931 to 1940 the volume of checks handled by the 12 Fed banks jumped from a daily average of 2,771,200 to 3,796,012 — an increase of 37 percent. As might be expected, the New York Fed handled nearly 20 percent of the total volume. With the computers of the 1990s this would be a light load, but in the 1930s checks were hand-sorted by drawee bank — a highly labor intensive job.

In the cash departments of the Feds, employees were busy paying out and receiving coin and currency. More than two billion pieces of currency were received and counted in 1931, and this amount held virtually unchanged throughout the decade. About the same number of coins were received and counted, and this volume remained nearly constant during the decade. Not surprisingly, the number of U.S. securities issued, redeemed or exchanged in the fiscal agency departments increased over 50 percent. Maintaining member bank reserve accounts and other deposit accounts did not require a lot of personnel, but it is significant that during the period 1931 to 1940 member bank reserve deposits skyrocketed from $2,433,310,000 to $11,985,385,000. These deposits bottomed to $1,907,477,000 in February 1932, remained fairly level until January 1934 and rose steadily the rest of the period. Federal Reserve note circulation was at $1,565,642,000 in January 1931 and rose continually to $4,870,578,000 in January 1940.

The number of employees involved in the collection and analysis of data steadily increased from a small beginning during World War I when the system was asked to help obtain data for use in the allocation of resources. More and more the demand for accurate data for developing monetary policy and for learning exactly what was happening in the nation's business and industry required more and more highly trained personnel. The system had always collected banking data in compliance with the Federal Reserve Act to "keep informed of the condition of member banks." But as the impact of monetary policy and the actions of the Fed expanded, so did the need to follow developments in the general economy. This facet of the system is discussed in more detail in the following chapter.

Net earnings of the 12 Fed banks fluctuated considerably during the decade. Changes in the volume of loans to member banks accounted for most of the fluctuation. In 1932 earnings from this source were $17,881,000 — nearly double the previous year and also the following year. Beginning in 1934 earnings from loans dropped to $1,241,000 and never approached that level for the next 20 years. Earnings from U.S. government securities more than made up the difference as holdings more than doubled during the decade. During the decade Fed banks made a profit, paid a dividend on their stock and in every year except 1931, 1933, and 1934, paid excess earnings to the Treasury (additional details in the Appendix).

Chapter 6
World War II and Its Aftermath (1941–1950)

Sunday morning, December 7, 1941, dawned as just another day to most Americans, but before the day was over, we were angry, disappointed, shocked and ready to fight. The events of that infamous day were unbelievable to most. Where was our air force? How could we be surprised? Couldn't we retaliate quickly and show the enemy who was boss? Gradually the nation realized that we were dangerously unprepared, ill equipped and without a trained, adequate fighting force.

What happened during the next four years was just as unbelievable. The nation's industrial machine tooled up and turned out more tanks, planes, trucks and other war materiel than seemed possible. Blessed with a large reservoir of labor, underutilized plant capacity and a determination to win, the country was united as never before. Those who lived during the 1940s watched sons, sweethearts and friends march off to training camps and then to places we were only dimly aware of. Guam, Guadalcanal, New Hebrides, Okinawa, Iwo Jima, Dunkirk, Bastogne soon became household words. At home, the big bands played at training camps, and Bob Hope took his entertainment group all over the nation and overseas.

WHAT ROLE FOR THE FED?
Very simply, the officials said whatever money it takes to win, it will be there. And interest rates will not rise. Presidents of the Fed banks served as chairmen for War Bond drives. Key personnel from the banks and the board left for military service. There was never any question as to the policy of the Fed. Officials knew full well that the nation was risking runaway inflation as spending exceeded income for the federal government and the federal debt jumped from $45.5 billion in 1941 to $263 billion when the enemy finally surrendered. But the life of the nation was at stake! So first things first. Win the war and then worry about inflation. Various means were used to contain personal debt and to direct resources into the war effort. Rationing of fuel, coffee, fats, and most industrial goods became a way of life. From December 7, 1941, to August 14, 1945, there was one goal — WIN!

CREDIT CONTROLS

During the war several direct credit controls were imposed on the economy. In 1941 Regulation W was issued by the Board of Governors, controlling most consumer credit. It specified minimum down payments and maximum lengths of payout. Price controls were placed on essential goods and the list of controlled prices expanded throughout the war. The opening paragraph of the board's 1942 Annual Report reflects the urgency of the situation: "The United States was [on December 7, 1941] abruptly confronted by unprecedented expenditures for total war. Taxation and measures for diverting the people's savings into the war effort were wholly inadequate for a war economy."

On April 6, 1942, Regulation V was issued by the board. This governed rules for making loans deemed by the armed forces and the Maritime Commission to be essential to the war effort. It greatly expanded production of war materiel as many small companies were able to obtain start-up funds. Most loans were made through commercial banks. In 1942, 2,700 applications were processed by the Fed banks for $2.7 billion. Twenty-seven percent of these were for loans under $25,000; 59 percent were for amounts under $100,000.

Financing the war required large sums of money, and it was needed quickly. The Treasury began issuing a variety of securities that were sold to the public—principally banks, insurance companies and other organizations that had funds to invest. As fiscal agent for the Treasury, Federal Reserve banks immediately experienced a tremendous increase in clerical work. Seeking help from every citizen, the Treasury embarked on a program of selling War Savings Bonds. These bonds issued in denominations as small as $25 were promoted through advertising and especially through payroll deduction plans at major employers. Everyone—schoolchildren and grandparents—joined in the effort to support the war effort.

Fed banks took on the task of qualifying "issuing agents" for War Bonds. Banks, savings and loan associations, credit unions and others that could qualify became salesmen for War Savings Bonds. Thousands of agents were qualified, and the paperwork grew by leaps and bounds at the Fed's fiscal agency departments. The number of pieces of paper handled jumped 700 percent, and in 1942 more than 12,000 persons—half of the total number of employees at the Fed banks—were involved in handling the fiscal agent work for the Treasury. In addition, the Fed banks assumed the handling of withholding taxes for the Treasury. Fed banks became involved in foreign asset control, and the San Francisco Fed assisted in handling the assets of displaced Japanese on the West Coast. Just to add another job, the Feds took over from the American Bankers Association the assembling of data on consumer loans.

Check volume and payment and receipt of currency and coin also increased steadily during the war years, but the increase was mild compared with the work load in the fiscal agency departments. Loans to member banks were virtually nonexistent.

PEACE ARRIVES

VE-Day, May 8, 1945, and VJ-Day, August 14, 1945, brought an end to nearly four years of some of the bitterest fighting known to man. Dropping of two atomic bombs on Japan brought an end to fighting in the Pacific and ushered in a new concept of fighting and a new era for mankind.

Beginning in late 1945 more than six million fighting men started the process of returning to civilian life. They looked forward to many things — seeing loved ones, getting married, going back to school, starting a home and not standing in line. I remember a friend who had married, rented a house and bought furniture showing friends who visited him his attitude by walking around the house hitting each piece of furniture and saying, "It's mine!" Those who had manned the home front had built up demands also. The war was won, now give us new cars, refrigerators, tires, houses and a multitude of other consumer goods, and let us have them NOW!

NOW LET'S DEAL WITH INFLATION

Of course, the nation's industrial plant could not shift from making tanks, trucks, and planes to cars, refrigerators and houses overnight. So there were shortages everywhere. People stood in line to buy a chance on a new car. Some items were still rationed — sugar, coffee and some meats. Now the danger of inflation was fueled by this enormous gap between demand and supply.

Chairman Eccles and other Fed officials were abundantly aware of this danger. But others influencing President Truman and the Treasury officials shouted back, "Remember the depression following World War I. Don't do anything to cause another depression. Above all don't do anything to increase the cost of carrying the national debt." Thus began a struggle for freedom for the Fed to act as it believed in the best interest of the nation. Let's look at some of the events in this drama that extended into the next decade.

Vitally concerned about the enormous buildup of spending power and the surging demand for goods, Chairman Eccles renewed his fight to get agreement from the Treasury to raise interest rates. The Fed was, for all intents and purposes, unable to act to forestall an impending surge of inflation. Raising member bank reserves, which it did, was ineffective as long as the Treasury insisted on keeping rates low. The Fed's pledge to keep rates low during the war was understandable. But now it was imperative, as far as the leadership at the Fed was concerned, to let rates seeks their normal level according to the demand and supply of credit.

A CHANGE OF PRESIDENTS

Harry Truman assumed the presidency upon the death of Franklin Roosevelt on April 12, 1945. He quickly sided with the Treasury and found the Fed's position unfriendly to the administration and "to close to the position of bankers." President Truman and the Treasury were adamant that the Fed not change—or as Secretary of the Treasury Frederick Vinson said at one point, "It does not seem wise to rock the boat during the transition to a peacetime economy." Chairman Eccles replied, "The continuance of the rate [the low rate] can no longer be of service to the Treasury's financing program nor to the maintenance of credit policy. Rather it is an element of weakness in our battle against inflation."

When Eccles's term as chairman expired January 31, 1948, President Truman refused to reappoint him. He did offer him the position of vice chairman, but after three months and no action, Eccles withdrew his name but continued to serve as a member of the board. President Truman's new secretary of the treasury, John Snyder, followed the president's position and refused to consider any changes in rates. Presidential assistant John Steelman is said to have felt that "not only was the administration uneasy about the specter of tight money but they felt that Eccles was too close to the bankers of the nation and not cooperative enough with the White House."

President Truman appointed Thomas B. McCabe, chairman of the board of directors of the Philadelphia Federal Reserve Bank, to the chairmanship of the Board of Governors April 15, 1948. The change of chairman did not reduce the pressure from banks for a break with the Treasury on rates. Freed from the chairmanship, Eccles redoubled his efforts to force a change that would permit the Fed to adjust rates more in line with the market.

UNEXPECTED SUPPORT FOR THE FED

In 1948, former president Herbert Hoover headed a commission to investigate the administration of the federal government. Although Hoover had had his problems with the Fed during the early 1930s when it refused to take any action to shore up the banking structure, the commission's report was sharply critical of the Treasury's domination of monetary policy and recommended that the Fed have an equal voice with the Treasury and a stronger role in the formation of credit policy. Attempts by Treasury Secretary Snyder to keep this recommendation out of the report were not successful.

As the struggle for independence continued, Eccles made a significant and effective point in a report to the Senate Subcommittee on Monetary Credit and Fiscal Policies. He emphasized that "it is not the Fed's policy to enforce its will on the administration for the final responsibility lies with the Congress." The message was not lost on the congressmen.

Late in 1949, Senator Paul Douglas (D-IL), chairman of the Senate Subcommittee on Monetary, Credit and Fiscal Policies and a respected economist and former university professor, swung his support behind Eccles and the Fed's fight to gain some independence of action. In his report he stated, "The freedom of the Federal Reserve to restrict credit and raise interest rates for general stabilization purposes should be restored even if the costs should prove to be a significant increase in the service charges on the Federal debt and a greater inconvenience to the Treasury." While the president and his staff, including the treasury secretary and the chairman of the Council of Economic Advisors, steadfastly held to the idea that interest rates must be kept low, Senator Douglas let it be known that Congress would not hesitate to intervene to forestall dominance of the Fed by the Treasury. The lines of conflict had been clearly drawn. Over the next several years cool heads, a willingness to negotiate and strong economic pressures resolved the conflict. How it was done is a fascinating story which will be described in the next chapter.

FED MAKES A FORMAL POLICY STATEMENT
In view of the widespread and heated discussion of the role of the Fed and the attitude of the Fed's leadership in subsequent years a statement in the Board of Governors' 1943 Annual Report is most interesting.

> **Monetary policy and inflation.** It is believed by many that inflation and deflation can be prevented by monetary action. The fact that the Federal Reserve System has the power, through changes in the discount rate, through open-market operations, and through modifications in reserve requirements, to make money dearer and scarcer in a boom and more abundant in a depression has been taken as an indication that monetary authorities are able, by their actions alone, to maintain economic stability. This is a greatly magnified view of the influence of monetary action on the course of economic life.
>
> In the past quarter century it has been demonstrated that policies regulating the quantity and cost of money can not by themselves produce economic stability, or even exert a powerful influence in that direction. The country has gone through boom conditions at times when monetary restraints were being exerted and interest rates were extremely high, and it has continued in depression at times when an active policy of monetary ease was in effect and money was both abundant and cheap. Economic stability depends on a complex of forces and policies, of which credit policy is only one. In order to be effective in bringing about stability the regulation of the availability and the cost of money must be integrated with a flexible fiscal policy and at critical times reinforced by direct controls over prices, wages, and supplies. Further experience with selective credit controls, which are discussed elsewhere in this Report, may also bring fruitful results.
>
> An important consideration at this time is that, while monetary policy can not by itself prevent inflation, inflationary conditions are certain to result in heavy upward pressure on money rates. When the buying power of money is declining, holders of money prefer to exchange it for commodities, equities or real estate, rather than invest it at a fixed rate of return, and others are willing to pay high rates for money to be used in speculation and speculative ventures. Consequently, money rates are always extremely high during inflation. This is an additional reason why,

in view of the enormous growth of our public debt, it will be vitally important to keep direct controls in effect after the war is ended, and thus hold the line on economic stability. These controls cannot be abandoned with safety until the flow of civilian goods from the reconverted industrial plant will be sufficient to meet the deferred and current demand of the people backed by their unprecedented holding of cash and liquid assets.

Direct controls were gradually relaxed, and Regulation W was allowed to expire June 30, 1949. The industrial plant was beginning to catch up with the demand for consumer goods, and price increases were moderating. The economy showed signs of leveling off with a reasonable balance between supply and demand. However, leadership at the Fed continued their efforts to break away from the "pegged" securities market.

ANOTHER SIDE TO THE FED

The battle for the Fed's freedom from dominance by the Treasury and its ability to act in monetary policy areas as it believed best were crucial to the life and effectiveness of the system. And it is well that attempts to resolve the differences persisted to a solution. Quite unnoticed by the general public and by many in the field of banking and economics, a major development was taking place in the Reserve banks. As additional responsibilities were placed on the system, the need for accurate and current data on the nation's economy as well as the banking structure became imperative. Section 4 of the Federal Reserve Act states that the Federal Reserve agent in each Fed bank will "make regular reports to the Federal Reserve Board." The agents took this requirement seriously, and some of the early reports are masterpieces in rhetoric and in content. Here are some examples.

From the Kansas City Federal Reserve Agent's report for 1916:

> At no time in the history of the section embraced within the boundaries of district No. 10 have general commercial conditions been so active and satisfactory as during the current year. Wholesalers, jobbers, and retailers have regularly reported unprecedented and increasing sales, with collections far above average. Manufacturing facilities have been generally taxed to capacity. Building permits and engineering activities were reported in increasing volume, while post-office receipts, bank clearings, and deposits have gone forward by leaps and bounds, each succeeding month adding to previous records. Mineral and oil industries have enjoyed record breaking prosperity.
>
> While agricultural production has not been as large as in previous years, increased market prices have more than offset the shortage and farmers have prospered as never before. Labor conditions have been satisfactory, except that a general shortage has existed in almost every line. Voluntary wage increases have been common and such differences as have occurred between labor and employers have been amicably adjusted through compromises. At livestock markets high prices have prevailed, many records being broken in receipts as well as in prices paid.

From the 1916 report of the New York Federal Reserve Agent:

> The resources of the member banks in this district increased from 3,326 million dollars on September 2, 1915, to 4,063 million dollars on September 12, 1916, a gain of 736 millions. . . . Liabilities to stock holders increased 80 millions, to depositors 12,250 millions. . . . Cash on hand, bank balances and cash items increased 186 millions and acceptances and letters of credit were 53 millions higher. . . . Except for the brief period in December when a severe stringency occurred in money on call, a good supply of loanable funds at low and stable rates has been available in this market throughout the last year, despite the unprecedented activity of trade and industry, the great volume of stock exchange business, and the negotiation from time to time of large loans to other countries.

The growth of the need for more data and the attitude of the management at the board and at the banks are interestingly and accurately related in a report prepared by Merritt Sherman, originally with the San Francisco Fed and later secretary to the Board of Governors in Washington, D.C. Here are significant excerpts and summaries from that report.

> From their inception in 1915, monthly business reports to the Federal Reserve Board from the Federal Reserve Agents related to regional conditions in the twelve Federal Reserve Districts. Where an industry or activity located in one district was of key importance in the national picture, the Reserve Agent might include comprehensive information regarding significant developments in that activity outside of his own district.
>
> The Federal Reserve Agents were alerted by the Board to the need for submitting frequent reports on regional business conditions as early as October 20–22, 1914, when all twelve agents attended a convention in Washington of about 100 Reserve Bank directors and all officers of the Board. By letter dated March 18, 1915, the Board outlined in specific terms its request for weekly and monthly reports to assist it in knowing about business conditions throughout the country. This procedure was consistent with the concept of the decentralized or regional central banking system embodied in the Federal Reserve Act. It also was in keeping with the availability — or lack of availability — of current statistical information relative to economic activities for the United States as a whole.

FEDERAL RESERVE BULLETIN BORN

The first issue of the *Federal Reserve Bulletin* (published by the Federal Reserve Board), dated May 1, 1915, announced that

> The Bulletin is intended to afford a general statement concerning business conditions and events in the Federal Reserve System that will be of interest to all member banks. . . . Brief comparative reports concerning operations of the Federal Reserve System in the several districts will also be published from time to time.
>
> Preparation by the Agents of monthly regional business reports, without the benefit of professionally staffed research departments, was continued through 1918.

On September 1, 1918, the Federal Reserve Board established a Division of Analysis and Research, with the director and staff located in the New York Bank. The Board's organization had not previously included a research division or office. There had been a statistician on its staff since November 1914, but the principal function of that office was to assemble banking data reported by the Reserve banks covering their operations and those of member banks.

As the Fed banks accumulated data on banks and on the economy of their districts, others became interested in seeing the data. Businessmen and industrial leaders also wanted to know what was going on in the business world. They were making projections for their own businesses and any information that would improve the accuracy of these projections was most welcome. Also, the Fed banks were learning that they needed to develop public relations programs, and the publishing of business and banking data was a tool readily available to them. Hence, each Fed soon began making information they collected available to member banks, businessmen and others in their districts. Sometimes the banks used an informal report, but others published the data in a *Monthly Business Review.* The Federal Reserve Board also made the *Federal Reserve Bulletin* available, which contained reports from all of the districts as well as information prepared by the board.

On December 17, 1918, the Federal Reserve Board announced that it would begin publishing its own summary of business conditions reflecting the national picture. These would be prepared from the agents' reports plus other data assembled by the board. District banks were encouraged to continue to make their reports available in the district and that the agents should continue to submit monthly reports to the board. By 1919 the board's staff was collecting data on retail trade and inventories. In addition, compilation of statistics on the volume of production, price movements, and other aspects of business was begun or expanded. Much of this expansion of data collection was done through the Federal Reserve agents, and those who had not already done so soon added personnel to assist in the task of collecting data. The additional personnel were not usually identified as workers in a research, statistical or report department, but the one in charge of the operation was sometimes called an Assistant Federal Reserve Agent. Only one or two banks employed a professionally trained economist.

The Conference of Federal Reserve Agents continued to take an active part in the development of monthly reviews, the research staffs of the banks and related publications. But the governors of the Reserve banks took little interest in the research activities partly because this activity was located in the office of the Federal Reserve agent rather than in the operations side of the bank where the governors had their primary responsibilities.

DON'T FORECAST!

An interesting event occurred in 1920 following the sharp peaking of commodity prices. The Fed had raised the discount rate to 7 percent, and when a sharp recession followed, the Fed came under severe criticism. Unfortunately, some of the district business reviews had contained comments on price developments and especially on prospects of future price trends. In other words, they did some forecasting. As a result, at a meeting in October 1920, the agents and Federal Reserve Board discussed the form and content of monthly reviews. Board member Dr. Adolph Miller made a lengthy statement on behalf of the board to the effect that the reviews should "avoid anything in the nature of forecast or prophecy as to the trend of prices or the trend of business until a change of conditions may make it advisable to make prognostications in the lines." His comments may not have been the first to express such sentiments, but for years after, even into the 1980s, it was a cardinal rule that in the preparation and editing of system research publications there should be no statement that could be interpreted as a forecast of future economic conditions, and especially interest rates.

During 1921 the secretary of commerce began publication of the *Survey of Current Business,* which duplicated some of the statistical data the system had been accumulating. In a discussion with the board it was agreed that the system would continue the series it had originated but that within the government there was agreement that there would not be a duplication of effort in preparing data. Whatever was developed by one agency would be shared with others, assuming it was of acceptable quality.

In 1922 the board's Analysis and Research Division was transferred from New York to Washington and a full-time director employed. Research work was expanded, and in 1922 the board published its first index of the physical volume of production, later to be known as the Index of Industrial Production. This soon became a widely used statistical tool for business and economic analysis. During this period, research was expanded to include analysis of the impact of bank reserves and to provide better understanding of the effect of open market purchases and sales of securities by the system. This was the beginning of research for use in the development of monetary policy that would be of increasing importance to the system and to the business and banking community. On July 1, 1923, the board's Division of Analysis and Research and the office of the statistician were combined under the title of Division of Research and Statistics, with Walter W. Stewart named as director (he had been director of research since September 15, 1922).

HOW MUCH DOES IT COST?

It will come as no surprise to most readers that the expansion of research and publications soon became a budget item. In 1924, following criticism by some board members, the board's Committee on Salaries, Expenditures, and Efficiency with the concurrence of its Committee on Research and

Statistics recommended "that all System research activities be reorganized, coordinated, and placed under unified direction and control and that yearly budgets for the function at the Board and at each Bank beginning with 1925 be submitted to the Board for prior approval."

Following a discussion at the November 1924 meeting of the Conference of Federal Reserve Agents, the board in December 1924 sent to all agents a statement of principles governing research, statistical, and publication activities of the Reserve banks and the board. The statement emphasized in formal terms the responsibility of the board, acting through its Division of Research and Statistics, for research activities and publications throughout the system.

Making sure that it retained full control over research and publication activities at the Reserve banks, the Federal Reserve Board in an August 1926 statement further stated:

> While research studies and scientific investigations may be undertaken on the initiative of the Federal Reserve banks or of the Federal Reserve Board, the Federal Reserve banks, before expense is incurred for their prosecution, shall secure the approval of the Federal Reserve Board. It is not intended, however, that approval be awaited before studies of small scope are undertaken which involve no considerable expense. In conducting research studies, the Director of the Board's Division of Research and Statistics may make assignments to one or more of the Federal Reserve banks of such portions as may seem desirable.
>
> All publications of the Federal Reserve banks dealing with matters of more than local interest and all educational material shall be submitted to the Federal Reserve Board prior to publication and shall be issued only with the approval of the Board. The monthly reviews, published by the Federal Reserve agents, shall be under the general editorial supervision of the Director of Research and Statistics of the Federal Reserve Board.
>
> The monthly reviews of the Federal Reserve banks shall not exceed eight pages. Free distribution of these reviews shall be confined to member banks, to other Federal Reserve banks, to the Federal Reserve Board, and to firms reporting statistical information, nonmember par list banks, and to such others as may be determined through the Board's Division of Research and Statistics in contact with a committee of the agents. For copies delivered in bulk for distribution, the Federal Reserve banks shall make a charge sufficient to cover costs.

On January 1, 1925, Dr. E.A. Goldenweiser succeeded Dr. Stewart as director of the Division of Research and Statistics at the board. Dr. Goldenweiser had been assistant statistician since March 1919 and continued as director of the Division of Research and Statistics until 1945. Under his direction, research at the board continued along lines marked by Dr. Stewart's service. Tools for measuring and analyzing economic activity were improved, and development of the professional staff continued both at the board and at the banks. During this period a majority of the members of the board and at least some of the operating heads of the banks felt the need for additional information to help in monetary policy formation and implementation, and that the research function could assist in providing such information. Although the board supported increased research for the system, some members felt that greater concentration of the functions at the board, with little other than data collection at the Reserve banks, would be more efficient and might well produce better reports, especially if most analytical work was done at the board.

A report prepared in 1957 for the Conference of Presidents provides a summary of the research operations during the period 1926-1935. While some of the ideas in the report are repetitious, it is quoted here as summary of the growth and development of research in the system.

> The scope of the research and statistical work varied from time to time and among Federal Reserve banks, depending upon circumstances. There were recurring periods when certain members of the Federal Reserve Board were dubious about the value of research activities and exerted their influence toward the restriction of the research and statistical work in the Board's division, as well as at Federal Reserve banks. There were economy waves growing out of special conditions which also had their effect upon the scope of activities. Moreover, conditions at Federal Reserve banks varied widely, depending upon the type of agents and governors who were administering the affairs of the institutions. Some of these executives merely took a passive attitude toward the statistical departments and more or less accepted the dictum of the Federal Reserve Board that statistical departments of the Reserve banks should constitute collection agencies to supply basic information to the Board's Division of Research. Some of them were sensitive to the Board's criticism of the scientific work of the research staffs and were cautious about proceeding with any projects which were likely to draw criticism. On the other hand, there were agents and governors who had a keen appreciation of the value of research and from the very beginning launched upon a program of research and endeavored to maintain an environment that would stimulate the activity of the research personnel. At some Reserve banks, one or more directors had a vital interest in economic developments and sponsored various research projects.
>
> In the second place, the operating departments of the Federal Reserve banks, under the supervision of the governor, often had relatively little access to the statistical department as a fact finding and research agency. This condition grew out of the fact that the governors in some Reserve banks found it difficult or unsatisfactory either to cut through the red tape and go directly to the statistical department or to go through the agent for the purposes of instituting a project in which he was interested, especially where the agent had accepted the restrictions placed upon the statistical department.

A revised Statement of Principles was issued by the Board of Governors following the reorganization of the system in accordance with the Banking Act of 1935. This statement essentially repeats the principles of the 1926 statement.

Mr. Sherman's summary statement brings the status of research in the system current with the end of the first 75 years of the system. Here are quotes from that summary.

> During and following World War II, the status and use of the research function evolved continuously and significantly, both at the Board and at the Reserve banks. Board responsibility for general supervision of the function continues in broad term, but this is shared with the presidents of the Reserve banks, and there is a substantial degree of regional autonomy.
>
> As for the monthly reviews of the Federal Reserve banks, many and extensive changes have taken place during the past several years. Some no longer issue a monthly review regularly but prepare and distribute other periodic releases. Content of some of the monthly reviews now being issued has shifted from matters relating to local business conditions to emphasis on special research studies having both regional and national—or international—significance. To be sure, the Board's needs are still served by the banks in gathering certain data. But regional research studies are serving the Reserve banks and their officers in carrying out their functions. They are serving the public, locally and often more widely, through providing various kinds of reports and research study results. And it seems safe to say that Reserve bank research and publication activities are playing a useful part in the over-all economic intelligence function that is so essential if the central banking system is to make its proper contribution to the public welfare.

At the end of the decade of the 1940s all Reserve banks had fully staffed, well organized research departments. The number involved in research at each bank varied with the emerging role of each bank in its district and in its involvement in the work load of the system. Each was headed by a person specially trained in research, and many held doctorate degrees from leading universities. By 1988, nearly 700 persons were employed in the Fed banks' research departments with over 200 holding doctorate degrees. In addition, the board's staff involved in developing and executing monetary and economic policies numbered just under 400.

WORK INCREASES AT FED BANKS

While all the debate on monetary policy continued at the "executive" level of the system, the volume of operations at the Fed banks continued to move steadily upward. In 1950 the 12 banks processed more than two billion checks—an 83 percent increase over 1941. Pieces of currency received and counted totaled just under four billion, an increase of 52 percent. Coin received and counted was over seven billion, an increase of 225 percent over 1941. The enormous jump in volume of U.S. securities handled has already been mentioned. It continued at levels just under the peak of war time volume. Personnel in the loan department were not very busy. The most loans made during the decade were 11 in 1947. Banks were afloat with liquidity and loans that were made were primarily to assist a member bank in meeting its reserve requirement overnight. Total employment at the 12 reserve banks totaled just under 18,000 persons, 335 officers.

A significant change was made in the check collection process in 1945. Work at the Federal Reserve offices in what was called the Transit Department involved receiving and sorting thousands of checks daily. In the early years, this was done manually with persons standing at a "sorting rack" which had compartments for each bank in the Fed office's territory. Each check would be picked up, the name of the drawee bank read and the check placed in the appropriate compartment. When the sorting was completed, a total of the amount of the checks would be determined by adding them on an adding machine.

Machines became available in the late 1940s that would automatically place the checks in the appropriate compartment on a large wheel as the operator punched the corresponding key. The machine automatically computed totals for each compartment and for all checks sorted. International Business Machines was the first to make such machines, and hundreds of them were leased or purchased by the Feds.

As an aid in identifying the drawee bank of a check and its geographic location, the American Bankers Association and the Federal Reserve System designed a fractional number to be printed in the upper right-hand corner of each check. The numerator of the fraction gave a number that indicated the state or city in which the bank was located and an official American Bankers Association number. The denominator gave the number of the Federal Reserve district and the Fed office in that district in which the bank was located and a number indicating the days before credit would be given to the depositing bank — 0 for immediate credit and 1 or 2 for days that it would be deferred. Thus, 30-9/1140 would be the Frost National Bank in San Antonio, Texas (30 for San Antonio and 9 for the bank's ABA number) located in the 11th (Dallas) Federal Reserve District served by the San Antonio Branch (4 for the fourth office of the Dallas district) and (0) the check would be given immediate credit.

This identification was helpful in sorting checks as the operator could at a glance know the name of the drawee bank and other information needed for properly sorting the check. Also, bankers receiving a check could know the location of the drawee bank and how long it would take to obtain payment. Later, as the process was placed on computers, the same numbering plan was encoded in magnetic ink at the bottom of the check and was read by the computer which made the necessary sort and computed totals.

So the decade closes with the dispute with the Treasury unresolved and leadership of the system still struggling to establish its position. Yet, under the reorganization following the Banking Act of 1935, the system continued to grow in size, in the volume of transactions handled and in its role as the central banking system of the nation. A depression following World War

II was avoided, and production of consumer goods and the nation's industrial plant quickly recovered from a wartime status. Thousands of veterans returned to colleges and universities with a seriousness of purpose that surprised the professors. Former D students became honor students. Living facilities for married students were hastily constructed. It was the best of times following the worst of times for many. Families with lost loved ones learned to recover. The nation was a leader in helping both enemy and friend rebuild governments and industrial plants. The dollar was *the* currency of the world, and the industrial giants of our country led the way in production of goods.

Chapter 7

The Fed Comes into Its Own (1950–1959)

Recovery from world war and the shock of the emergence of atomic energy was progressing smoothly when an event on the other side of the world jarred the nation. North Korea invaded South Korea, and on June 25, 1950, President Truman declared that this invasion must be stopped. Working through the United Nations, armed forces were quickly mobilized and sent to aid the South Koreans.

With memories of shortages during World War II still fresh in the minds of everyone, consumer goods were snapped up without regard to cost. In September Regulation W was reinstated, and Regulation X governing real estate transactions was imposed. Also, Regulation V was reactivated. While the military action in Korea was labeled a police action, it had all the implications of war to U.S. citizens, and they reacted accordingly. Financing of the police action brought additional pressure from the Treasury to "keep interest rates low" to avoid raising the cost of refinancing the debt from World War II and providing funds for the Korean Conflict.

The police action dragged on. General Eisenhower was wanted by both parties to run for president. The Republicans won, and he was elected in 1952 on a promise to end the conflict in Korea. The specter of inflation reared its ugly head, and the Fed stepped up efforts to gain control of interest rates — and its own destiny.

Chairman of the Board of Governors Thomas B. McCabe resigned March 31, 1951, and President Truman wanted to appoint Harry McDonald, chairman of the Securities and Exchange Commission, in his place. But he learned at the last minute that McDonald was ineligible as the board already had a member from McDonald's district. Secretary of the Treasury Snyder favored William McChesney "Bill" Martin, then assistant secretary of the treasury. Since McDonald was ineligible, President Truman appointed Martin on April 2, 1951, to fill the unexpired term of McCabe. This proved to be a most fortunate choice. Bill Martin had been one of the architects, with the board, in developing a way out of the stalemate on "pegged" interest rates. Now he was given the chance to make it work.

Here is some background information on Bill Martin. His father served as Federal Reserve agent, governor and president of the St. Louis Fed from 1914 to 1940. In 1929, at age 23, Bill joined the stock brokerage firm of A.G. Edwards. He was named a partner in the firm in 1931 and operated on the floor of the New York Stock Exchange for seven years. His record was so impressive that he was named governor of the exchange in 1935 and its first paid president in 1938. During World War II he moved up the ranks of the military from private to colonel, and following military service, President Truman was so impressed with Martin's record that he named him assistant secretary of the treasury in 1948.

From a background of finance and experience in the Treasury Department, Bill Martin was uniquely qualified to reconcile differences with the Treasury and to lead the Fed into its new role in the nation. Some Fed officials may have feared that his sympathy would be with the Treasury, and President Truman hoped he had placed a loyalist within the enemy's walls. Both were to find that Bill Martin had a mind of his own and that he had a firm idea of what was right and the direction the Fed should go. He would not be at the beck and call of any group or persons. He would carve out his own path and soon won the respect of the financial and political leadership of the nation and the world.

WHAT WAS THE ACCORD?

On March 3, 1951, following intense negotiations by staff members of the board and the Treasury, a joint announcement said, "The Treasury and the Federal Reserve System have reached full accord with respect to debt management and monetary policies to be pursued in furthering the common purpose to assure the successful financing of the Government's requirements and, at the same time, to minimize monetization of the public debt."

What this meant was known only to the participants. But later events disclosed four parts to the agreement. First, the Treasury agreed to exchange marketable 2½ percent bonds for nonmarketable 2¾ percent bonds with a maturity of 29 years. Second, the Fed agreed to use its open market operations to keep the market orderly while it adjusted to the new rate. Third, the Fed agreed to keep its discount rate at 1¾ percent and not to change it without consulting with the Treasury. Finally, the Fed and the Treasury agreed to consult in setting the strategy for financing the debt. To ease the transition to an unpegged market, the Fed would support the market for a short period with an indefinite amount of money.

It worked. With Bill Martin's steady hand at the helm and close liaison with the Treasury, the Fed emerged in control of its own destiny. Market rates were gradually permitted to seek a realistic level, and the Treasury was assured that its financing would not fail. The road to a free market was not without its bumps. After nearly 20 years of a "pegged" market price, it took time for the industry to adjust. Also, the Treasury found it had to evaluate

William McChesney "Bill" Martin, Jr. Chairman of the Board of Governors, Federal Reserve System, April 2, 1951–January 31, 1970. He was a key player in developing the "accord" with the Treasury and served longer as chairman than any other person named to that position. Courtesy Board of Governors of Federal Reserve System.

the market carefully before announcing rates on a new issue or rollover transaction. By consulting with key institutions and personnel in the market, the Treasury was reasonably successful in issuing securities at rates that were compatible with the market. In some cases it missed substantially, and when it did, it either had an issue fail to sell quickly or gave speculators an opportunity to make a quick profit.

For example, in early June 1952, the Treasury announced that it would go to the market for at least $3.5 billion in new money, offering a bond due in six months with a coupon rate of 2⅜ percent. The books were opened June 16 and closed June 17 with subscriptions nearly three times the amount the Treasury wanted. On June 18, the issue was traded on the market on a "when issued" basis at 100 14/32 asked. It was announced on June 20 that nonbidding subscribers would be allotted, at par, the full amount for which they subscribed. The market price continued above par for several days so subscribers could sell the bonds they were awarded at a profit and never put up any money. The following quote from the June 20 *Wall Street Journal* describes one of the problems facing the Treasury and the Fed in achieving an orderly market. Referring to the 2⅜ percent bond, the *Journal* reported: "Nonbank subscribers of the bonds included a lot of 'free riders' — individuals who subscribed for the bonds with the intention of selling them immediately in order to realize a quick profit. They were able to do this because the bonds are now quoted at a level fractionally higher than the subscription price of par."

This ability to make a quick profit without putting up any money continued to a greater or lesser degree until June 1958. Subscriptions for non-bank persons submitted for their account by a bank were not required to pay any money until settlement day for the securities — usually three to five days after the allotment was announced. Some banks submitted pages of names of customers — many who were not aware of the danger but were assured by their bank that it would be a "good deal." On June 4, 1958, the Treasury announced an offering of a 3¼ percent bond due May 15, 1985. On June 5 the market price on the bond was quoted 100 24/32 bid and 101 asked. The market price of the bond remained above par for several days, enabling anyone to sell at a profit without taking possession of the bonds.

All of this activity came to a screeching halt when an issue of 2⅝ percent bonds due February 15, 1965, was issued June 15, 1958. With memory of the profit on the 3¼ bonds a few days earlier fresh, subscriptions for the 2⅝ bonds were strong. Unfortunately, the market suddenly decided to go the other way, and by settlement day they were selling below par, and those "free riders" were forced to come up with money to pay for the bonds for which they had subscribed or take a loss by selling on the market. The market became so unsettled that the Fed stepped in and bought a substantial amount directly to stabilize the market.

As the Treasury gained experience, it moved to an auction procedure for all of its securities. This eliminated the need to guess at the market rate and also stopped the "free riders."

ENTER CONGRESSMAN PATMAN

It is now time to introduce a salty, dyed-in-the-wool Populist who will become well known to Chairman Martin and other Fed personnel. Wright Patman, Democratic congressman from northeast Texas, became a thorn in the side of Fed personnel from Washington to San Francisco. He first came on the scene as chairman of a Joint Economic Committee in March 1952. The purpose of the committee: to determine the meaning of independence for the Fed. Senator Paul Douglas (D–IL) was a member of the committee.

To set the stage for the role that Congressman Patman would have in the growing independence and leadership of the Fed, it is necessary to remember that he came from a part of Texas that was largely farming — and not very prosperous farming — and that he was a product of the Depression years and in economics and politics he was a confirmed Populist. To illustrate, he is quoted as saying that any interest rate above 4 percent was too high. His "needling" of Fed officials during hearings before his committee is well chronicled. At one point he requested a list of *all* expenditures of *all* Federal Reserve banks and branches. After his staff had reviewed the lists, he requested a detailed explanation of selected items.

Employees of the banks spent hours, even days, preparing the requested material. Of course, the items selected for detailed explanation were the ones most difficult to explain.

In fairness to Congressman Patman, his efforts did reveal some expenditures that were questionable, and the result was a review of policies and customs regarding expenditures by the Fed banks. Personnel at the banks came to look at any questionable expense with the thought that it might have to be explained to a congressman. Since earnings of the Fed banks over and above expenses and additions to surplus were paid to the general fund of the U.S. Treasury, it was argued that expenses of the system were in effect paid for by taxpayers' money. The lower the expense, the more money to the Treasury and hence a lower need for taxes. The reasoning might be questioned, but it did make for sharp evaluation of expenses. Fed officials attending bankers' conventions certainly could not charge the expense of their wives who accompanied them, even though not to have his wife with him was out of keeping with other delegates, most of whom brought their wives at their bank's expense. Congressman Patman was a dedicated politician, knowledgeable and not about to have Congress assume the responsibility for monetary policy, but neither was he going to abandon his Populist theme.

REFINING "INDEPENDENCE"

Out of the joint committee headed by Congressman Patman came some firming of the meaning of independence of the Fed. During the congressional hearings Chairman Martin, responding to a question as to the relationship of the Fed to the Treasury, said, "I do not think you should subordinate the Treasury to the Federal Reserve or the Federal to the Treasury. I think they have both got to be equal." Pressed for an answer if there was conflict between the two, Chairman Martin replied, "We would sit around the table and hammer it out."

Many member of Congress, including Congressman Patman and Senator Paul Douglas, were unhappy that the Treasury had dominated the Fed during the war years. To them it raised the worrisome question about the executive and the congressional roles in determining monetary policy. Allan Sprowl, president of the Federal Reserve Bank of New York, brought an idea to the hearings that was generally satisfactory to all parties. He said: "The Fed's independence does not mean independence from government but independence within government." He insisted further that "in performing its major task — the administration of monetary policy — the Federal Reserve System is an agency of Congress set up in a special form to bear the responsibility for that particular task which constitutionally belongs to the legislative branch of the government. The Fed would inevitably have to coordinate its decisions closely with the Treasury, since it dealt largely in the Treasury's own obligations. It was to Congress, however, that the Fed was ultimately answerable."

While the committee agreed that the Fed should be responsive to Congress, it could not agree on what goals the Fed should pursue. It did agree that it was unmistakably clear that Congress would not allow the executive branch of government to have free sway over monetary policy. After all, Congress was given the authority to coin money, and it would not accept domination of that function by the Treasury. Also, the committee's hearings brought the Congress into the picture of monetary policy and overview of the Fed. After 40 years of silence it was again concerned about the Fed. However, it frequently did not agree with or even want to assume the burden of determining what monetary policy should be. That was left to the Fed, and the Congress would feel free to criticize whatever decision the Fed made. Thus began a new period of congressional oversight that would expand over the next 30 years.

With the accord well in place and a reasonable definition of "independence" established, the task of the Fed was to show leadership in the formation of monetary policy and forge a niche in government that would fulfill its obligation to the Congress and to the nation. Fortunately, Bill Martin was chairman of the Board of Governors until 1970 — nearly 20 years — a period long enough to gain stability of the Fed's position. (He completed a part of McCabe's unexpired term plus his own.)

POWER OF THE FED RECOGNIZED

The role of the Fed became increasingly important to the nation's economy and to the administrative branch of the government. A jump in the federal debt from $42.1 billion in 1940 to $278 billion at the end of 1945 enlarged the market for government securities. The Fed's open market operation was its most flexible and easily managed "tool" in executing monetary policy, and this enormous market now gave the Fed more leverage in influencing the cost and availability of credit. Although the debt dropped to about $251 billion in 1948, it then began a steady climb, and by the end of the 1950s it stood at $289 billion. The need for the U.S. Treasury continually to roll over its debt and to raise new money made it imperative that the Treasury and the Fed coordinate their activities.

Another factor now entered the picture, and it did not make the Fed's task any easier. Politicians quickly saw the role the Fed could play in keeping money and credit "cheap" or "dear," and what president — or congressman — would want the economy to be slowing down or, heaven forbid, drop in a depression while he was campaigning for reelection. Thus, pressure came at the Fed leadership from several directions. The built-in inflationary pressure of the continually growing federal debt required close attention to keep the lid on the economy. This meant keeping interest rates low enough so that business and consumers could obtain necessary financing but not so easy as to encourage speculation and overspending. Being a "creature of Congress," the Fed could not long act contrary to the wishes of the nation as expressed in contacts with constituents. Interpreting this pressure and measuring its validity were constant tasks of the Fed's leadership. Sometimes it was a fine line between too "loose" and too "tight."

Chairman Martin expressed the position of the Fed this way: "Our purpose is to lean against the winds of deflation or inflation, whichever way they are blowing." This allowed considerable discretion as the Fed would determine which way and how hard the wind was blowing and take appropriate action to slow it down or speed it up. To do so required that the Fed be free from political pressure, and that meant having equal footing with the Treasury. Martin was careful to maintain a position of independence from the executive branch but not from Congress. I have heard Chairman Martin in a question-and-answer session repeat that the Fed must "do all within its power to promote steady economic growth, encouraging investment through low interest rates when needed and to put on the brakes if inflation threatens. But in the long run, the Fed cannot act contrary to the wishes of the rank and file of the nation as expressed through their elected officials." The Fed can "take away the punch bowl" just as the party gets interesting, but it must eventually bow to the wishes of the people.

CHALLENGES WITHIN THE SYSTEM

Internal pressures also required Chairman Martin's attention. Effective leadership at the board had not been consistent since its creation in 1914. As pointed out earlier, Benjamin Strong, governor of the New York Fed, was the dominant leader until his death in 1928. Warburg and Harding were capable men, but the role of the Fed was so indefinite and the position of the Board so unsure that they were overshadowed by Strong's aggressiveness and firm belief in what he felt was best for the nation and the Fed. Eccles capably brought badly needed reorganization to the system and through his close relation with President Roosevelt laid the foundation for a strong and effective organization. When Roosevelt died, the working relationship between the Fed and the president came to a screeching halt. President Truman did not trust Eccles, and Eccles was not noted for his diplomacy. Lacking cooperation from the Treasury, McCabe found his job nearly impossible. Thus, Chairman Martin came into an organization that had 12 horses in addition to the seven members of the board, most of whom had their own ideas as to what should be done.

Most persistent in challenging the leadership of Chairman Martin was Allen Sprowl, president of the New York Fed. Sprowl had been with the New York bank since graduation in 1919, and he had worked under the strong leadership of Benjamin Strong. The New York bank was accused by some other Fed leaders of wanting to be the "head of the System." Operating at the heart of the nation's and later the world's money market, officials of the New York bank may have felt that they were in the best position to know what should be done. To his credit, Sprowl was most helpful in firming the position of the system in its relations to the Treasury and to Congress. But it took time for Chairman Martin to bring about harmony within the Fed.

One of Martin's moves was to encourage open discussion in determining monetary policy. At meetings of the Open Market Committee all Fed bank presidents were invited to attend and to express their views. Although only 5 could vote (this on a rotating basis), all 12 had an opportunity to provide input and to express the views and feelings from their districts. At these meetings, Chairman Martin always spoke last and respected the opinions of other participants. This open discussion of the subjects at hand usually resulted in unanimous decisions rather than split votes and hurt feelings. However, a review of the minutes of the meetings emphasizes the willingness of participants to vote against the majority opinion.

CHAIRMAN MARTIN AND WASHINGTON POLITICS

Within the Washington scene, Chairman Martin's relationship with the president, if not cordial, was without antagonism. At one point in 1955 as President Eisenhower was campaigning for reelection, the economy was slipping, and a recession was a real prospect. The president urged Secretary of the Treasury George Humphrey to put pressure on Martin to ease money. This Humphrey did, but Martin resisted, not wanting to weaken the Fed's position so soon after the accord. But he did not feel the Fed could go against a direct plea from the White House. However, rather than use open market operations to ease credit, the Fed reduced reserve requirements of member banks. The impact was about the same, but it sent a message that the Fed would act independently.

During the campaign, President Eisenhower repeatedly refused to chastise the Fed publicly. Replying to questions at one point, he said, "Well, I think the only comment I can logically make is this: the Federal Reserve Board (meaning the Board of Governors) is set up as a separate agency of the government. It is not under the authority of the president, and I really believe it would be a mistake to make it definitely and directly responsible to the political head of state. Certain individuals have viewpoints on the other side of the fence. But I do have this confidence in the Federal Reserve Board: they are watching this situation day by day." This position of the president gave strength to the Fed's independent role.

Also important to teamwork in Washington was a practice of talking to each other. Under Chairman Martin's initiative, a routine was developed that brought Martin, the secretary of the treasury, and the chairman of the President's Council of Economic Advisors in touch with each other on a regular basis. Chairman Martin had lunch at the Treasury once each week, and the secretary of the treasury met at the board for lunch weekly. Other regular meetings were held with the chairman of the President's Council of Economic Advisors and the vice chairman of the board. President Eisenhower suggested that the chairman of the Fed, chairman of the Council of Economic Advisors and the secretary of the treasury meet on a regular basis to forestall speculation that there was a crisis if they met only occasionally. This arrangement continued and was helpful in exchanging ideas and blunting disputes that might arise.

The meetings of leaders in the area of monetary policy came to be known as the Quadriad. It had its beginning during Roosevelt's administration when the president established an informal group consisting of the chairman of the Board of Governors, secretary of the treasury as chairman, the director of the budget and chairman of the then Advisory Commission on Natural Resources. Meetings were discontinued during World War II and were sporadic until Chairman Martin came into the picture. President Eisenhower encouraged resumption of the meetings, and they have continued to be an important communication vehicle between the administration and the Fed.

From the prospect of 75 years of history, the 1950s was a decade of growing and maturing for the Federal Reserve System. Begun in 1914 as an "automatic" system that would stabilize the currency and provide restraint on overexpansion and offer encouragement when business declined, it had struggled for leadership and purpose for nearly 50 years. Much needed and critical reorganization made under the leadership of Chairman Eccles and President Roosevelt gave the Fed direction and a stabilized structure. But it took another 20 years for the system to achieve its proper place in the role of government. Until the "accord" with the Treasury, it was not possible to function objectively. Now in the 1950s it began to play the role of a true central bank. Its independence within the government and its relation to the Congress defined and reinforced both by President Eisenhower and the Congress, it was able to assume the role of a guardian of the currency, a lender of last resort and a modifier of business and economic trends. Not by itself could it dictate the direction of the economy, but through exerting influence on the cost and availability of credit it was a strong partner with the Treasury, the Congress and the administrative branch of the federal government.

BEHIND THE SCENES AT FOMC

Reference was made in Chapter 4 to the three tools of the Fed. With the much larger federal debt, the use of purchases and sales of government securities had become the most frequently used tool. It is convenient, can be executed quickly and its action reversed easily if needed. It is an hour-by-hour tool for influencing the availability and cost of credit. It was and is a powerful tool. By executing a purchase or sale, the Fed can change the availability of funds and the psychology of the market. Fed "watchers" follow closely these transactions for clues as to the intent of the Fed.

Because it is so vital to the market and the trend of Fed policy, it is worthwhile to look more closely at the way decisions are made to use this tool. The Banking Act of 1935 established the Federal Open Market Committee—usually referred to as the FOMC or the committee—as the body to direct the purchases and sales of securities for the 12 Reserve banks. The amount in the Fed's portfolio and the earnings from it are shared by each bank approximately on the basis of their capital structures. This allocation is essentially a matter of bookkeeping although without the earnings from the securities, it would be difficult to cover the expenses of the banks. Earnings from loans to member banks are often small or nonexistent.

The members of the FOMC are the seven members of the Board of Governors and five representatives of the Reserve banks who serve on a rotating basis except that the representative of the New York Fed is a permanent member. The other four representatives (almost always the president, but the act says, "president or first vice president") are selected annually by the boards of directors of the Reserve banks. Dallas, St. Louis and Atlanta banks rotate, each serving one year at a time. Boston, Philadelphia and Richmond alternate; Chicago and Cleveland alternate and San Francisco, Kansas City and Minneapolis rotate on the committee. The act does not specify that they must rotate, but by custom they do. The boards of directors also elect an alternate representative who usually becomes the representative the following year. The presidents of all 12 banks sit with the committee but do not have a vote unless they are a voting member at the time.

The committee meets with the Board of Governors in Washington every six to seven weeks. It also occasionally meets by conference telephone

as circumstances dictate. At the regular meetings, the committee members usually have their chief economist with them as an advisor. These persons sit with the committee but do not participate in the discussion except in unusual situations. They are there to give counsel to their president if needed. As mentioned earlier, during the term of Chairman Martin, each president, whether a voting member or not, was asked to give a brief review of the economic and banking situation in his district. It might include statistical data on employment and banking trends. It would stress any new developments that are not being reflected in statistical data, apparent developing trends and any other information that would give a picture of the economy in the district. Prior to the meeting the presidents confer with their economic staffs and have the benefit of comments by members of their boards of directors who represent a cross section of their districts. The board's staff, together with the staff of the New York Fed, give a presentation on national and international trends and problems and a report on open market activities.

A free and open discussion follows on the most effective monetary policy for the next several weeks. If it is the time that the chairman is preparing to give a required report to Congress, the estimates will include the next several months and the subsequent year. While the discussion often includes opinion on the use of the discount rate and reserve requirements, the basic decisions are on open market operations.

At the end of the session a directive is framed to give direction to the manager of the "desk" at the New York Fed where purchases and sales of securities are executed. This directive gives general instructions. Also, the "desk" makes a telephone call each morning to the board so that they can stay in touch with the developments in the market. In order that the manager have a "feel" for the intent of the committee, he sits with the committee and hears the discussion. In accordance with Section 10 of the Federal Reserve Act, a record of the decisions of the committee, including each member's vote, is published in the Annual Report of the Board of Governors. A record of each meeting is made public immediately after the subsequent meeting is completed. These directives of the committee are quite lengthy. A sample is given in the Appendix.

THE "DESK"

Instructions of the FOMC with respect to purchases and sales of securities are carried out by personnel at the New York Fed. Referred to as the "desk," it actually is a room with a maze of telephones, computers,

Opposite: **Federal Open Market Committee (FOMC) meeting at the Board of Governors offices in Washington, D.C. Includes the seven members of the Board of Governors, presidents of the 12 Reserve banks (five of whom are voting members of the committee), secretary and financial staff and advisors. Photo by F. Harlan Hambright & Associates. Courtesy Board of Governors.**

chalkboards and other communication paraphernalia. During the time that the market is open, the manager of the desk and his staff are in constant touch with the market. Dealers approved by the Fed to make purchases and sales through the Fed are contacted when a decision is made to execute a transaction. Bids are taken, and sales or purchases usually are made on the basis of the best bid. An effort is made to "spread the business" if possible, but usually it is the best bid that gets the business. The transaction may be split between more than one dealer if the bids are the same. Sometimes the desk simply declines to make the trade if the prices quoted do not accomplish its purpose. It is a very sensitive nerve of the market, and a simple telephone contact with a dealer can start rumors in the market. Any action by the desk is known almost immediately throughout the market. We discussed the way funds are spread or absorbed through the banking system in Chapter 4.

The FOMC is a powerful institution. Its decisions impact on all business and financial institutions. The qualifications of the persons who sit on this committee are important to the nation. Under the Federal Reserve Act, members of the Board of Governors are appointed by the president, by and with the advice and consent of the Senate. The term of office is 14 years, and they cannot be reappointed after serving a full term. During their term of office and for a period of two years after serving, they cannot hold any office, position or employment in any member bank, except that the two-year restriction does not apply if the member has served a full term. They cannot own any bank stock, they cannot speculate in the stock market and they cannot hold any marketable U.S. securities.

Salaries are not competitive in the market, so anyone accepting a position as member of the board does so at a financial sacrifice and usually does so out of a sense of responsibility to be of service. Most members of the board do not serve the full 14 years but move on to other endeavors after serving several years. Presidents of the Reserve banks are under similar restrictions, although their salaries are more competitive. Every effort is made to eliminate any possible conflict of interest so that no member of the committee is in a position to profit from the decisions of the committee. In 1988 a former director of the New York Fed was indicted for passing information to an associate that supposedly resulted in a profit. He did not have access to the FOMC but reported a discussion at the meeting of the board of directors of the bank. This is the only time such a "leak" has been reported in the 75-year history of the system involving hundreds of directors and officers and board and bank personnel.

Opposite: **The Trading Desk at the Federal Reserve Bank of New York. Specialists carry out instructions from the Federal Open Market Committee to buy and sell U.S. marketable securities. They also assess conditions in the government securities market throughout the day. They maintain a telephone link with about three dozen dealers in U.S. securities. Courtesy Federal Reserve Bank of New York.**

OPERATIONAL STUDIES IN THE SYSTEM

A side of the Fed System that is generally omitted from a discussion of the system is the day-to-day operations and the employees studying ways of improving these operations. Economists, politicians and presidents of banks become deeply engrossed in talking about monetary policy, fiscal restraints, impact of gold and a multitude of other problems and theories—and it is right that they should, for that is their responsibility. But in the "back rooms" of the Fed banks are thousands of employees doing the work of sorting and mailing out checks, paying out and receiving coin and currency and performing functions as fiscal agent of the Treasury. Millions of pieces of paper must be handled each day, and the transactions must be done accurately and timely. A delay in presenting checks to a drawee bank can result in losses of thousands of dollars. Fed banks have the reputation of being accurate. Some are better than others, but generally they are correct in their handling of thousands of transactions.

Early in the history of the system, even before the banks opened for business, the governors of the banks, primarily under the leadership of Benjamin Strong, governor of the New York Fed, met periodically to discuss mutual problems. At one point the Federal Reserve Board intervened to restrain the activities of the Conference of Governors as the board thought the conference was acting in areas that the act gave to the board. Closer cooperation between the conference and the board resulted, and after the reorganization of the system in 1935 and the change of titles to president, the Conference of Presidents met regularly with the board. They did not always agree with each other but there was an interchange of ideas, and it provided a means for the presidents to present problems they faced and to give the board input on problems in the districts.

Within the Conference of Presidents there is a substructure of committees assigned specific areas of operations. There is a subcommittee on check collection, a committee on currency and coin, a committee working with the Treasury on problems involving fiscal agency activities. Other committees—some standing committees and some ad hoc—struggle with problems of law, loans and discounts and research.

WHAT TO DO WITH ALL THOSE CHECKS

One of the accomplishments of the committee on check collection was the setting up of a cooperative study by the system and the American Bankers Association on the handling of the soaring volume of checks. In 1952 the system assumed the collection of postal money orders, and of course it had been handling government checks for the Treasury since the early 1920s. In 1951 the volume of checks processed each day by the Fed banks averaged 9,750,000. By 1955 it had grown to 13,440,061. Although the operation had been partially mechanized, it still required manual handling of each check. Banks added machines and people, but they were running out of space in which to put them. Commercial banks were facing a similar problem.

Top: Amount encoding machine used by Federal Reserve banks, larger commercial banks and some business organizations to encode in magnetic ink the dollar amount on checks in the lower right-hand corner. *Bottom:* A computerized check sorter used by Federal Reserve banks to process checks. The machine reads the magnetic ink numbers on the check, sorts according to drawee banks, endorses, adds the amounts and totals at the rate of more than 100,000 items per hour.

The study group reviewed every possible way of changing the operation so the checks could be read by a machine. Computers were fast becoming capable of performing many functions, and it was hoped at one time that a machine would be available to read the handwriting and printing on a check. That reality was many years away. The Bank of America had done some experimenting with placing symbols on the back of the check, and there was considerable sentiment for using that position. But this area was being used for bank endorsement stamps, and that made reading the back of the check vulnerable to errors. At one point an attempt was made to require that checks be of uniform size. That met with stubborn resistance from commercial banks which had their own idea as to the appearance of their checks, including their size.

In 1956, the study group recommended the adoption of a legend on the bottom half inch of the check to be printed in magnetically impregnated ink. The characters were to be in Arabic so they could be ready by humans as well as machines. The uniform placement of encoding on the check made machine reading possible. The encoding included the ABA number of the drawee bank, the routing symbol to show which Federal Reserve district it was in, the customer's account number, room for coding by each bank and the amount of the check. The report was accepted by the American Bankers Association and the Federal Reserve System. But it remained a super selling job to convince commercial banks to incur the expense of having the codes on their checks, for printers to improve their accuracy of printing and customers to accept "those funny figures" on the bottom of their checks. Also, for years most banks had placed their checks with merchants, in their own lobby and in many other convenient places. Known as "counter checks" because they were usually on the "counter," they were used by thousands of customers rather than a check book. Obviously, these would not have the customer's account number on them. But more importantly, some left spaces for writing in the name of the bank so that no information could be preprinted on the printed check.

The sheer weight of the volume of checks and the delays caused when each one had to be manually handled gradually sold the program to the bankers and slowly but surely to their customers. Counter checks disappeared from stores and bank lobbies. Customers reluctantly paid a small fee to have their own checks preprinted. By the end of the decade the daily average of nearly 16 million checks were being processed by Fed banks in a timely manner and without a major increase in staff or machines. Computers had arrived at banks to stay.

COUNTING ALL THAT MONEY

Counting and sorting currency were another major task of the Fed banks. Every piece of currency that was returned to the Fed had to be individually sorted as being fit for further circulation or unfit and thus to be destroyed. In addition, because each Federal Reserve note issued by each of the 12 Fed

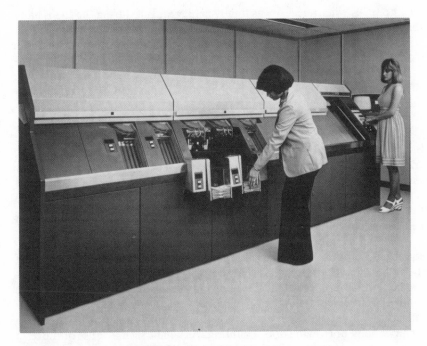

High-speed currency sorting machine. This machine counts and sorts currency according to fitness and checks for counterfeits.

banks was a liability of that bank, these notes had to be sorted by the bank of issue and returned to that bank. In 1954 Congress amended the Federal Reserve Act to permit Fed banks to pay out Federal Reserve notes of other Fed banks. This reduced the work load of processing currency. But it was still necessary to handle each piece of currency manually.

A major problem in mechanization of the process was the need to watch for counterfeits. As long as each bill was observed as it was counted, employees became experts at detecting counterfeit bills. The different "feel" of a counterfeit and the overall impression of the quality of engraving were two telltale indicators. "Sorters," as they were called, fed bills into a counting machine at the rate of as much as a thousand an hour and rarely missed a counterfeit. Also, it was difficult to design a machine that would accurately determine the fitness of a piece of currency.

Still another cost of handling currency was the need to ship unfit currency to the Treasury for destruction. Bills had to be kept under dual control, cut in half to destroy their value if found accidentally during shipping or handling and when a shipment of halves had arrived for destruction, the remaining halves were shipped. Daily average volume of pieces handled was 15,641,000 in 1951 and 18,256,000 in 1960.

Work on a design of a machine to perform this function continued into the late 1970s when success was finally achieved. But during the 1950s hand sorting was a major cost to the system. Development of the machine that was finally accepted was done under the direction of a subcommittee of the Conference of Presidents. This is another example of the network of committees that functioned within the system to solve operational problems. Other committees worked with problems of implementing regulations of the system.

CHANGING ROLE OF THE DISCOUNT WINDOW

Businesses often develop their own set of expressions regarding operations, and these are usually strange to outsiders. The "discount window," or sometimes just "the window," is such an expression in the Fed System. It is short for going to a teller's window at the Fed and offering commercial paper for discounting. Put more simply, it is a member bank going to the Fed for a loan.

Founding fathers of the Federal Reserve System envisioned the discounting of commercial paper by member banks as the heart and soul of the system. It was to be virtually automatic. In 35 years, needs of commercial banks changed as well as the environment in which they operated. The following statement from the Board of Governors' Annual Report for 1957 reflects these changes and sets forth the system's policy with regard to member bank borrowing or discounting. As will be seen, the use of the term "discount" was somewhat misleading in the 1950s.

> The more frequent use of the discount rate is a further step in the evolving process, which began seven years ago when the Treasury—Federal Reserve Accord reactivated the flexibility of monetary policy. It is the purpose of this section of the Annual Report to outline the role of the discount function as an instrument of monetary policy under present-day conditions.
>
> Federal Reserve Bank lending to member banks has taken the form chiefly of advances secured by United States Government Securities rather than discounts of commercial paper as envisaged in the original Federal Reserve Act. Following active utilization of the discount mechanism in the early years of the System, this facility was little used from 1934 to 1952. During most of the 1930s when member banks had large excess reserves, the discount mechanism had mainly a standby significance. During the war and until early 1951, member banks generally found it advantageous to replenish their reserves by disposing of United States Government securities rather than borrowing at the Federal Reserve Banks. They held large amounts of such securities, the prices of which were supported by the Federal Reserve.
>
> After the spring of 1951, however when the support policy was discontinued, market prices of Government securities became responsive to supply and demand forces. Thenceforth, when banks, in order to replenish their reserves, sold Government securities, yields were free to rise. When yields on short-term Government securities rose above the discount rate, the discount window at Federal Reserve Banks became in terms of

cost an attractive alternative to security sales as a means of making reserve adjustments.

In 1952–53, as credit demands expanded and Federal Reserve policy limited the amount of reserves made available through open market operations, pressure on bank reserves increased, and member bank borrowing from the Reserve Banks rose rapidly. During this initial revival of the discount mechanism after a generation of disuse numerous problems arose, including uncertainty among many member banks about what was an appropriate use of the discount privilege. A special circumstance was that the then-existing excess profits tax made borrowing from the Reserve Banks profitable to banks subject to the tax. Nevertheless, revival of member bank borrowing demands served to refamiliarize member banks and the Federal Reserve System with the discount mechanism and its role in credit and monetary management.

As one result of these developments, the System re-examined historical experience, notably in the 1920s, with member bank borrowing under prevailing provisions of the law. In the light of practices shown by experience to be appropriate and sound and also in the light of statutory provisions now governing Reserve Bank discounts and advances to member banks, the Board of Governors revised its Regulation A. The revised Regulation, effective in February 1955, set forth the following general guiding principles applicable to both the extension of advances and discounts by Reserve Banks and the use by member banks of the discount privilege:

Federal Reserve credit is generally extended on a short-time basis to a member bank in order to enable it to adjust its asset position when necessary because of developments such as sudden withdrawal of deposits or seasonal requirements for credit beyond those which can reasonably be met by use of the bank's own resources. Federal Reserve credit is also available for a longer period when necessary in order to assist member banks in meeting unusual situations, such as may result from national, regional, or local difficulties, or from exceptional circumstances involving only particular member banks. Under ordinary conditions, the continuous use of Federal Reserve credit by a member bank over a considerable period of time is not regarded as appropriate.

In considering a request for credit accommodation, each Reserve Bank gives due regard to the purpose of the credit and to its probable effects upon the maintenance of sound credit conditions both as to the individual institution and the economy generally. It keeps informed of and takes into account the general character and amount of loans and investments of the member bank. It considers whether the bank is borrowing principally for the purpose of obtaining a tax advantage or profiting from rate differentials and whether the bank is extending an undue amount of credit for the speculative carrying of or trading in securities, real estate, or commodities, or otherwise.

This statement must have been written either by an economist or a lawyer — maybe both. However, a careful reading discloses a flexible policy with the opportunity for a strict interpretation. In other words, if a member bank is really in trouble, and that not of its own making, the Fed stands ready to help it recover, not for just a few weeks but for months if necessary. If the member bank is in trouble because of its own mismanagement, the Fed will help, but it will monitor the member bank's operations carefully. The one clear point is that the Fed will not support excessive lending and especially lending for speculative ventures.

This was a major move from the original idea of discounting. Even today some member banks consider membership in the Fed as a *right* to borrow for any purpose. It was my privilege to be in charge of a Federal Reserve office during the time when this policy was in place. From personal experience I can say it was a flexible policy yet one that took a hard line on mismanagement or using the Fed for funds to invest in securities or excess loans. I well remember a small country bank with less than three million dollars in deposits that found it needed help to adjust to new economic conditions. Management was capable and cooperative. Loans were made to the bank for nearly two years. In another case, the bank, not much larger, wanted to borrow to invest in government securities and management saw no reason why the Fed should not loan as much as the member bank could collateralize. I was called "uncooperative," "selfish" and insisting on a policy that was illegal.

It was not an easy policy to administer. It called for subject judgments, and bankers who wanted to borrow at a low rate from the discount window were not always understanding. Managements of the larger member banks were generally aware of the policy and needed only a suggestion that it was "time to get out of the window for a while" to pay off their loan from the Fed. A few used the rate differential between the discount rate and the rate for federal funds — a term used for the sale of balances between banks — to arbitrage occasionally, but again a suggestion was usually all that was needed to obtain compliance with the Fed policy.

An amusing incident that shows the close management of funds and the need for constant attention occurred when the officer at a member bank went to lunch late and returned to the bank to find he had sold more federal funds than he had available. It was late in the day and past the regular closing time at the Fed. Again, an exception was made and a loan arranged to take the member bank out of an embarrassing situation.

LOOKING BACK
The end of the decade of the 1950s found the Federal Reserve System firmly established as a major player in the nation's economic picture with recognition of its dominant — almost exclusive — role in the area of monetary policy. Its ability to influence the cost and availability of credit was unquestioned. The administrative branch of the government recognized the "independence" of the system although it often went to great lengths to influence decisions at the Fed in order to improve its own political position. Chairman Martin had guided the system through its "accord" with the Treasury and smoothed the relationships within the system. Discussions with Congress, while not always congenial, were on an acceptable basis. It

was agreed that the Fed should make the difficult decisions on monetary policy but should never forget that it was a "creature of Congress" and subject to its oversight. The nation had experienced a decade of general prosperity with steadily expanding industrial development, relatively stable prices, low unemployment, slightly higher but not excessive interest rates, and the "police action" in Korea had ended. Underneath all was the knowledge by many that inflation was slowing emerging, and the steadily growing federal debt posed a problem that would not go away.

Chapter 8

The Public Discovers
the Fed (1960–1969)

What a decade! The Bay of Pigs debacle, the Cuban missile crisis, President Kennedy assassinated, the Gulf of Tonkin resolution, the Vietnam War, a "guns and butter" policy at the White House and the Fed banks prepare for possible atomic attack. Inflation becomes a growing threat to economic stability, and the general public discovers that the Fed causes changes in interest rates—and that such changes impact their pocketbooks.

On the economic front, inflation continued to rear its ugly head. Each year the federal government ran a deficit in its operations, and the federal debt steadily increased. Wholesale prices crept upward. But prosperity seemed assured as the gross national product also increased steadily, incomes rose and all seemed right with the world—except for that nasty conflict in Vietnam. Bank deposits increased, and all financial institutions solicited the ballooning and very profitable consumer credit field.

At the Fed, Chairman Martin continued to hold a steady course and further solidify the system's position as an independent yet responsive institution. Fears of uncontrolled inflation clouded the picture of prosperity. Knowledgeable men in finance could not help but be concerned with the growing debt and the slowly but stubbornly increasing level of prices. The wholesale price index rose 17 percent during the decade, and the Fed's discount rate doubled.

Under the leadership of the chairman of the House Banking Committee, Wright Patman (D–TX), Congress increased its probing of Federal Reserve policies and activities. Dialog between Congressman Patman and Chairman Martin was frank and at times amusing. The congressman was not about to assume responsibility for setting monetary policy, but he pursued his Populist philosophy in being critical of any move to raise interest rates or make credit less available. In the Senate, under the leadership of Senator Paul Douglas (D–IL) the Fed found a more sympathetic ear. The election of John Kennedy to the presidency in 1960 suggested an administration that would be more receptive to "liberal" economic and political policies than had been the case during the previous decade.

130

However, world events took over the spotlight before domestic policies could be formed. The ill-fated attempt to overthrow Fidel Castro and the disaster at the Bay of Pigs were soon followed by an attempt by the Soviet Union to move offensive weapons into Cuba. President Kennedy's challenge to the Soviets resulted in a reversal of their move, but it threw a scare into the nation that saw frantic attempts to prepare for a possible atomic attack.

THE FED'S ROLE

The threat of an atomic attack had a significant impact on the Federal Reserve System. As the holder of reserve supplies of currency and a major player in any recovery of the financial structure of the nation, steps were immediately taken to develop emergency plans. These plans were based on assumptions furnished by the Department of Defense and ranged from probable knock-out of some Fed banks to "maybe survival." The destruction in Japan by the two bombs dropped to end World War II left no doubt that an atomic attack would cause damages unheard of before. Cities were classified as "probable direct hits," "probable major damage" and "possibly escape from direct hits but likely to suffer from drifting radiation." Fed buildings were examined as possible fallout shelters. A direct hit was assumed to destroy everything, and everybody within a mile or more from ground zero.

Some Fed banks stocked their lower vaults with food and water. Officers and employees were classified by who would move to "relocation sites" if time permitted and who would stay behind. Duplicate records were prepared daily and sent to at least one probable relocation site. The Board of Governors established a relocation site in the mountains at Culpepper, Virginia. Also, Fed officers were assigned to a relocation site of the federal government for periods of two weeks, the theory being that in case of attack, those officers would assume control of the monetary system and proceed to reconstruct the economy. The site was deep in the hills and supposedly safe from even a direct hit. Security was tight, and Top Secret clearance was needed to participate in the knowledge of the site's location. A stock of currency was stored for use in the event of an attack. Periodically, Fed banks would reconstruct the balance sheet of the bank from the duplicate records sent from each office.

Much speculation occurred as to what would actually happen. Some Fed offices were designated as "fallout shelters" for their community. Question: Who decides who can come in? and Suppose the shelter is full and people still want in? Within the bank: Should employees be forced to remain in the shelter rather than try to reach their families? To what extent should the bank go in enforcing evacuation plans? Should violators be shot?

All this seems unnecessary from the viewpoint of the 1990s, but at the time there were real concerns and unanswered questions. Fortunately, answers did not have to be found. Duplication of records continues even into 1990. Computers now perform the laborious task of making duplicate records, and there is less talk of "relocating" employees and officers. The Fed, as a major player in the nation's government and a key player in any possible attempt to recover financially from such an attack, moved quickly to establish procedures for continuing a financial structure if an attack occurred.

The assassination of President John Kennedy in Dallas, Texas, on November 22, 1963, shocked the nation and the world. Not since President William McKinley's death by an assassin on September 6, 1901, had such a tragedy hit the nation. The snuffing out of the life of a young, energetic man who showed great promise as a leader was a loss rarely experienced by any nation. Vice President Lyndon Johnson was sworn in as president in Air Force One before leaving Dallas. Fear of a larger conspiracy sent security to a high point, and every effort was taken to assure the continuation of the government.

POLITICS AS USUAL AGAIN

At the Fed, the change of presidents was taken in stride. Chairman Martin continued to work with the administration and the Congress. However, President Johnson, Gardner Ackley, chairman of the President's Council of Economic Advisors (CEA) and Secretary of the Treasury Henry Fowler were not sure that Chairman Martin was "on their side" in matters of stimulating the economy. Meetings of the Quadriad were frequently used to pressure Martin to take or not to take certain action that might jeopardize the political scene. The increasing threat of inflation and the continued deficit in the federal budget were a growing concern of Chairman Martin and others at the Fed. Throughout the decade pressure from both Presidents Kennedy and Johnson urged Martin to keep interest rates low and to stimulate the economy. Unemployment in the area of 6 percent was unyielding to efforts to lower it. The administration felt the Fed should take action to stimulate the economy. Most of the leadership at the Fed believed the unemployment was "structural," not cyclical, and were inclined to urge caution in any stimulative effort for fear of setting off greater inflation.

At one point, the Fed agreed to abandon its longtime policy of buying only bills in the government security market. The theory was that it should not attempt to influence the rate curve but take action only in short-term securities. Finally, Martin agreed to move into the longer-term market and attempt to keep long-term rates low so as not to impact on the construction industry but to raise the short-term rates to stem the flow of gold out of the country and at least partially restrain inflation. The procedure became known as "operation nudge," meaning to nudge rates in a given direction.

This failed to accomplish what the administration wanted. Unemployment remained high. The flow of gold was slowed, but greater pressure was needed to stimulate the economy according to the president's advisors.

Martin responded by moving somewhat heavily in the longer-term market, and the name soon changed to "operation twist." In all of these actions, Chairman Martin carefully maintained the right of the Fed to make its own decisions. While listening to the pleas of the administration — and sometimes to men in his own organization — not to take action, he would find a way of meeting the request partway but not with the same tool suggested. It was a constant game of leadership, recognizing that the Fed could not long act completely against the wishes of the administration for it was after all a part of government. But he carefully avoided giving the appearance of yielding to the pressure and found another way of meeting the pressure partway, still retaining the Fed's right to the decision.

FED'S INDEPENDENCE CHALLENGED AGAIN

Congressman Patman continued to probe the activities of the system and used every opportunity to push for easier money. It bothered him that the Fed did not have to come to Congress for an appropriation, but he saw little possibility of that happening. But he did ask that the Fed's budget be submitted to Congress for review. Also, he questioned every expenditure. He also wanted the General Accounting Office (GAO) to examine the Fed's books. In fact, the GOA had audited the Federal Reserve Board. When the GAO was created in 1921, auditing of the Board was transferred from the Treasury to the GAO. However, the Banking Act of 1933 specifically provided that the board's funds "shall not be construed to be government funds or appropriated money." This was done to strengthen the board at a time when the system was badly in need of a boost.

In spite of Congressman Patman's heckling and complaints, it was generally recognized that neither the congressman nor the Congress really wanted to make the hard decisions on monetary policy facing the system. Nevertheless, criticizing the Fed and its "tight money" policy and its supposed friendliness to the "bankers" made good copy for home consumption and "kept the Fed on its toes." Pressure for control or at least close oversight of the Fed continued to grow, and in the next decade several modifications were made in the exposure of the Fed's actions to the general public.

President Johnson's theme of "guns and butter" as the Vietnam War escalated brought increasing pressure on prices and a growing federal deficit. Inflationary pressures built up, and Chairman Martin and other leadership at the Fed were increasingly concerned about the possibility of runaway inflation. Chairman Martin was forced to keep a running "battle" with the administration over the need to restrain spending. President Johnson tried his well-known "strong-arm" approach on Martin but with little effect. The chairman was not intimidated, and although he was very careful not to oppose the president openly, he did not acquiesce to his demands for action that would make money easier. He steadfastly pursued a course that would lead to restraint.

A classic example was the decision to increase the discount rate on

December 6, 1965. Martin had warned the administration as early as October that he believed an increase was necessary. Market rates were as much as a point above the discount rate, and Martin believed the discount rate should be more in line with market forces. As late as December 3 he mentioned to Secretary of the Treasury Fowler that he expected an increase in the discount rate. And on December 6, the board approved a request of the New York and Chicago Reserve banks for an increase of a half point.

President Johnson was furious. He had scheduled a meeting of the Quadriad at the LBJ ranch in early December, and he expected Martin to wait until that meeting before taking any action. Martin, however, made discussion a moot point since approval for an increase had already been given to two Reserve banks. It was another example of Martin's ability to maneuver through a maze of diverging opinions and pursue his own objective. He jealously guarded the system's right to independence and would not let it become a slave to the administration.

More and more people were now aware that there was a Federal Reserve System. Even the evening news might include an item about the Fed — a short item, but it was getting attention. University professors were being heard to discuss the system in public as well as in the classroom. Most people, even most bankers, did not understand the ramifications of monetary policy, but they were aware that what the Fed did might directly or indirectly affect them.

A case in point. In January 1964 William D. Bryan filed suit against the Fed claiming that the delegation of power to the FOMC by Congress was unconstitutional. The suit was dismissed by the U.S. District Court for Montana. But it illustrates that people were watching the Fed. It was no longer in the "closet" but on the front page — certainly of the *Wall Street Journal* if not the *New York Times*.

PROBLEMS WITH CURRENCY

A new and generally unforeseen problem in currency developed in the mid-1950s. Silver certificates in denominations of $1, $5 and $10 had been in circulation for nearly 100 years. These certificates were redeemable in silver at the Treasury. But as industrial demand for silver expanded, the price of silver crept upward. By 1961 it had reached 92 cents per ounce, and by the end of 1962 it was $1.08. Anticipation of still higher prices fueled a boom in the demand for silver bullion. The Treasury was deluged with requests to redeem silver certificates, and for a time those requests were met. It soon became evident that the Treasury would run out of silver, so notice was given that after a certain date silver certificates would no longer be redeemed in silver and that they would be removed from circulation as they were turned in to Federal Reserve banks. People scrambled to get uncirculated silver certificates as collector's items.

Since Federal Reserve notes had not been authorized in denominations of less than $5, it was necessary for Congress to authorize their issuance.

It also authorized $2 notes, but none were issued at first. It was the job of the Fed banks to retire all silver certificates coming into their possession and to begin issuing their own $1 notes. In a short time Federal Reserve notes were the only currency in circulation. A few U.S. notes were around, but consumers soon became suspicious of them as they had a red seal on the face of the bill instead of a green one.

GREATER PROBLEMS WITH COIN

The higher price of silver created a more serious problem with coin. All coin except pennies contained some silver, and as the value of the silver content of a coin exceeded its face value, it became profitable to melt the coin and sell the silver. It was unlawful to melt coins, but the profit became so enticing that the nation's coin supply was threatened. Quickly, the U.S. Mint obtained authority to change the metal content in coins, first the dollar coins, then all others. Even the pennies were hit with a higher price of copper, so all coins were changed and made of cheaper metals in the now familiar "sandwich" coin. Again, the Federal Reserve banks were the vehicle for making the change. Millions of pieces of coin were received, and at times it was necessary to ration new coin until the mints could catch up with the demand. The number of pieces of coin received and counted by the Federal Reserve banks jumped from 4.5 billion in 1964 to 10.9 billion in 1967.

NEWS ON THE INTERNATIONAL FRONT

Remember Governor Benjamin Strong (New York Fed) and Montagu Norman (governor of the Bank of England)? They were prominent in the picture of the system in the 1920s. Strong believed that the system should have strong ties with foreign central banks, especially the Bank of England. He and Governor Norman were close friends and completed many international transactions involving the Fed. Many criticized him for being concerned about relations across the Atlantic. But in the 1960s international problems literally forced their attention on leadership in the Fed as well as all persons involved in the monetary system of the world.

Gold was no longer in sufficient supply to provide the reserve that current regulations and law required. In September 1949, gold reserves held by the United States reached a peak of $24.7 billion. By the end of 1960 they had dropped to $17.8 billion and continued to decline to $11.7 by the end of 1970. Reserves held by Federal Reserve banks against note circulation and deposits reached 37.9 percent in 1960—below the required 40 percent.

What to do? The founders of the system would have said, "Get more gold or reduce your note liability." To do otherwise would to them have been a disaster—a violation of the "gold standard"—an admission of a devalued currency. But ideas had changed since 1914, and it was obvious to the leadership of financial institutions in 1960 that there simply was not enough gold in the world to support the currencies of the world at the level designated in law.

Answer? Change the regulation and the law. On March 3, 1965, Congress authorized a reduction ratio of required reserves to 25 percent. This did not solve the problem very long, and on March 18, 1965, Congress amended Section 16 of the Federal Reserve Act, eliminating the reserve provision entirely. The nation now had a truly "managed" currency. The sole backing of Federal Reserve notes and reserves against deposits was the assets of the Federal Reserve banks, primarily U.S. government securities. Paul Warburg and Carter Glass would have cried "shame, shame" (see Warburg's statement in Chapter 3).

A SUBSTITUTE FOR GOLD?

Leadership of the world's financial institutions was not taken by surprise by the problem of gold reserves. In the Board of Governors Annual Report for 1964, 30 pages are devoted to the growing problem of currency reserves. The 1965 report used 17 pages to discuss the problem of world currencies and the role that the Federal Reserve System might play in the solution of the problem. In November 1966 the following met in Washington, D.C. to discuss possible solutions: Chairman Martin of the Board of Governors of the Federal Reserve System; Secretary of the Treasury Henry H. Fowler; Pierre-Paul Schwitzer, executive director of the International Monetary Fund (IMF); and the deputy ministers of the central banks of the "Group of Ten" (England, France, West Germany, Italy, Belgium, Japan, Canada, Sweden, the Netherlands and the United States). The meeting was continued in London in January 1967. The principal topic of discussion was how to devise in the future a way of creating reserve assets that would supplement gold as a reserve currency.

The meeting was successful in achieving its objective, and at a meeting of the Board of Governors of the IMF in Rio de Janeiro in September the Outline Plan was adopted. It set forth the principles for guiding the creation, distribution and use of Special Drawing Rights (SDRs). It is not my purpose in this history of the system to explain the details of SDRs, but it is important that the system is now deeply involved in world currencies and methods of making international settlement of accounts. It no longer is concerned only with domestic problems of monetary policy and currencies but must take an active — in most cases a leading — part in the development of means for maintaining order in the world of finance and business. Accelerating totals of all currencies involved in the world's business and the lack of adequate supply of gold to continue it as the only reserve made it imperative that alternate means be created. SDRs were the answer to that problem, and Chairman Martin and Secretary of the Treasury Henry Fowler were leaders in the process of developing this alternative.

Market forces left little time to implement the new plan. In March 1968 the market price of gold in London reached $40 per ounce, compared with the official price in England and the United States of $35. The result was a two-market system for gold. Central banks agreed to utilize a "gold pool" to attempt to stabilize the price. On Friday, March 16, 1968, the Bank of England was forced to close the London gold market. Over the weekend governors of the central banks met in Washington and on March 17 issued a communiqué terminating the sale of gold to private markets. The following comments from the Board of Governors' Annual Report for 1968 gives further explanation of the action:

> The gold policy of stabilizing the market price of gold had been based on the belief that if the market price diverged too widely from the official price, doubts about the viability of the official price might arise abroad even in official circles. The fact that by mid March 1968 the SDR plan was close to adoption meant that the monetary authorities of the world, taken as a group, would soon have available a means for increasing reserves that do not depend upon either additional stocks of gold or an increase in the value of existing stocks of gold. With the establishment of the SDR system there would therefore be less and less reason to question the possibility of maintaining the official price of gold at $35 per ounce. As a result there would also be much less reason than before for concern about the price of gold in free markets.
>
> Establishment of the two-market system for gold in March 1968, although done under the pressure of a speculative crisis, was a logical step in the evolution of the international monetary system away from dependence on gold. As the Governor of the Bank of Italy pointed out in his annual report for 1967, "The Washington decision, while meeting current needs, forms part of the continuous process which has been reducing the monetary function of gold, first within individual economies, and then on an international plane." To say that the monetary functions of gold will be further reduced under the SDR system is not to argue that gold should be, or will be, demonetized. It simply means that if, as may be reasonably expected, the bulk of future additions to international reserves consist of SDR's, the size of the gold component, relative to total reserves, will gradually decline over time.

On June 6, 1968, the Congress passed the "SDR Act" authorizing the United States' participation in the plan for the creation and use of SDRs. Let us leave the topic at this point with the observation that future events will only strengthen the need for this action.

The decade of the 1960s came to a close with the horizon marred by an escalating war in Vietnam, a continued adverse trade balance and the tenth year out of the past 20 that the federal budget had been in deficit and the federal debt at an unheard level of $382.6 billion. Inflationary pressures were building, and a day of reckoning must soon be dealt with—and the Fed would have to shoulder the bulk of the responsibility for an action sure to be unpleasant.

Also, the decade brought to an end the term of William McChesney "Bill" Martin as a member and chairman of the Board of Governors of the Federal Reserve System. He had completed a yeoman task of bringing the system into a state of independence heretofore unknown. His unique ability to work with the administration, the Congress and leadership within the system had been unequaled. That he was able to counter efforts of each group with his own brand of quiet diplomacy and achieve the goals he believed vital to the system are a tribute to him that will long be remembered by those who worked with or against him. His contribution to the system was invaluable, and while its independence would again be challenged, the work he accomplished enabled the system to withstand determined efforts to weaken its ability to steer the nation's and the world's monetary policies to a stability many thought impossible.

Chapter 9
The Soaring Seventies (1970–1979)

What a decade! The discount rate tripled. Gasoline prices sky-rocketed. The federal debt more than doubled! At long last the Vietnam War wound down, and our armed forces began returning home. Negotiating for the release of prisoners was partially successful. Tragedy again hit the nation as the embarrassing story of Watergate spread like wildfire and Richard Nixon resigned in disgrace. Adding to the nation's sorrow was the taking of 45 hostages by Iran.

The amazing resilience of our great nation was exhibited once again as we continued to grow, to buy and sell, to love and to march onward to become a stronger and wiser people.

Leadership at the Fed changed as Dr. Arthur Burns replaced Bill Martin whose term had expired. Dr. Burns had been economic adviser to former President Eisenhower and had headed the Economic Advisory Council. As Burns took office, President Nixon joked, "I respect [Burns's] independence. However, I hope that independently he will conclude that my views are the ones that should be followed."

The comment was not lost on the Fed leadership, but subsequent events suggested that Chairman Burns was indeed independent. Events of the 1970s were difficult for the Fed in several ways. Congress looked for ways of curbing the independence of the Fed or at least forcing it to reveal its policies and goals in more specific terms. And the stubborn problem of inflation would not go away.

A NEW STYLE OF LEADERSHIP AT THE FED
It is worthwhile to look at the change that the new chairman brought to the Fed and to its relations with Congress and the administration. Bill Martin had been a superb diplomat who worked for a consensus in any discussion. At meetings of the FOMC he was the last to speak, and rarely was the committee's decision split. True, one or two might file a minority opinion, but the directive to the manager of the "desk" at the New York Fed was always clear. Chairman Burns on the other hand was firm in his opinions, and as far as he was concerned, he was right. Appearing before congressional committees, he seemed to assume the position of a professor teaching the congressmen a lesson in economics. At meetings of the FOMC he spoke

first and dared others to change his mind. He worked closely with the president and was accused, but never proved, of playing politics.

DIFFICULT ECONOMIC PROBLEMS

Chairman Burns's attitude towards the Congress may have exacerbated congressmen's determination to "get the Fed." In any event, legislation was soon introduced that would substantially alter the Fed's position in decision making. In addition, he came to the board at a time when inflation was accelerating and economists and politicians could not agree on solutions. Unemployment continued around 7 percent, and prices ratcheted upward. It was not supposed to work that way. According to the classic economic theory, when prices went up, unemployment was supposed to go down as the economy would be working at full speed. The higher prices were supposed to slow the demand for goods and thus cause industry to retrench; unemployment would increase, and thus the cycle would repeat itself. But it was not working that way, and the Fed among others was at a loss to find a workable solution. Out of this dilemma came the term "stagflation," meaning inflation and a stagnated economy.

Early leaders in the Fed such as W.P.G. Harding, Paul Warburg and Benjamin Strong might have said the problems of the economy were not the problems of the Fed. Let economic forces work themselves out. But by 1970 the Fed had evolved into a major player in the business cycle, and it was expected to have a solution to the problems of unemployment, high prices and expensive credit. It was true that the Fed now held a dominant position in the world of economics and politics. Action taken by the Fed influenced the entire nation directly or indirectly. The Fed was now a powerful influence in the money market and in determining the cost and availability of credit. By the end of the decade its portfolio included more than $100 billion of the federal government's securities — nearly 24 percent of all marketable securities of the U.S. government. An order to buy or sell these securities in the market sent an immediate signal to everyone in the financial world. And with this powerful tool as well as control of the discount rate and within limits the percent of reserves required by member banks, it was indeed a force to be reckoned with and respected.

Thus, it was understandable that presidents and the Congress were anxious to have a say as to what action the Fed anticipated taking. The president, as he prepared for reelection, wanted the economy to be running smoothly, even booming, to enhance his chances of being reelected. Congressmen up for reelection were anxious for "good times." Many congressmen were followers of Congressman Patman or at least sympathetic with his ideas of cheap credit and lots of it. In many ways it was the age-old conflict between the "haves" and the "have nots" expressed in terms that called for more help to all except the "rich bankers" and other "selfish rich." The expedient action was that which would help today. Worry about tomorrow later.

The task of taking a long look and trying to prevent problems that were certain to occur later fell to the Fed, and its spokesman was Chairman Burns. He not only enjoyed the role but "relished" it. A man born in Austria who worked his way through Columbia University and later became a professor of economics at that institution, he was a pragmatic man married to no special theory except the one that works in a given situation. His mannerism of "talking down" to congressmen did not endear him or his policies to them.

CONGRESS WANTS TO KNOW NOW

The struggle for independence of the Fed hit the "front burner" again during the 1970s. Congressman Patman lost his position as chairman of the House Banking Committee when the election of 1974 swept out many Democrats. But the new chairman, Henry Reuss (D–WI), and his counterpart, Senator William Proxmire (D–WI), took up the fight and were even more aggressive in determining how and what the Fed did and why they did it. Four separate attempts were made to force the Fed to divulge its goals and its action. Congress wanted to know the Fed's goals for interest rates and the probable impact of its action on the economy. Also, they wanted any discussion, especially in the FOMC, made open to the public.

The first action by Congress was the passing of House Concurrent Resolution 133 on March 25, 1975. This was a watered-down version of Congressman Reuss's original proposal. It called for the Fed to consult with Congress four times each year, twice with each banking committee of each house and report the Fed's objectives and plans with respect to the ranges of growth or diminution of monetary and credit aggregates in the coming 12 months. It fell short of demanding a forecast of interest rates.

EVASIVE ACTION BY THE FED

In complying with the resolution, Chairman Burns and his staff used several measures of monetary growth. They added to M-1 and M-2, measures already in use, M-3, M-4 and M-5 (see Glossary in Appendix for definitions). These were broader measures of the monetary base and gave the Fed more chances for setting objectives. Also, the Fed adopted the practice of using a moving base. In other words, at each time of projection of goals it used the most recent point in time as the base. This resulted in only a three months' projection. Congressmen were not happy with this kind of reporting. They wanted the Fed policy stated clearly and not with a moving base, and they wanted the Fed to define the link between the policy and expected performance of the economy. Chairman Burns refused to be that specific.

In 1977 Congress passed the Federal Reserve Reform Act, which reiterated the requirement for quarterly reports to Congress by the Fed "concerning the ranges of monetary and credit aggregates for the upcoming 12 months." Also, it prohibited discrimination "on the basis of race, creed, color, sex or national origin in the selection of Class B and C Reserve Bank director." In another sign of the times, it provided that the selection of these directors should be made "such that directors represent the public and shall be chosen with due but not exclusive consideration given to the interests of agriculture, commerce, industry, services, labor and consumers." The original Federal Reserve Act omitted mention of services, labor and consumers. The act also provided for Senate confirmation of the selection of chairman and vice chairman of the Board of Governors and extended criminal conflict-of-interest provisions for federal employees to Federal Reserve Bank directors, officers and employees. Other provisions of the act related to board action in handling bank holding company cases.

In 1978 Congress passed the Full Employment and Balanced Growth Act of 1978, known as the Humphrey-Hawkins bill. This bill required the Fed to send to the Congress (1) the Fed's own monetary policy goals and (2) how these related to the short-term objectives in the president's report, this to be done within 30 days after the president released his Economic Report to the Congress.

The casual reader may wonder why all this debate about disclosing the Fed's goal and objectives. It was not solely a question of "guarding one's turf." Congress understandably wanted to know the plans of the Fed because the Fed's action impacted directly and indirectly on the business activity of the nation. Also, Congress was charged with the responsibility of overseeing the Fed. Leadership at the Fed did not guard their action out of jealousy or wanting to be "secretive," but they felt deeply that not only was it impossible to foretell the future but if the Fed was forced to make its views public, it would create conditions in the market that would insure that the projections would be in error. Knowing the Fed's policy in detail would enable "sharp" operators in the market to take action that would be highly profitable and might neutralize the action of the Fed. Giving a few persons an advantage when most citizens could not utilize the information also would not be in the public interest.

LET THE SUNSHINE IN?

Next came the Government in Sunshine Act. In the wake of the Watergate scandal there was strong support for eliminating any possible "secrecy" in government agencies. Under a proposal put forth by Senator Abraham Ribicoff (D–CT) the Fed would have been required to open its meetings to the public, to keep full transcripts of its deliberations and release them immediately. Chairman Burns did not think this was a good idea.

The biggest problem to the Fed was the possibility of having to keep and release immediately, transcriptions of discussion of monetary policy. Since 1936 the Fed had kept detailed memoranda of such discussions. In the mid-1960s Congressman Patman launched a campaign to have these released, and in 1965 the Fed decided to release all relating to discussions that occurred before 1960 and announced that others would be released after a five-year delay. Decisions of the FOMC were released 90 days after the meeting, and in 1975 this was shortened to 45 days.

Further complicating the situation, in 1976 a Georgetown University law student filed suit challenging the Fed's right to refuse immediate release. And the federal district court agreed. As a result a decision was made to release the memoranda of discussion immediately following the next meeting of the FOMC.

The Government in Sunshine Act provided for several exemptions, including paragraph 9, which reads as follows:

> (9) disclose information the premature disclosure of which would – (A) in the case of an agency which regulates currencies, securities, commodities, or financial institutions, be likely to (i) lead to significant financial speculation in currencies, securities, or commodities, or (ii) significantly endanger the stability of any financial institution; or (B) in the case of any agency, be likely to significantly frustrate implementation of a proposed agency action.

These exemptions, and others not mentioned but included in the act, gave the Federal Reserve System and especially the Board of Governors leeway to avoid disclosing sensitive action. That it did impact the Board is shown by the following quote from the board's 1978 Annual Report:

> Under the Government in the Sunshine Act . . . which became effective March 12, 1977, the Board opened more than a third of its meetings in 1978 to public observation, either entirely or in part. Items considered in closed sessions under exemptions in the Act related primarily to monetary policy (premature disclosure of which could cause financial speculation) and to supervision of banks and bank holding companies (discussion of which generally involve information from bank examination reports or confidential commercial and financial information). To illustrate, more than half of the agenda items since March 1977 involved applications by individual banks and bank holding companies; in these discussions the Board is required by law to consider financial and managerial information, which it obtains, chiefly from bank examination reports.
>
> To aid the public in obtaining the maximum possible benefit from the Board's open meetings, copies of most staff memoranda considered by the Board at open meetings are made available to the public and an agenda summarizing the issues to be discussed is provided at each meeting. A pamphlet has been prepared explaining the applicability of the act to the Board's proceedings. Photographs of the Board members and seating charts are available in the Board Room. For those unable to attend, a recording of the discussion is retained in cassette form in the Board's Freedom of Information Office; copies may also be purchased at a nominal fee.
>
> The Board maintains a Sunshine mailing list to insure that interested members of the public learn of meetings in a timely manner. Besides announcements in the *Federal Register,* notices of meetings are made available at the Board's Freedom of Information and Public Affairs Offices and at the Treasury Department's press room.

A record, including either minutes or recordings, of each closed Board meeting is provided in the Freedom of Information Office, unless the Board has voted to withhold part or all of the discussion under the act's exemptions. This material is released when exemptions no longer apply.

HOW ABOUT A GAO AUDIT?

For years Congressman Patman had argued that the Fed should be subjected to audit by the U.S. General Accounting Office (GAO), the audit arm of Congress. In fact, the Fed had been subject to government audit until 1933. When Congress created the GAO in 1921, auditing of the Federal Reserve Board was transferred from the Treasury Department to the GAO. But in the Banking Act of 1933, in an effort to strengthen the Fed, the act provided that the board's funds "shall not be construed to be government funds or appropriated moneys." The Board of Governors had, however, hired private audit firms to audit its books and to review the board's audits of the Federal Reserve banks.

Congressman Patman had no confidence in the private audits and pushed for bringing the system under the GAO. He viewed the interest payments by the Treasury on government securities held by the Fed to be a subsidy to the Fed. Now he and other congressmen saw an opportunity to bring the Fed under an audit by the GAO. With the shadow of Watergate hanging over the capital, Congressman Patman went all out to win his point. "Why should any agency be exempt?" he asked. Legislation was drafted to accomplish his goal.

Leadership at the Fed believed such an audit was unnecessary as the private audits were made independently and were probably more thorough than a GAO audit would be. More importantly, a GAO audit would divulge important and sensitive decisions on monetary policy and in the handling of international transactions. For example, to execute appropriate monetary policy, it might be necessary to buy a given security in the market one day and sell it the following day. Such action probably would be viewed as "churning" to make a profit. The board was well aware that a GAO audit would make it almost impossible to conduct monetary policy without giving watchers of the Fed an advantage in the market, an advantage not available to everyone. It would be impossible to segregate "administrative" expenses from those required to execute monetary policy. In effect, the GAO could, and probably would, be directing monetary policy.

CHAIRMAN BURNS CALLS IN THE RESERVES

Chairman Burns, in his effort to defeat a GAO audit, trod very closely to the political line. He enlisted the help of the more than 300 directors of the Reserve banks and their branches, and he personally lobbied many congressmen and sought the support of leaders through the financial community. When Chairman Reuss accused him of "behind-the-scenes manipulations," Chairman Burns replied in part and almost parenthetically, "My impression is that the members of Congress want to hear from their constituents."

The end result was provision for "limited" GAO audits of the Fed. Chairman Burns and his staff had fought a hard and at times bitter battle. But they escaped a defeat that would have rendered the Fed ineffective in its pursuit of suitable monetary policy. Its independence had been bruised but not broken.

LEADERSHIP CHANGES AGAIN

The presidential election in November 1976 swept the Democratic party into power and Jimmy Carter into the White House. President Carter was eager to have the economy stimulated and the ups and downs that had plagued the nation during the past years eliminated. The fact that inflationary pressures were building rapidly was overlooked. Chairman Burns was not excited about the new administration. Candidate Carter had made comments about the Fed that the chairman disliked, and he did not share the idea that the economy needed stimulation.

As a result, President Carter did not reappoint Burns as chairman but nominated G. William Miller, chairman of the board of the Textron Corporation, as Burns's replacement. It would have been difficult to have brought about a sharper contrast in management styles. Miller was an activist and proceeded to conduct the board meetings as if they were meetings of the board of a commercial corporation. He posted No Smoking signs in the boardroom in contrast to Burns's pipe-smoking habit. He limited discussion to three minutes and even voted against the majority of the board on a request to raise the discount rate. The financial community was an enthusiastic supporter of Miller at first but soon recognized his lack of understanding of the economic and fiscal problems facing the nation. His term of office was only 18 months. In 1979 President Carter asked him to take the position of secretary of the treasury and began looking for a new chairman of the Board of Governors. Paul Volcker, president of the Federal Reserve Bank of New York, became his choice. (More on Mr. Volcker later.)

ANOTHER FIRST AT THE BOARD

On September 18, 1978, Nancy Hays Teeters was sworn in as the first woman member of the Board of Governors of the Federal Reserve System. She was named to fill the unexpired term of Chairman Burns, although she represented the Chicago rather than New York district. Mrs. Teeters was no stranger to the Fed. She had served as a staff economist at the board for nine years. She also had served as economist for the President's Council of Economic Advisors. Her publications included a series of studies on "Setting National Priorities," of which she was coauthor.

An interesting conversation is reported to have taken place between Teeters and Chairman Burns as she was about to join the board:

Teeters: "Arthur, you don't want somebody with known Democratic connections."

Chairman Burns: "It doesn't matter, Nancy. After six months [on the Board] everybody is a central banker."

Governor Teeters was replaced at the end of her term by Martha R. Segar from Michigan, also a representative from the Chicago district. Segar also spent time at the board prior to her appointment, serving as a financial economist from 1964 to 1967. While not specifically designated as such, both women gave additional emphasis to representation of consumers on the board. Governor Segar's term as a member of the Board of Governors expires January 31, 1998.

INCREASING IMPORTANCE OF INTERNATIONAL FACTORS

Rapidly expanding communications and transportation facilities were drawing all nations closer together. Financial transactions between nations and between businesses in different nations were expanding almost daily. The major industrial nations of the United States, Canada, United Kingdom, France, West Germany, Italy, the Netherlands, Belgium and Japan were in many respects one large market. Exchange rates for currencies were critical to profits and stability of economies.

In December 1973 the Committee of Twenty of the International Monetary Fund (IMF) met in Rio de Janeiro to discuss the mutual problems of currency exchange and a reserve base for all currencies. The meeting was continued in Washington in January 1974. Also of importance to the representatives at the meeting was the growing energy crisis. The following paragraph from the 1973 Annual Report of the Board of Governors illustrates the critical importance of international developments to the Fed:

> By early July (1973) exchange markets for the dollar against EEC (European Economic Community) currencies had become disorderly. Beginning July 10 the Federal Reserve undertook intervention to stabilize the exchange rate for the dollar, drawing on recently enlarged swap lines (swapping various currencies by buying and selling in the market), and sold $273 million of foreign currencies (marks, French francs and Belgium francs) by the end of the month. This action was reinforced by purchases of dollars by the German Federal Bank and a relaxation of a credit squeeze in the German interbank market. The appearance of central bank intervention, together with the joint statement on July 18 of the Chairman of the Federal Reserve Board of Governors and the Secretary of the Treasury that intervention would take place "in whatever amounts are appropriate for maintaining orderly market conditions," helped to restore exchange markets to more normal functioning.

The 1976 Annual Report of the Board of Governors devoted 17 pages to the international situation. On October 10, 1978, Congress amended the

Bretton Woods Agreement Act of 1945 to authorize the subscription to 1.45 billion in SDRs (Special Drawing Rights). More and more decisions at the board had to take into consideration the impact on the international scene. More and more time was required for meetings and consultations with leaders of other industrial nations' central banks. It was a new role but an essential one as the value of the dollar in world markets had become important to domestic business.

THE CONSUMER DEMANDS ATTENTION

Whether it resulted from more intense and rapid communication or was in part a sign of the affluence of the nation (we now had time and money for such things), consumers demanded to be taken seriously. They insisted on quality products, the ability to seek redress for errors, access to more information and insistence that the government do something. Inflation and its erosion of the value of the dollar were the most immediate complaints.

In an attempt to slow inflation a three-pronged program was announced by the administration in August 1971: (1) a 90-day freeze on wages and prices, (2) suspension of the convertibility of the dollar into gold and (3) a temporary 10 percent tax on dutiable imports. High rates of interest resulted in the appointment of the Committee on Interest and Dividends with Chairman Burns as chairman. These actions were not entirely successful. The wholesale price index increased 4 percent during the following 12 months.

Responding in part at least to consumer demands, Congress passed 14 acts, including the Equal Credit Opportunity Act on October 28, 1974; the Home Mortgage Disclosure Act on December 31, 1975; the Financial Institutions Regulatory and Interest Rate Control Act on November 10, 1978; the Truth in Lending Act on May 29, 1968, with a variety of amendments in the 1970s; the Magnuson-Moss Federal Trade Commission Improvement Act on January 4, 1975; the Community Reinvestment Act on October 12, 1977; the Fair Housing Act, amending the Civil Rights Act of 1968, and the Fair Credit Reporting Act on October 26, 1970; the Fair Debt Collection Act on September 20, 1977; and the Right to Financial Privacy Act on November 10, 1978.

And guess who got to administer most of these acts? The Board of Governors of the Federal Reserve System. The workload on the board was staggering. The number of employees increased from 901 to 1,572 during the decade, with most of them requiring special training such as lawyers, economists and statisticians.

Each of the Reserve banks also had a role to play in the administration of most of these acts. The complete and almost immediate coverage of the nation was possible through the 12 Reserve banks and the 25 branches. Usually, personnel already employed by the banks were available for special assignment, but in several areas where specialized training was needed, additional professional persons were hired. But the total number of employees at the Reserve banks increased only from nearly 20,000 to 22,000, with many of these working in operating sections of the bank clearing checks and handling currency and coin.

BANK OPERATIONS CHANGING TOO
Technology and legislation hit the operations side of the system also. One of the most sweeping pieces of legislation impacting the banking industry was the Bank Holding Company Act of 1970. The act of 1956 was important, but the new act brought one-bank holding companies into the fold, and it was a major change in the organization of commercial banks. For example, in 1973 the Board of Governors considered 1,499 cases involving the Bank Holding Company Act. In the board's Annual Report for 1976 14 pages are devoted to a review of litigation surrounding the question of bank holding companies.

Check collection had been a major operation of the Reserve banks since their organization. Receiving, sorting and collecting millions of checks required a substantial part of the staff of the Reserve banks. As checking accounts became more popular and the volume of business transacted with checks expanded, so did the volume of checks sent to the Reserve banks. Mention was made in the discussion of the decade of the 1950s of the study to make checks readable by machines. This program was a giant step toward automation. In the 1970s computers came to the Feds, and checks were among the first operations to utilize the new technology. The 1979 volume of checks handled by the Reserve banks had reached 33 million *daily* with a value of $3.75 billion, compared with 3.3 million and $1.66 billion in 1970. Something had to be done. Reserve banks were running out of physical room to add more of the older machines. Progress continued in a search for a machine that would handle currency, sorting, counting it and checking for counterfeits.

CHANGES OUTSIDE THE FED
Other changes were taking place in the world of money that would impact the Fed. A revolution was in the making in the financial world. Long-established practices and policies were being challenged and changed. New terminology was emerging. NOW accounts (negotiable orders of withdrawal) were replacing the customary checking account. Interest could be paid on these accounts but not on checking accounts. Consumers were quick to capitalize on the change. Savings and loan associations began to abandon their primary role of financing construction of houses. Credit unions joined the chase for more deposits, abandoning their traditional role of serving only "members." The requirement still held that customers must be members, but the membership rules were broadened substantially. It was jokingly said that if you drove through a town where a credit union was located, you could become a member.

"Disintermediation" became a buzz word. What did it mean? Different things to different people. But basically it was the movement of deposit funds away from the traditional banks and into a variety of organizations offering to pay interest or offering a probable increase in value of the depositors' funds. Insurance companies, brokerage houses and even business corporations such as Sears joined the game.

All of these changes diluted statistical data on deposits and made the task of evaluating a given situation more difficult. As mentioned earlier, the Board of Governors had expanded their measures of the money supply by adding to M-1 (demand deposits) M-2, M-3, M-4 and M-5. Also, the newcomers to the "deposit" game were not under the control of the Federal Reserve System, the Federal Home Loan Board or the Exchange Commission. In fact, they could do about as they pleased, much to the concern of banks and savings and loan associations.

Still more changes were taking place in the world of financial transactions. One involved the rapid movement of money across the country or to the next town by use of "wire transfers." For many years the Federal Reserve System had provided telegraphic transfer of member bank balances, but it was used only by banks and in a limited way. "Bank drafts"—checks by one bank on another—sent through the mail were the more likely way for money to move from one bank to another. Again, improvements in communications made faster movement possible, and the opportunity to earn interest on idle funds accelerated the shift to wire transfers. Using the Fed's wire system or the bank system operated by commercial banks, money could be moved anywhere in a matter of minutes. With interest rates moving higher and higher, the incentive to make maximum use of funds was good business. Corporations as well as banks joined in the race to see how efficiently they could be in utilizing the funds available to them. At the Feds, the number of wire transfers handled jumped from 21 million in 1976 to 353 million in 1979. The dollar value of these transfers rose from $35.6 trillion to $64.2 trillion during the same period.

REMOTE DISBURSEMENTS A PROBLEM

Imagine you are the treasurer of a large corporation with headquarters in Dallas, Texas. Assume that you have a weekly payroll of $1 million. If you write your payroll checks on a Dallas bank, they will clear in a day or two as most of your employees live in the Dallas area. That doesn't give you much "float"—the amount of money you can use against which you have written checks but which have not been charged to your account. Now assume that you have been reading the trade journals for your industry and picked up an idea. Move your payroll account to a small bank in Montana and write your payroll checks on that account. It will take nearly a week for the checks to be charged to your account, and you will have that $1 million to "sell" at maybe 8 percent for several days. That should earn you a promotion. But wait—how do you know that bank in Montana is able to handle your million-dollar payroll? No problem. Open the account for a minimum balance the bank will agree to and tell the bank to call you when the payroll checks reach it. You will immediately wire-transfer money to cover the checks. No risk, and you have made the company money. It should earn you a raise.

These operations were not pleasing to the leadership of the Federal Reserve System. On January 11, 1979, the Federal Reserve Board issued a policy statement intended to discourage the use of remote disbursement arrangements. A portion of that statement follows:

> The Board has the following principal concerns with respect to remote disbursement: (1) it can expose both the bank involved and recipients of the remotely disbursed payments to risk of loss ... that they may not be aware of ... during the deliberately prolonged clearing time. (2) Consumers and small businesses — may be denied prompt access to funds due them. (3) Remote disbursement could result in unsafe or unsound banking practice if the funds at the remote disbursing bank are not sufficient to cover the customers' checks. This would result in unsecured extension of credit by the bank to the customer. Such extensions of credit might not be warranted as a matter of loan policy. In the case of small banks, such loans might exceed the legal limit for lending to any one customer.... The Board believes the banking industry has a public responsibility not to design, offer, promote or otherwise encourage the use of a service expressly intended to delay final settlement and which exposes payment recipients to greater than ordinary risks.

The board proceeded to take whatever action was available to discourage the use of remote disbursement arrangements and the practice gradually was curtailed by most banks.

One of the reasons for establishing the system was to make the collection of checks more efficient. Circuitous routing of checks had been a problem for decades. And the Fed set up its check clearing service to make it possible to clear checks promptly. Why bother? Some people have argued that "float" never hurt anyone. Two parties have the use of the same money at the same time. If every check writer were honest and there were no "bad" checks, the argument might have merit. But that is not the case in the real world. Two major problems are involved. A delay in check clearing makes it difficult for the payee of a check to know when it has been finally collected. If you deposit a check on Monday and two weeks later you are told that it was not paid because the maker did not have enough money in his account, you have been inconvenienced to say the least. A more critical problem with float is the opportunity for fraud. Check "kiting" is an old scheme for defrauding banks. If a person can write a check drawn on one bank, deposit it in a second bank, and before it reaches the drawee bank write a check on a third bank to cover the first one, it is possible to build up a large balance in one bank, then withdraw the cash from the account and leave town. Someone will not be able to collect the last check written. It has happened many times, and the answer to this fraud is to make check collection rapid so there is not time to cover one check with another one.

Float presents still another problem to banks. Giving credit for checks deposited by a customer before they are collected from the drawee bank results in the first bank making money available that it does not have. If the checks deposited are returned unpaid, then the bank has to collect from the customer — not a pleasant thing to do, especially if the customer has already spent the money. Federal Reserve banks adopted a policy in the early years of their operation of giving credit to member banks for checks deposited for collection on a deferred basis, using their experience of the average time for collection of checks in a given geographic area. For example, credit for checks drawn on out-of-town banks was delayed one or two days, depending on the probable time of collection. Some checks would not be collected in the time credit was deferred, resulting in the bank "carrying the float." Float carried by Fed banks grew into the millions of dollars. On December 31, 1979, it was over $6 billion.

WHAT CAN THE FED DO?

Leadership at the Board of Governors and at the Reserve banks were very concerned about the trend in shifting deposits and the increasing delay in collection of checks. For several years the board had recommended to the Congress that authority be given to require reserves against deposits at all organizations offering checking privileges. Within the system efforts were begun to speed up the collection of checks. In 1975 the Atlanta Fed opened a branch in Miami, Florida, to facilitate collections and better serve member banks in the Miami area. Pursuant to the board's policy statement of July 17, 1971, 24 regional check clearing offices were opened in 1972, and 15 more were scheduled to open by mid-1973. These facilities, most operating at night, reduced time for checks to reach the drawee bank. Reserve banks stepped up efforts to speed the handling of checks by permitting later deposit of checks for collection and speeding dispatch of the checks by use of over-the-road carriers rather than mail.

In 1978 the use of automated clearinghouses was encouraged, and the Fed banks began utilizing their wire facilities to process transactions by wire wherever possible. Social Security payments and other regular government payments were among the first to take advantage of these facilities. By sending a magnetic signal over the wires, a computer tape was created that could be sent to the member bank and fed directly into its computer system. Commercial firms were encouraged to use the ACHs for payrolls and other regular payments. This procedure permitted immediate credit with no float involved. Volume built slowly as payers were reluctant to give up the float. But it was obviously a forward step and a more efficient way of handling regular payments.

Congress began to look at the huge float carried by Fed banks and questioned the policy that would permit such unauthorized "loans" to member banks. Float was in effect a loan to the depositing bank. Also, Congress questioned the Fed's giving of services to member banks. No charge was made for clearing checks, and transportation was paid for delivering and receiving currency and coin from member banks. Bank-to-bank wire transfers were also free. Transfers involving a third party did involve a fee.

Pressure was building to make significant changes in the financial structure of the nation as well as the Fed. As will be seen in the next chapter, Congress was about to make a major move.

MORE BUILDINGS NEEDED

More programs for the Fed to execute meant the need for more personnel and space. The number of officers at the Reserve banks jumped from 558 to 716 during the decade of the 1970s. Many of these were professional persons needed to handle the growing load of technical and legal questions. At the Reserve banks the number of employees grew modestly from 22,079 to 24,208. Most of the Reserve banks added space by renting or building new buildings. Most were finding it necessary to consider new headquarters for the bank.

At the Board of Governors the new Martin Building was constructed, and on November 19, 1974, the building was dedicated with former Chairman Martin as the honored guest.

Moving into the decade of the 1980s, the Fed faced many problems. Paramount in the thinking of its leadership was the growing threat of uncontrolled inflation. The wholesale price index had doubled during the 1970s. The discount rate had moved from 5½ to 12 percent. The prime rate jumped from 4.25 percent to 13. The federal deficit had more than doubled. The following paragraph from the 1979 Annual Report summarizes the attitude of most financial leaders:

> At year-end, the short-term outlook for inflation remained bleak. Inflationary pressures seem likely to continue intense, not only because of a further boost in oil prices, but because past increases in costs and prices will still be working their way through the economy. In these circumstances, the urgent task of policy is to make sure that inflation is not exacerbated by the development of excessive demands on the economy or by unrealistic expectations as to the future strength of markets.

Chapter 10
Another Banking Evolution (1980–1989)

The economy emerged from the soaring seventies with inflation unchecked and the financial industry in turmoil. However, by the end of the decade, unbelievable progress had been made in containing inflation and correcting inequities in the banking world. The Federal Reserve System was a major player in changes that rivaled those of the 1930s in banking. During the 1980s inflation tumbled to a mere 3 percent. The cost of gasoline at the pump dropped below $1. Inventories stopped soaring in value, and the construction and real estate boom came to a screeching halt. The nation watched (mostly in vain) for a glimpse of Halley's comet and marveled at scenes from the sunken *Titanic*. The mood at the nation's colleges and universities became generally nonviolent and conservative.

Financial markets around the world were uneasy about the changes taking place in President Carter's cabinet and especially the vacancy at the Fed. G. William Miller had accepted the position of secretary of the treasury, leaving the Fed without a chairman. With no chairman at the Fed, the dollar quickly weakened in world markets. Looking for a replacement at the Fed, President Carter was hopeful of finding someone who would not be too independent from the administration but one who would be acceptable to the financial community.

WELCOME, PAUL VOLCKER
"There is a tide in the affairs of men, which, if taken at the flood, leads on to fortune." In retrospect this quotation from Shakespeare's *Julius Caesar* seems apropos to the selection of Paul Volcker, president of the New York Fed, to head the Federal Reserve System at this time in history. He was well educated in the field of economics and banking with a master's degree from Harvard University and time as a student at the London School of Economics. He had been associated with the system since being a summer employee at the New York Fed. He had served in the Treasury as director of financial analysis and as deputy under secretary. He had experience in commercial banking at the Chase Manhattan Bank in New York and served as principal negotiator in the development of a new international monetary

system. He was a natural for the job of chairman of the Board of Governors of the Federal Reserve System. His nomination was quickly approved by the Senate, and the financial world breathed a sigh of relief when he was sworn in on August 6, 1979.

A "WARM" WELCOME FOR THE NEW CHAIRMAN

It was far from quiet on the financial front in the early days of the 1980s. Events of the preceding two decades finally forced major adjustments in the banking community. Inflation was roaring upward at exponential speed. The prime rate jumped to 21 percent. The discount rate reached a new record high at 14 percent. The world watched with concern as the nation struggled to bring inflation under control. Chairman Volcker had no doubts about the seriousness of the situation, and he was determined to pull the plug on this runaway inflationary binge.

For years the Fed had been using interest rates as the key to measuring conditions in the market for money. It was well known that this was the key indicator used, and those adhering to the monetarist theory of monetary policy were shouting for the Fed to do something—like looking at the money supply as a measure of economic activity.

Only two months after assuming the chairmanship, Paul Volcker took a daring step. He called the FOMC to a special Saturday meeting. An unheard-of event. It was reported that Chairman Volcker didn't waste a lot of time in discussions. His staff had prepared information over the past several weeks, and he was ready for action. What his words were on that Saturday morning, October 6, 1979, was not recorded, but I heard from one who was present that there was no question about what decisions were going to be made. Following the meeting at a press conference the chairman announced that the board would allow the Reserve banks to increase the discount rate from 11 to 12 percent, new higher reserve requirements would be set for member banks and the system would no longer look only at interest rates in setting monetary policy but would look primarily at the money supply. You could hear the monetarists cheer and say, "About time." The bold move settled the markets and gave further evidence that the Fed would do what was necessary to halt the inflationary spiral.

It was a tough battle. As the Fed began to wring out the inflationary psychology and slow the skyrocketing prices, the economy reacted as the classical economist would have expected. Interest rates skyrocketed. The prime rate rose from 9.06 percent in 1978, to 12.67 percent in 1979, to 15.27, and during 1980 it jumped repeatedly, reaching 15 percent, then 19 percent, and in January of 1981 to 20.5 percent! Mortgage rates rose to 15.89 percent in May of 1982. And the Fed's discount rate hit 14 percent in June 1981 as the Fed applied the brakes. The result was not unexpected. New housing starts dropped from over 2 million in 1978 to 846,000 in August 1981. Who was to blame? The Fed, of course. The construction industry, particularly hard hit, struck back with threats and warnings that the nation was going

Paul A. Volcker, chairman of the Board of Governors, Federal Reserve System, August 6, 1979–August 11, 1987. A strong leader who led the fight to break the accelerating inflation of the early 1980s. Courtesy Board of Governors of Federal Reserve System.

into a depression worse than the 1930s. Chairman Volcker caught the brunt of the criticism. Contractors mailed the chairman two-by-fours to emphasize their plight.

INFLATION SLOWED

But the Fed hung tough. Chairman Volcker and others in leadership roles knew that to give in now would only renew the inflation. So they held their ground, and by September 1981 the prime rate dropped one point. The upward momentum had been broken. It remained to be seen if the Fed could hold out long enough to bring rates on down and convince the public that inflation had been knocked down and maybe knocked out. At least there was promise of more stability. But it took another four years to bring interest rates down to their earlier, more reasonable level. In 1985 the prime rate dropped below 10 percent, and in 1987 mortgage rates dropped to 9.3 percent.

The psychology that said prices always went up had been proved wrong. But the battle was not without its price. Loans made with great confidence suddenly were in default. Real estate values tumbled to more realistic levels — disastrous levels in some cases. The number of commercial banks closed because of financial difficulties, which for decades had been fewer than 10 each year, jumped to 42 in 1982 and in 1988 to 200. And the trend continued in 1989.

Savings and loan associations fared even worse. Inflated real estate loans, insider "deals" and fraud racked the industry. Hundreds of associations were declared insolvent, but the insurance fund of the Federal Savings and Loan Insurance Corporation (FSLIC) was insufficient to pay depositors with insured deposits. As a result many remained open, hoping to work out of a very difficult situation. Estimates of the cost to liquidate the insolvent associations were as high as $500 billion. President Bush's proposal to solve the problems of the savings and loan industry, presented to Congress in February 1989, carried a price tag to taxpayers of at least $50 billion, and many analysts believed this was too low.

MAJOR CHANGES FOR THE FED
AND THE BANKING INDUSTRY

Increased sophistication in monetary affairs on the part of the average citizen, entrance of nonbank corporations into the field of checking accounts, improved communications permitting almost instantaneous execution of transactions and easy access to the markets of the world completely disrupted the usual patterns of banking.

Writing in the Federal Reserve Bank of Dallas's *Economic Review* of May 1989, economists Harvey Rosenblum and W. Michael Cox stated,

> Over the past decade, the banking and monetary system of the United States has fundamentally and perhaps irrevocably changed. There are clearly many major differences in the financial environment today as compared with only a few years ago. Perhaps the greatest of these differences is the way in which people hold money and wealth. As recently as 10 years ago, individuals used chiefly currency and demand deposits for transaction balances, while they preferred savings accounts, interest-bearing securities, and other assets as stores of value. In this old regulated financial environment, checkable bank deposits were prohibited from paying interest, and rates on savings deposits were limited to a maximum of 5½ percent.

These developments plus a growing interest on the part of Congress resulted in the passage of the Financial Institutions Deregulation and Monetary Control Act of 1980. Passed by Congress on March 30, 1980, it reshuffled the entire financial community. In its impact on banking and the

Federal Reserve System it ranks with the Federal Reserve Act itself and the Banking Acts of 1933 and 1935. Rosenblum and Cox expressed it this way: "Understanding the likely macroeconomic effects of financial deregulation is clearly important to the Federal Reserve in view of the direct linkage to monetary policy. The selection of a monetary aggregate, of an operating procedure, and of policy indicators or guidelines must all be reexamined in the light of the new and deregulated financial environment."

Features of this act, which used 85 pages of small print to cover its provisions, are numerous and far-reaching. From the standpoint of the Fed, three features stand out:

1. It required all depository institutions that maintain transaction (checking) accounts or nonpersonal time deposits to maintain reserves with the Fed, but only to the extent necessary for the conduct of monetary policy.
2. It opened the facilities, including the discount window, of the Fed banks to *all* banks, including savings and loan associations and credit unions.
3. It required the Fed to price its services to banks and to recover its cost for providing these services by charging fees—not only to recover its direct and indirect costs but also an amount it would have paid in taxes and interest on invested capital if it had been a private for-profit organization.

The services for which fees were to be charged were spelled out in the legislation and included furnishing currency and coin, clearing and collection of checks, wire transfers of funds, automated clearinghouse transactions, balance settlements for banks, safekeeping of securities, noncash collections, Federal Reserve float and any new services that might be initiated.

Another provision that pleased Fed personnel was a requirement that ceilings on interest rates paid by banks and savings and loan associations be phased out. This control of interest paid on savings deposits—an outgrowth of the 1935 Banking Act—probably stimulated more questions and interpretations than any other topic requiring the attention of personnel of the board and the Fed banks. Originally, uncontrolled payment of interest on deposits, especially demand deposits, was thought to have been one of the causes of the failure of banks in the late 1920s and the 1930s. In the past 50 years this conclusion had been questioned and now even controls on interest on demand deposits were thrown away.

Other major provisions of the Act:

- permitted automatic transfers from savings accounts to other accounts and debts;
- made Negotiable Orders of Withdrawal (NOW) accounts permissible nationwide (formerly permitted in some states by state action);
- raised insurance of deposits to $100,000 per depositor at commercial banks and savings and loan associations;

- overrode state usury laws with some exceptions;
- added an amendment to the Truth in Lending Act affecting national banking laws;
- removed collateral requirement for Federal Reserve notes held in vaults of Fed banks;
- expanded eligible collateral for Federal Reserve notes to include securities guaranteed by the U.S. Treasury and other assets eligible for purchase by Federal Reserve banks;
- allowed member banks to deposit an amount up to 10 percent of their capital and surplus with any depository institution that is authorized to have access to Federal Reserve advances;
- eliminated the penalty rate for borrowing from the Fed using certain collateral;
- authorized savings and loan associations to invest up to 20 percent of assets in commercial paper, consumer loans and corporate debt;
- authorized the Treasury to issue long-term debt up to $70 billion;
- authorized the Treasury to increase the rate of interest on Savings Bonds above 5½ percent;
- made numerous changes in operations of savings and loan associations and credit unions that were peculiar to them.

CHANGES WELCOMED BY CONSUMERS

Most consumers probably welcomed these changes. The most obvious change to them was that their bank would now pay interest on their checking accounts, something they believed should have been done long ago. And their deposits were now insured up to $100,000. However, most of the changes had little direct impact on the consumer, at least in the beginning. They were little interested in who could borrow from the Fed or whether the Fed had to charge for its services. Besides, they now had a smorgasbord of financial services available to them from many organizations.

But the impact on the financial community was dramatic. For generations savings and loan associations had followed the theme that created them and loaned almost exclusively to homeowners and contractors building homes or apartments. They loaned "long," and their deposits were considered "stable" even though interest rates paid to depositors often were in line with short-term rates. Now they were in many ways in the same ball game with commercial banks. Unfortunately, they had long-term loans outstanding at low rates and soon found themselves competing for deposits at higher short-term rates. Also, as they moved into the arena of checking accounts, they found that their personnel were unfamiliar with the problems and procedures in handling such accounts. The competition for persons trained in this area was fierce in some communities.

Credit unions also found themselves in a new ball game. Released from strict membership rules, they solicited business from the entire community. Their loan portfolio did not suffer the same restructuring experienced by savings and loan associations, but they did venture into a broader range of loans, including some real estate development. Access to services of the Fed was welcome, but they did not see an immediate need for use of the discount window. Check clearing with the Fed was a possibility. Their currency and coin needs were small.

IMPACT ON THE FED

Two things hit the Fed banks almost immediately. First, their clientele was suddenly expanded to include all depository institutions offering checking accounts. Clearing arrangements had to be made. In some cases clearing accounts were opened at the Fed and in others, arrangements were made through a correspondent bank. At the board, regulations had to be written governing the transition to reserve accounts for savings and loan associations and credit unions. The law said these reserves should be imposed "solely for the purpose of implementing monetary policy." How much was needed for this purpose? How would it be administered, and how was the transition to be made?

The board realized that there must be time for the new "customers" to adjust to leaving part of their money with the Fed. Also, reserves for the very small institutions were not necessary for the implementation of monetary policy. Over a period of six years the requirement was installed. Eventually, very small institutions were exempt from reserve requirements. Provisions also were made to impose "emergency" reserves if deemed necessary. Reserve requirements were based on the size of the institution as reflected in the amount of demand deposits held. Rates originally ranged from 7 to 16¼ percent on demand deposits. Rates on savings and time deposits ranged from 3 to 6 percent, with NOW accounts generally requiring 12 percent.

A second and even more complicated procedure was the establishment of fees for services. Costs of providing services could be quite easily determined from records of the Fed banks. But what would happen when the Fed started charging? Would banks shift to other sources of the services? Correspondent banks had for years offered check clearing facilities and loans to banks keeping accounts with them. Could they do it cheaper than the Fed? No one knew.

Perhaps a more difficult question was how to change the attitude of Fed personnel. For generations they had been trained to "give" services and to solicit business on the basis of services being "free." Officials of the Fed banks visited commercial banks and invited them to make use of the Fed's free services. They visited nonmember banks and pointed out the advantages of membership and the free services available. Now the same personnel were faced with being competitive and soliciting customers on the basis of offering services "cheaper" than were available from correspondent banks. Membership in the Fed System had little appeal. Everyone had access to the services. Why be a member and tie up more funds in purchasing

Fed stock which would pay a maximum dividend of 6 percent (the maximum permitted by the Federal Reserve Act)? The only advantage of membership now was the right to elect some of the directors of the Fed banks—a right of questionable value in the eyes of most bankers. After all, the real power was in Washington at the Board of Governors.

THE FED ADJUSTS

It is a tribute to the quality and training of Fed personnel that the adjustment was made without major problems, and by 1984 the goal of breaking even on services was achieved. The "private sector adjustment factor" was set at 16 percent. This was the amount the Fed banks added to their direct and indirect costs in arriving at their true competitive costs. Some hard decisions had to be made in reducing personnel in some cases, and the fees had to be adjusted several times. Check volume did drop slightly the first year fees were imposed, but by the following year the volume was again on the increase. The amount of float being absorbed by the Fed dropped from a daily average of $6.7 billion in 1979 to $4.2 in 1980 and to $2.8 in 1981. Over the next several years it was reduced further and in 1989 was averaging about $1 billion.

Several internal changes were made at the Fed banks in an effort to improve their services and to reduce float. Installation of computer terminals in member banks greatly improved the ability of member banks to transfer funds. Banks were able to initiate transactions in-house that were cleared through the Fed network. In 1982 this program was expanded to include smaller country banks. It not only improved the service for the commercial banks but reduced the clerical load at the Feds. Banks could now receive and send transfers as needed without calling or writing the Fed. The use of the wire facilities was now a vital part of the banking industry.

Both the Fed's and the commercial banks' "bank wire" were keys to efficient use of available funds. No bank wanted to have idle funds, even overnight. And the market was broad enough that funds could be sold any time—at a price. Transactions were originated by telephone conversation or by prearranged time schedules, and the dollar volume was unbelievable. In 1980 the amount going through the Fed's wire system exceeded $78 trillion for a daily average of $302 billion. By 1988 it had reached a daily average of more than $600 billion.

DAYLIGHT OVERDRAFTS

With four time zones in the continental United States and the commercial banks' goal of utilizing every available dollar, officers in charge of maintaining the bank's cash position had to be on their toes. For example, a bank officer in a bank in Chicago evaluating his position at 10:00 A.M. might expect to have $10 million in excess funds for the day. After making arrangements to sell that much, he might find that some anticipated deposits did not materialize or that an unexpected withdrawal reduced the surplus so that he might have to buy funds to meet his daily reserve requirement at the Fed. If these developments occurred late in the day, the New York banks might be closed, and he would need to seek a source farther west.

Because banks planned to keep surplus funds to a minimum, it could happen that a bank would sell more than it should, and the result at the end of the day would be a deficiency in its reserve account, or worse, an overdraft. Also, banks that were very active in this "Fed Funds" market could and sometimes did oversell during the day anticipating that they would balance out — have adequate reserves at the Fed — by the close of business. In other words, for a period of time during the day the bank could be "overdrawn" at the Fed. The Fed was concerned about these "daylight overdrafts," for if a bank should become insolvent or unable to recover its reserve position, the Fed would be exposed to a loss. Overdrafts did occur, and in 1985 the board issued procedures for avoiding them. Banks active in the funds market were required to establish parameters within which they would operate so that overdrafts would not occur. Even "daylight overdrafts" were to be avoided, and penalties were assessed against violators.

REMOTE DISBURSEMENTS — A NEW CHECK COLLECTION PROBLEM

Delays in returning dishonored (unpaid) checks had been a problem in the banking industry for years. According to the Uniform Commercial Code, a drawee bank has until midnight of the business day following receipt to decide whether to pay a check. If it delays returning the check beyond that time, the check is considered paid. It is not uncommon for a check to pass through two, three or more banks before it reaches the drawee bank. So even if the drawee bank complies with this requirement, it may take several days for the returned check to reach the bank of first deposit — the bank where the payee deposited the check. Customarily, the check would be returned through the same channels it was cleared, and that could take days. If the delay is too long, the funds may already have been spent by the payee, and the bank of first deposit will have difficulty recovering the amount of the check. Customers are not happy being notified a week after they deposit a check that it is not good.

Banks struggled with this problem for years. Drawee banks have been reluctant to return a check written by a good customer. So they give the customer every opportunity to "cover" the check (make it good). And banks receiving a returned check unpaid are equally unhappy about "dishonored" (unpaid) checks. Wire notification to the bank of first deposit that a check for a large amount is being returned was one procedure that helped. At least the bank would know the check was coming back and could notify its customer. In 1988 the Fed initiated a procedure for sending the returned check directly to the bank of first deposit. This improved the situation and added to the services provided by the Fed.

Delay in giving a customer credit for a check deposited also was a problem in collecting checks. Some banks followed a policy of delaying credit until they were sure the check was paid by the drawee bank. As we have seen, this could be several days. A particular problem involved checks drawn on the federal government. It was not easy for a customer to see why he should not have immediate credit for depositing a government check such as a Social Security check. From the bank's viewpoint it could not be certain that the check would not be returned. The government reserved the right to return a check at any time—years later. In other words, a government check could never be considered absolutely paid. The deposit of checks written to deceased persons, stolen checks, forged endorsements were some of the problems facing banks. In 1987 Congress enacted the Competitive Equality Banking Act, which among other things required depository institutions to make deposited funds available to depositors within specific time schedules that were based on several factors, including the type of deposit and relative location of the depository and paying banks. Also, the bank's policy on this procedure had to be disclosed to customers.

CONSUMERS AND THE FED

The decade of the 1980s saw a continuing emphasis on the rights of consumers. The board established a Consumer Advisory Council which met regularly and passed on to the board ideas and suggestions for improving service to consumers and protecting their rights. One indication of the board's concern for the rights of consumers was its publication and distribution of more than one million copies of a booklet entitled *Consumers Handbook to Credit Protection Laws.* Videotapes also were prepared, and every effort was made to let the customer know his rights and how to protect them. In the board's Annual Report special attention was given to customers' problems and how they were dealt with. The table on the next page from the 1984 report illustrates the wide range of complaints received at the board.

By 1980 use of credit cards had become one of the most frequent methods of paying for goods and services. On July 27, 1981, Congress passed the Cash Discount Act, which directed the Fed to prepare a study on the effect that charge card transactions have on card issuers, merchants and consumers. The pressure for this action came from the fact that some merchants were offering cash discounts to customers who paid cash rather than use a credit card. The practice made sense as the merchant paid a discount to the bank that reimbursed him for credit card charges. Also, stolen credit cards were a problem and in some cases resulted in substantial losses to merchants. To protect holders of credit cards, a limit of $50 was placed on their liability for the use of a stolen credit card if the holder gave prompt notice to the issuer that the card had been stolen. The board's lengthy report, issued in 1983, gave a broad description of the use of credit cards. It confirmed their growing importance to consumers and did not find their use to have any adverse impact on consumers or merchants.

Consumer Complaints Received by the
Federal Reserve System, by subject, 1984

Subject	Number
Regulation B (Equal Credit Opportunity)	166
Regulation C (Home Mortgage Disclosure)	18
Regulation E (Electronic Fund Transfers)	80
Regulation M (Consumer Leasing)	2
Regulation Q (Interest on Deposits)	118
Regulation X (Borrowers of Securities credit)	0
Regulation Z (Truth in Lending)	461
Regulation BB (Community Reinvestment)	1
Fair Credit Reporting Act	65
Fair Debt Collection Practices	10
Fair Housing Act	3
Holder in Due Course	3
Real Estate Settlement Procedures Act (RESPA)	2
Transfer Agents	3
Municipal Securities Dealer regulation	2
Unregulated bank practice	1,351
Other*	52
Total	2,337

"Other" refers primarily to miscellaneous complaints against business entities.

INTERNATIONAL DEVELOPMENTS

With the shift of the United States from a creditor to a debtor nation the importance of international financial transactions required the Fed to devote more attention to the position of the dollar in international exchange rate markets. Close cooperation with other industrial nations — particularly the United Kingdom, West Germany, France and Japan — was essential on an hour-to-hour basis. The Fed now had to give consideration to the dollar's position internationally as well as to all domestic factors. Intervention in the exchange markets was not unusual although it was done only if necessary. Assembling of data by the system became critical as it expanded its sources for information and sought to stay well informed about past and future developments both economically and politically.

The importance of international developments to the Fed is illustrated by the following lead story in the May 23, 1989, issue of the *Wall Street Journal*:

> Some Fed officials have begun to consider easing credit to stem the dollar's surge, government officials said. Though the Fed's policy committee (FOMC) decided last week to leave credit unchanged, the dollar's surprising strength has led to a growing sentiment for reducing short-term rates. No decision has been made yet. The dollar continued to soar, and central banks (including the Federal Reserve) appeared powerless to halt its advance. The currency's rally boosted bonds but depressed commodity markets. Stocks edged up.

LEGISLATION

Congress's continued interest in the Fed is shown by the legislation passed in every session. The Fed's reputation for implementing difficult programs—especially those that were not politically palatable—made it the recipient of many new programs. The nationwide network of the system made it suitable to execute national policies, and Congress was most willing to give them to the Fed, even though it might complain about the way the Fed handled them. On October 15, 1982, Congress passed the Garn–St. Germain Depository Institutions Act, which among other things modified the authority of the Federal Deposit Insurance Corporation (FDIC) and the Federal Savings and Loan Insurance Corporation (FSLIC) to assist banks and savings and loan associations that were in trouble, raised the limit of a national bank's loan to one borrower to 15 from 10 percent of the bank's capital and surplus. The act also designated the older Federal Reserve Board building in Washington, D.C., as the Marriner S. Eccles Federal Reserve Board Building. The more recently constructed building for the Fed is known as the Martin Building.

On December 21, 1982, Congress passed the Further Continuing Appropriations Act, which among other things declared "the sense of Congress to be that the Federal Reserve, with due regard to inflation, take such action as necessary to achieve and maintain a level of interest low enough to generate sufficient economic growth to reduce the current intolerable level of unemployment." This is another example of Congress's desire to achieve an economic goal and to tell the Fed to do it but not to tell them how. Of course, such directives were subject to varied interpretations, but the intent of Congress was clear.

Each year the Board of Governors submitted to Congress recommendations for legislation. With the broadening of the Fed's involvement in the financial community, the board has recommended an increase from three to five Class C directors at the reserve banks. It also has recommended that authority be given to extend reserve requirements to nonbank organizations that were offering checking accounts. Mutual funds and a variety of other sources were available to customers, but there was a complete lack of supervision of these accounts. Lack of deposit insurance on these accounts did not deter consumers from investing in them as the additional income from interest or from possible appreciation of equity investments was enticing. But as the decade ended, Congress had not acted on these requests.

VOLCKER LEAVES THE FED

In the spring of 1987 rumors began circulating that Chairman Volcker would not be reappointed when his term expired in August 1987. Although his term as a member of the Board of Governors did not end until January 31, 1992, his term as chairman expired August 6, 1987. Appointment as chairman was for a period of four years, and on August 6 he would complete his second four-year term as chairman. The financial community did not like the prospect of Volcker's leaving the Fed. His leadership had taken the Fed and the business community through some perilous times, and he was greatly respected as a leader in a complicated and changing industry.

On June 3, 1987, President Reagan announced that he was nominating Alan Greenspan to replace Paul Volcker as chairman of the Board of Governors of the Federal Reserve System. The announcement was well received as Greenspan was a known and a respected leader in the field of finance. He had served as chairman of the President's Council of Economic Advisors under President Ford and as a member of President Reagan's Economic Policy Advisory Board. In addition, he had been senior advisor to the Brookings Panel on Economic Activity and consultant to the Congressional Budget Office. A native of New York City and a summa cum laude graduate of New York University, he was amply qualified for the chairmanship of the Fed.

The announcement of his appointment raised questions about why Paul Volcker had chosen not to accept reappointment. President Reagan would have reappointed him if Volcker had been receptive. From comments made by Mr. Volcker it was quite clear that personal reasons, rather than any conflict with the administration or the Fed, led to his decision. In his letter of resignation dated June 1, 1987, he said, "After eight years as chairman, a natural time has now come for me to return to private life as soon as reasonably convenient and consistent with an orderly transition." At a press conference he stated that "a variety of considerations" entered into his decision. His wife had not been well for many years, and no doubt that was one factor in his decision. Largely because of her poor health, he had commuted from New York City during his time at the Fed rather than move to Washington.

Thus ended a period of service by another strong, decisive leader of the Federal Reserve System. Along with Carter Glass, Marriner Eccles, and William McChesney Martin, Paul Volcker will be remembered as a man who guided the Fed through major changes and times of question about its ability to act in accordance with the public interest of the nation. In his place Alan Greenspan faced the task of establishing his leadership and his credibility. He was soon tested as the economy showed signs of strong resurgence in early 1989 and the Fed was faced with the need to cool down the economy, maintain stability of the dollar in world markets and yet keep the nation from falling into a recession. With a huge and growing federal debt and an unfavorable balance of payments, the nation could ill afford a slowdown in business activity that would reduce federal tax revenue and exacerbate the trade deficit. Not only was the Fed forced to evaluate domestic trends carefully, but the entire world faced uncertain trends in inflation and in trade positions. Founders of the system would be appalled at the magnitude of the questions facing the Fed as it charts its course week by week and even hour by hour.

Alan Greenspan, appointed chairman of the Board of Governors, August 11, 1987; meeting the challenge of maintaining stability in the face of threatened depression and inflation in the late 1980s. Courtesy Board of Governors of Federal Reserve System.

As the decade of the 1980s came to a close, old questions erupted in the halls of Congress. No fewer than six bills and one joint resolution were introduced during the first session of the 101st Congress. Some proposed needed changes, changes that the Board of Governors have been requesting. Others resurrected old ideas that have been discussed for most of the history of the system. Some probably reflect a politician's desire to have a more direct and forceful impact on the action of the Fed. Here is a summary of the bills as they stood in late 1989. All have been referred to the appropriate committees for consideration and possible hearings. Their passage in this session of the Congress is at best questionable.

House Bill 3066: "A bill to strengthen the political responsibility and accountability of the Federal Reserve System." Introduced by Congressman

Lane Evans (D–IL), the bill would increase the number of Class C directors at the Reserve banks from three to six. One would be required to have a background in agricultural, one a background in small business, one would represent the interests of labor and one the interests of consumers (makes what is now implied specific). The Fed has wanted an increase in the number of Class C directors for several years. Six may be too many, but certainly a case can be made for enlarging representation on the boards of directors.

House Bill 844: "A bill to authorize and direct the General Accounting Office to audit the Federal Reserve Board, the Federal Advisory Council, the Federal Open Market Committee, and Federal Reserve banks and branches." Introduced by Congressman Philip Crane (R–IL). This is not new. See Chapters 8 and 9 under "General Accounting Office." I believe this will be vigorously opposed by the system.

Senate Bill 734: A companion bill to H.R. 844, introduced by Senator Harry Reid (D–NV).

House Bill 2795: "A bill to modernize the Federal Reserve System and to provide prompt disclosure of certain decisions of the Federal Open Market Committee." Introduced by Congressman Byron L. Dorgan (D–ND), this piece of legislation would add the secretary of the treasury to the Board of Governors; call for the term of the chairman and vice chairman of the Federal Reserve Board to expire on January 31 of the first calender year beginning after the term of the president who appointed them; require the immediate disclosure of any change in the board's intermediate targets, meaning monetary aggregates, credit aggregates, prices, interest rates or bank reserves; require the General Accounting Office to audit any communications between or among members of the Board of Governors or officers and employees of the Federal Reserve System relating to any of the items mentioned above and finally, to require the Board of Governors to submit estimated expenditures and proposed appropriations for the board and all Federal Reserve banks for the current year and two succeeding years, such estimates to be presented to the president by October 16 of each year. The use of the term "appropriations" is either an error or used for lack of knowledge of how the system works. No appropriations are made for the system. It is anticipated that the system will vigorously oppose this bill in its entirety.

House Bill 2914: "A bill to provide for the retirement of all $100 Federal Reserve notes and the replacement of such notes with new $100 Federal Reserve notes of a different design." Introduced by Congressman Charles B. Rangel (D–NY), this is an effort to help law enforcement agencies in criminal investigation or prosecution. This would involve considerable expense, but the board is not likely to object seriously.

House Bill 843: "A bill to provide that all Federal Reserve notes and other currencies of the United States be redeemable in gold." Introduced by Congressman Phillip M. Crane (R–IL), the bill would require redemption in either gold coins or gold bullion. Coins would be denominated in grams, not dollars, and would not bear any designation of value except the weight of gold contained therein. Probably not a practical idea. See discussion in Chapter 5.

Joint resolution directing the Federal Open Market Committee of the Federal Reserve System "to adopt and pursue monetary policies leading to and the maintaining of, zero inflation." This joint resolution, introduced by Congressman Stephen L. Neal (D–NC) on August 1, 1989, and on September 25, 1989, calls for what the board has been striving for for several decades. However, the resolution does not say how to do it. The second version of the resolution calls for zero inflation to be achieved in five years and for the board to report at its semiannual report to the Congress how it plans to accomplish this objective. This appears to be a political move for attention, but no one expects the Congress to assume the duty of making it come about. It is much more astute politically to have the Fed to blame for any failure.

Whether these bills arose from a sincere desire to give stability to the economy or whether they reflect political goals is not for this author to say. It would seem that a review of history would discourage proposals to give specific directives on monetary policies. As pointed out in earlier chapters, there is serious question as to whether the Fed could exert complete control of the economy. Fiscal policies, foreign trade, the psychology of the masses and the fragility of data impact on the ability of the Fed to "be in control." And the experience of 75 years confirms the Fed's unsure hand in fine-tuning the economy.

A LOOK BACK
As the first 75 years of the Federal Reserve System came to a close in 1989, it could take pride in that it had even survived through a period that saw two world wars; a depression during which values dropped 50 percent, unemployment reached 25 percent, one-half of the nation's banks failed; two so-called police actions and two internal structural and policy revolutions. It also grew from an "automatic" regulator of currency and bank reserves to an institution charged with attempting to eliminate the business cycle and please all politicians. It has been praised by presidents, damned by presidents, threatened with extermination by Congress, examined, audited and called the banker's friend and an enemy of the people. Books have been written calling it a tool in the hands of international bankers (whoever they are). It has been accused of being secretive and unwilling to tell the world or Congress what it intended to do. Bankers have praised its

willingness to help them and damned its refusal to be more receptive to their wants.

At the end of 75 years, the system is firmly ingrained in the fabric of the nation. It plays a vital role in attempting to regulate the nation's economy to prevent depression and inflation. Its leadership stubbornly refuses to be told how to run its business, yet it is responsive to directives from its parents, the Congress. Its role in international financial policy is well recognized. As with any institution, people have been the key to its achievements. Without the strong and persistent support of Carter Glass and President Woodrow Wilson, the system might never have been born. Benjamin Strong, governor of the New York Fed, provided the necessary spark of vision and leadership through the early days of the system. Marriner Eccles came to Washington in the 1930s with little knowledge of the Fed, but his perceptive approach to desperately needed reorganization gave strength to the system. Bill Martin charted the difficult path to an "accord" with the U.S. Treasury and a return to open markets in government securities. Paul Volcker, a giant of a man physically, proved to have that necessary stubbornness and finesse needed at a special time in history as he led the nation in restoring confidence in markets and halting the threat of runaway inflation. The strength of a regional system has been validated many times as the nation has grown and expanded, so that today every part is important to the health and well-being of the nation's total economy.

What will the next 75 years bring? Will the managed currency the world uses lead to a disaster in the future? Will the warning of Paul Warburg against such a currency prove correct? Can a democracy that depends on an educated and informed constituency make the hard decisions necessary for survival, or will we "pay ourselves" into a debt that cannot be repaid and see our nation follow the path of destruction suffered by other great nations?

Only the future can answer such questions, but in the meantime the leadership in the Federal Reserve System will continue to play a critical role in trends and actions that shape the future. The words of Chairman Martin seem appropriate for the leadership of the Fed to remember: "The Fed cannot, in the long run, act contrary to the wishes of the people as expressed through their elected officials."

Appendixes

Glossary

Accord. An agreement between the U.S. Treasury and the Board of Governors of the Federal Reserve System to gradually make the market for government securities subject to supply and demand — to discontinue the artificial pegging of prices by the Federal Reserve System.

Board. As used in this book, the term refers to the Federal Reserve Board of the Federal Reserve System or the Board of Governors of the Federal Reserve System. The name was changed to Board of Governors by the Banking act of 1935.

Clearinghouse. An organization of banks in a community for the purpose of exchanging checks drawn on each other.

The "committee." Usually a reference to the Federal Open Market Committee of the Federal Reserve System. During organization of the system it was sometimes used to refer to the Organization Committee charged with the responsibility of organizing the system.

Deregulation. Reducing or eliminating the control over the banking system by the federal government. Also used in referring to control over other business by government.

Desk. A term used to indicate the U.S. government securities trading desk at the New York Federal Reserve Bank where government securities are bought and sold for the 12 Federal Reserve banks at the direction of the Federal Open Market Committee of the system.

Discount. Refers to borrowing from a Federal Reserve bank by a depository institution — usually a bank.

Discount rate. The rate of interest charged by a Federal Reserve bank when lending to a depository institution.

FDIC. Federal Deposit Insurance Corporation, which insures deposits in commercial banks.

Fed or the Fed. A broad term referring to a Federal Reserve bank or the Federal Reserve System.

171

Float. The amount of money that is credited to a depositor's account before it is charged to the payor's account.

FOMC. Federal Open Market Committee of the Federal Reserve System.

FSLIC. Federal Savings and Loan Insurance Corporation. Insures deposits in savings and loan associations.

GAO. General Accounting Office. Congress's auditing arm. Audits most government agencies and others at the direction of Congress.

GNP. Gross National Product. The total dollar value of all of the goods and services produced in the United States over a given period.

Gold Standard. A measure of the value of a money in gold, e.g. one dollar is equal to 1/1000 of an ounce of gold.

Governor. Title of the operating officer of a Federal Reserve bank prior to 1935. Also, title of a member of the Board of Governors of the Federal Reserve System.

Market. A term sometimes used to refer to the market for money or for government securities.

Money supply. A measure of the amount of money in the nation available for spending. Several measures are used. **M-1** = the sum of currency and coin in circulation, demand deposits, traveler's checks and other checkable deposits. **M-2** = M-1 plus money market fund balances, saving and small time deposits, overnight repurchase agreements and Eurodollars and money market mutual funds. **M-3** = M-1, M-2 and large time deposits, term repurchase agreements, term Eurodollars and institutions' money market mutual funds. **L** = all of the above plus other liquid assets.

Pegged prices. A price that is fixed at a given level. In this book referred to the Fed supporting the price of U.S. government securities at par.

Rediscount. Expression referring to borrowing from a Federal Reserve bank. It assumes that the note or bill presented by the borrowing bank was discounted by the bank and hence the term "*re*discount." Not a correct description of borrowing from a Federal Reserve bank since the 1920s.

Sandwich coins. Coins made of two or more kinds of metal "sandwiched" together. Applies to coins struck since the early 1960s.

Stagflation. A term used to describe economic conditions when inflation is high and the economy is stagnant, as in the 1970s.

Wildcat banks. A term used to describe banks that were harder to find than a wildcat. Particularly during the period 1836 to 1863 a bank sometimes issued a substantial amount of its own currency and then located in a place hard to find so no one could present the currency for redemption.

The Federal Reserve Act
(As enacted December 23, 1913)

Copies of the currently amended Act with Other Statutory Provisions affecting the Federal Reserve System can be obtained from any Federal Reserve Bank or the Board of Governors, Federal Reserve System, Washington, D.C. 20551, for a small fee.

An Act To provide for the establishment of Federal reserve banks, to furnish an elastic currency, to afford means of rediscounting commercial paper, to establish a more effective supervision of banking in the United States, and for other purposes.

Be it enacted by the Senate and House of Representatives of the United States of America in Congress assembled, That the short title of this Act shall be the "Federal Reserve Act."

Wherever the word "bank" is used in this Act, the word shall be held to include State bank, banking association, and trust company, except where national banks or Federal reserve banks are specifically referred to.

The terms "national bank" and "national banking association" used in this Act shall be held to be synonymous and interchangeable. The term "member bank" shall be held to mean any national bank, State bank, or bank or trust company which has become a member of one of the reserve banks created by this Act. The term "board" shall be held to mean Federal Reserve Board; the term "district" shall be held to mean Federal reserve district; the term "reserve bank" shall be held to mean Federal reserve bank.

FEDERAL RESERVE DISTRICTS

SEC. 2. As soon as practicable, the Secretary of the Treasury, the Secretary of Agriculture and the Comptroller of the Currency, acting as "The Reserve Bank Organization Committee," shall designate not less than eight nor more than twelve cities to be known as Federal reserve cities, and shall divide the continental United States, excluding Alaska, into districts, each district to contain only one of such Federal reserve cities. The determination of said organization committee shall not be subject to review except by the Federal Reserve Board when organized: *Provided,* That the districts shall be apportioned with due regard to the convenience and customary course of business and shall not necessarily be coterminous with any State or States. The districts thus created may be readjusted and new districts may from time to time be created by the Federal Reserve Board, not to exceed twelve in all. Such districts shall be known as Federal reserve districts and may be designated by number. A majority of the organization committee shall constitute a quorum with authority to act.

Said organization committee shall be authorized to employ counsel and expert aid, to take testimony, to send for persons and papers, to administer oaths, and to make such investigation as may be deemed necessary by the said committee in determining the reserve districts and in designating the cities within such districts where such Federal reserve banks shall be severally located. The said committee shall supervise the organization in each of the cities designated of a Federal reserve bank, which shall include in its title the name of the city in which it is situated, as "Federal Reserve Bank of Chicago."

Under regulations to be prescribed by the organization committee, every national banking association in the United States is hereby required, and every eligible bank in the United States and every trust company within the District of Columbia, is hereby authorized to signify in writing, within sixty days after the passage of this Act, its acceptance of the terms and provisions hereof. When the organization committee shall have designated the cities in which Federal reserve banks are to be organized, and fixed the geographical limits of the Federal reserve districts, every national banking association within that district shall be required within thirty days after notice from the organization committee, to subscribe to the capital stock of such Federal reserve bank in a sum equal to six per centum of the paid-up capital stock and surplus of such bank, one-sixth of the subscription to be payable on call of the organization committee or of the Federal Reserve Board, one-sixth within three months and one-sixth within six months thereafter, and the remainder of the subscription, or any part thereof, shall be subject to call when deemed necessary by the Federal Reserve Board, said payments to be in gold or gold certificates.

The shareholders of every Federal reserve bank shall be held individually responsible, equally and ratably, and not one for another, for all contracts, debts, and engagements of such bank to the extent of the amount of their subscriptions to such stock at the par value thereof in addition to the amount subscribed, whether such subscriptions have been paid up in whole or in part, under the provisions of this Act.

Any national bank failing to signify its acceptance of the terms of this Act within the sixty days aforesaid, shall cease to act as a reserve agent, upon thirty days' notice, to be given within the discretion of the said organization committee or of the Federal Reserve Board.

Should any national banking association in the United States now organized fail within one year after the passage of this Act to become a member bank or fail to comply with any of the provisions of this Act applicable thereto, all of the rights, privileges, and franchises of such association granted to it under the national-bank Act, or under the provisions of this Act, shall be thereby forfeited. Any noncompliance with or violation of this Act shall, however, be determined and adjudged by any court of the United States of competent jurisdiction in a suit brought for that purpose in the district or territory in which such bank is located, under direction of the Federal Reserve Board, by the Comptroller of the Currency in his own name before the association shall be declared dissolved. In cases of such noncompliance or violation, other than the failure to become a member bank under the provisions of this Act, every director who participated in or assented to the same shall be held liable in his personal or individual capacity for all damages which said bank, its shareholders, or any other person shall have sustained in consequence of such violation.

Such dissolution shall not take away or impair any remedy against such corporation, its stockholders or officers, for any liability or penalty which shall have been previously incurred.

Should the subscriptions by banks to the stock of said Federal reserve banks or any one or more of them be, in the judgment of the organization committee, insufficient to provide the amount of capital required therefor, then and in that event the said organization committee may, under conditions and regulations to be prescribed by it, offer to public subscription at par such an amount of stock in said Federal reserve banks, or any one or more of them, as said committee shall determine, subject to the same conditions as to payment and stock liability as provided for member banks.

No individual, copartnership, or corporation other than a member bank of its district shall be permitted to subscribe for or to hold at any time more than $25,000 par value of stock in any Federal reserve bank. Such stock shall be known as public stock and may be transferred on the books of the Federal reserve bank by the chairman of the board of directors of such bank.

Should the total subscriptions by banks and the public to the stock of said Federal reserve banks, or any one or more of them, be, in the judgment of the organization committee, insufficient to provide the amount of capital required therefor, then and in that event the said organization committee shall allot to the United States such an amount of said stock as said committee shall determine. Said United States stock shall be paid for at par out of any money in the Treasury not otherwise appropriated, and shall be held by the Secretary of the Treasury and disposed of for the benefit of the United States in such manner, at such times, and at such price, not less than par, as the Secretary of the Treasury shall determine.

Stock not held by member banks shall not be entitled to voting power.

The Federal Reserve Board is hereby empowered to adopt and promulgate rules and regulations governing the transfers of said stock.

No Federal reserve bank shall commence business with a subscribed capital less than $4,000,000. The organization of reserve districts and Federal reserve cities shall not be construed as changing the present status of reserve cities and central reserve cities, except in so far as this Act changes the amount of reserves that may be carried with approved reserve agents located therein. The organization committee shall have power to appoint such assistants and incur such expenses in carrying out the provisions of this Act as it shall deem necessary, and such expenses shall be payable by the Treasurer of the United States upon voucher approved by the Secretary of the Treasury, and the sum of $100,000, or so much thereof as may be necessary, is hereby appropriated, out of any moneys in the Treasury not otherwise appropriated, for the payment of such expenses.

BRANCH OFFICES

SEC. 3. Each Federal reserve bank shall establish branch banks within the Federal reserve district in which it is located and may do so in the district of any Federal reserve bank which may have been suspended. Such branches shall be operated by a board of directors under rules and regulations approved by the Federal Reserve Board. Directors of branch banks shall possess the same qualifications as directors of the Federal reserve banks. Four of said directors shall be selected by the reserve bank and three by the Federal Reserve Board, and they shall hold office during the pleasure, respectively, of the parent bank and the Federal Reserve Board. The reserve bank shall designate one of the directors as manager.

FEDERAL RESERVE BANKS

SEC. 4. When the organization committee shall have established Federal reserve districts as provided in section two of this Act, a certificate shall be filed with the Comptroller of the Currency showing the geographical limits of such districts and the Federal reserve city designated in each of such districts. The Comptroller of the Currency shall thereupon cause to be forwarded to each national bank located in each district, and to such other banks declared to be eligible by the organization committee which may apply therefor, an application blank in form to be approved by the organization committee, which blank shall contain a resolution to be adopted by the board of directors of each bank executing such application, authorizing a subscription to the capital stock of the Federal reserve bank organizing in that district in accordance with the provisions of this Act.

When the minimum amount of capital stock prescribed by this Act for the organization of any Federal reserve bank shall have been subscribed and allotted, the organization committee shall designate any five banks of those whose applications have been received, to execute a certificate of organization, and thereupon the banks so designated shall, under their seals, make an organization certificate which shall specifically state the name of such Federal reserve bank, the territorial extent of the district over which the operations of such Federal reserve bank are to be carried on, the city and State in which said bank is to be located, the amount of capital stock and the number of shares into which the same is divided,' the name and place of doing business of each bank executing such certificate, and of all banks which have subscribed to the capital stock of such Federal reserve bank and the number of shares subscribed by each, and the fact that the certificate is made to enable those banks executing same, and all banks which have subscribed or may thereafter subscribe to the capital stock of such Federal reserve bank, to avail themselves of the advantages of this Act.

The said organization certificate shall be acknowledged before a judge of some court of record or notary public; and shall be, together with the acknowledgment thereof, authenticated by the seal of such court, or notary, transmitted to the Comptroller of the Currency, who shall file, record and carefully preserve the same in his office.

Upon the filing of such certificate with the Comptroller of the Currency as aforesaid, the said Federal reserve bank shall become a body corporate and as such, and in the name designated in such organization certificate, shall have power—

First. To adopt and use a corporate seal.

Second. To have succession for a period of twenty years from its organization unless it is sooner dissolved by an Act of Congress, or unless its franchise becomes forfeited by some violation of law.

Third. To make contracts.

Fourth. To sue and be sued, complain and defend, in any court of law or equity.

Fifth. To appoint by its board of directors, such officers and employees as are not otherwise provided for in this Act, to define their duties, require bonds of them and fix the penalty thereof, and to dismiss at pleasure such officers or employees.

Sixth. To prescribe by its board of directors, by-laws not inconsistent with law, regulating the manner in which its general business may be conducted, and the privileges granted to it by law may be exercised and enjoyed.

Seventh. To exercise by its board of directors, or duly authorized officers or agents, all powers specifically granted by the provisions of this Act and such incidental powers as shall be necessary to carry on the business of banking within the limitations prescribed by this Act.

Eighth. Upon deposit with the Treasurer of the United States of any bonds of the United States in the manner provided by existing law relating to national banks, to receive from the Comptroller of the Currency circulating notes in blank, registered and countersigned as provided by law, equal in amount to the par value of the bonds so deposited, such notes to be issued under the same conditions and provisions of law as relate to the issue of circulating notes of national banks secured by bonds of the United States bearing the circulating privilege, except that the issue of such notes shall not be limited to the capital stock of such Federal reserve bank.

But no Federal reserve bank shall transact any business except such as is incidental and necessarily preliminary to its· organization until it has been authorized by the Comptroller of the Currency to commence business under the provisions of this Act.

Every Federal reserve bank shall be conducted under the supervision and control of a board of directors.

The board of directors shall perform the duties usually appertaining to the office of directors of banking associations and all such duties as are prescribed by law.

Said board shall administer the affairs of said bank fairly and impartially and without discrimination in favor of or against any member bank or banks and shall, subject to the provisions of law and the orders of the Federal Reserve Board, extend to each member bank such discounts, advancements and accommodations as may be safely and reasonably made with due regard for the claims and demands of other member banks.

Such board of directors shall be selected as hereinafter specified and shall consist of nine members, holding office for three years, and divided into three classes, designated as classes A, B, and C.

Class A shall consist of three members, who shall be chosen by and be representative of the stock-holding banks.

Class B shall consist of three members, who at the time of their election shall be actively engaged in their district in commerce, agriculture or some other industrial pursuit.

Class C shall consist of three members who shall be designated by the Federal Reserve Board. When the necessary subscriptions to the capital stock have been obtained for the organization of any Federal reserve bank, the Federal Reserve Board shall appoint the class C directors and shall designate one of such directors as chairman of the board to be selected. Pending the designation of such chairman, the organization committee shall exercise the powers and duties appertaining to the office of chairman in the organization of such Federal reserve bank.

No Senator or Representative in Congress shall be a member of the Federal Reserve Board or an officer or a director of a Federal reserve bank.

No director of class B shall be an officer, director, or employee of any bank.

No director of class C shall be an officer, director, employee, or stockholder of any bank.

Directors of class A and class B shall be chosen in the following manner:

The chairman of the board of directors of the Federal reserve bank of the district in which the bank is situated or, pending the appointment of such chairman, the organization committee shall classify the member banks of the district into three general groups or divisions. Each group shall contain as nearly as may be one-third of the aggregate number of the member banks of the district and shall consist, as nearly as may be, of banks of similar capitalization. The groups shall be designated by number by the chairman.

At a regularly called meeting of the board of directors of each member bank in the district it shall elect by ballot a district reserve elector and shall certify his name to the chairman of the board of directors of the Federal reserve bank of the district. The chairman shall make lists of the district reserve electors thus named by banks in each of the aforesaid three groups and shall transmit one list to each elector in each group.

Each member bank shall be permitted to nominate to the chairman one candidate for director of class A and one candidate for director of class B. The candidates so nominated shall be listed by the chairman, indicating by whom nominated, and a copy of said list shall, within fifteen days after its completion, be furnished by the chairman to each elector.

Every elector shall, within fifteen days after the receipt of the said list, certify to the chairman his first, second, and other choices of a director of class A and class B, respectively, upon a preferential ballot, on a form furnished by the chairman of the board of directors of the Federal reserve bank of the district. Each elector shall make a cross opposite the name of the first, second, and other choices for a director of class A and for a director of class B, but shall not vote more than one choice for any one candidate.

Any candidate having a majority of all votes cast in the column of first choice shall be declared elected. If no candidate have a majority of all the votes in the first column, then there shall be added together the votes cast by the electors for such candidates in the second column and the votes cast for the several candidates in the first column. If any candidate then have a majority of the electors voting, by adding together the first and second choices, he shall be declared elected. If no candidate have a majority of electors voting when the first and second choices shall have been added, then the votes cast in the third column for other choices shall be added together in like manner, and the candidate then having the highest number of votes shall be declared elected. An immediate report of election shall be declared.

Class C directors shall be appointed by the Federal Reserve Board. They shall have been for at least two years residents of the district for which they are appointed, one of whom shall be designated by said board as chairman of the board of directors of the Federal reserve bank and as "Federal reserve agent." He shall be a person of tested banking experience; and in addition to his duties as chairman of the board of directors of the Federal reserve bank he shall be required to maintain under regulations to be established by the Federal Reserve Board a local office of said board on the premises of the Federal reserve bank. He shall make regular reports to the Federal Reserve Board, and shall act as its official representative for the performance of the functions conferred upon it by this

Act. He shall receive an annual compensation to be fixed by the Federal Reserve Board and paid monthly by the Federal reserve bank to which he is designated. One of the directors of class C, who shall be a person of tested banking experience, shall be appointed by the Federal Reserve Board as deputy chairman and deputy Federal reserve agent to exercise the powers of the chairman of the board and Federal reserve agent in case of absence or disability of his principal.

Directors of Federal reserve banks shall receive, in addition to any compensation otherwise provided, a reasonable allowance for necessary expenses in attending meetings of their respective boards, which amount shall be paid by the respective Federal reserve banks. Any compensation that may be provided by boards of directors of Federal reserve banks for directors, officers or employees shall be subject to the approval of the Federal Reserve Board.

The Reserve Bank Organization Committee may, in organizing Federal reserve banks, call such meetings of bank directors in the several districts as may be necessary to carry out the purposes of this Act, and may exercise the functions herein conferred upon the chairman of the board of directors of each Federal reserve bank pending the complete organization of such bank.

At the first meeting of the full board of directors of each Federal reserve bank, it shall be the duty of the directors of classes A, B and C, respectively, to designate one of the members of each class whose term of office shall expire in one year from the first of January nearest to date of such meeting, one whose term of office shall expire at the end of two years from said date, and one whose term of office shall expire at the end of three years from said date. Thereafter every director of a Federal reserve bank chosen as hereinbefore provided shall hold office for a term of three years. Vacancies that may occur in the several classes of directors of Federal reserve banks may be filled in the manner provided for the original selection of such directors, such appointees to hold office for the unexpired terms of their predecessors.

STOCK ISSUES; INCREASE AND DECREASE OF CAPITAL

SEC. 5. The capital stock of each Federal reserve bank shall be divided into shares of $100 each. The outstanding capital stock shall be increased from time to time as member banks increase their capital stock and surplus or as additional banks become members, and may be decreased as member banks reduce their capital stock or surplus or cease to be members. Shares of the capital stock of Federal reserve banks owned by member banks shall not be transferred or hypothecated. When a member bank increases its capital stock or surplus, it shall thereupon subscribe for an additional amount of capital stock of the Federal reserve bank of its district equal to six per centum of the said increase, one-half of said subscription to be paid in the manner hereinbefore provided for original subscription, and one-half subject to call of the Federal Reserve Board. A bank applying for stock in a Federal reserve bank at any time after the organization thereof must subscribe for an amount of the capital stock of the Federal reserve bank equal to six per centum of the paid-up capital stock and surplus of said applicant bank, paying therefor its par value plus one-half of one per centum a month from the period of the last dividend. When the capital stock of any Federal reserve bank shall have been increased either on account of the increase of capital stock of member banks or on account of the increase in the number of member banks, the board of directors shall cause to be executed a certificate to the Comptroller of the Currency showing the increase in capital stock, the amount paid in, and by whom paid. When a member bank reduces its capital stock it shall surrender a proportionate amount of its holdings in the capital of said Federal reserve bank, and when a member bank voluntarily liquidates it shall surrender all of its holdings of the capital stock of said Federal reserve bank and be released from its stock subscription not previously called. In either case the shares surrendered shall be canceled and the member bank shall receive in payment therefor, under regulations to be prescribed by the Federal Reserve Board, a sum equal to its cash-paid subscriptions on the shares surrendered and one-half of one per centum a month from the period of the last dividend, not to exceed the book value thereof, less any liability of such member bank to the Federal reserve bank.

SEC. 6. If any member bank shall be declared insolvent and a receiver appointed therefor, the stock held by it in said Federal reserve bank shall be canceled, without impairment of its liability, and all cash-paid subscriptions on said stock, with one-half of one per centum per month from the period of last dividend, not to exceed the book value thereof, shall be first applied to all debts of the insolvent member bank to the Federal reserve bank, and the balance, if any, shall be paid to the receiver of the insolvent bank. Whenever the capital stock of a Federal reserve bank is reduced, either on account of a reduction in capital stock of any member bank or of the liquidation or insolvency of such bank, the board of directors shall cause to be executed a certificate to the Comptroller of the Currency showing such reduction of capital stock and the amount repaid to such bank.

DIVISION OF EARNINGS

SEC. 7. After all necessary expenses of a Federal reserve bank have been paid or provided for, the stockholders shall be entitled to receive an annual dividend of six per centum on the paid-in capital stock, which dividend shall be cumulative. After the aforesaid dividend claims have been fully met, all the net earnings shall be paid to the United States as a franchise tax, except that one-half of such net earnings shall be paid into a surplus fund until it shall amount to forty per centum of the paid-in capital stock of such bank.

The net earnings derived by the United States from Federal reserve banks shall, in the discretion of the Secretary, be used to supplement the gold reserve held against outstanding United States notes, or shall be applied to the reduction of the outstanding bonded indebtedness of the United States under regulations to be prescribed by the Secretary of the Treasury. Should a Federal reserve bank be dissolved or go into liquidation, any surplus remaining, after the payment of all debts, dividend requirements as hereinbefore provided, and the par value of the stock, shall be paid to and become the property of the United States and shall be similarly applied.

Federal reserve banks, including the capital stock and surplus therein, and the income derived therefrom shall be exempt from Federal, State, and local taxation, except taxes upon real estate.

SEC. 8. Section fifty-one hundred and fifty-four, United States Revised Statutes, is hereby amended to read as follows:

Any bank incorporated by special law of any State or of the United States or organized under the general laws of any State or of the United States and having an unimpaired capital sufficient to entitle it to become a national banking association under the provisions of the existing laws may, by the vote of the shareholders owning not less than fifty-one per centum of the capital stock of such bank or banking association, with the approval of the Comptroller of the Currency be converted into a national banking association, with any name approved by the Comptroller of the Currency:

Provided, however, That said conversion shall not be in contravention of the State law. In such case the articles of association and organization certificate may be executed by a majority of the directors of the bank or banking institution, and the certificate shall declare that the owners of fifty-one per centum of the capital stock have authorized the directors to make such certificate and to change or convert the bank or banking institution into a national association. A majority of the directors, after executing the articles of association and the organization certificate, shall have power to execute all other papers and to do whatever may be required to make its organization perfect and complete as a national association. The shares of any such bank may continue to be for the same amount each as they were before the conversion, and the directors may continue to be directors of the association until others are elected or appointed in accordance with the provisions of the statutes of the United States. When the comptroller has given to such bank or banking association a certificate that the provisions of this Act have been complied with, such bank or banking association, and all its stockholders, officers, and employees, shall have the same powers and privileges, and shall be subject to the same duties, liabilities, and regulations, in all respects, as shall have been prescribed by the Federal Reserve

Act and by the national banking Act for associations originally organized as national banking associations.

STATE BANKS AS MEMBERS

SEC. 9. Any bank incorporated by special law of any State, or organized under the general laws of any State or of the United States, may make application to the reserve bank organization committee, pending organization, and thereafter to the Federal Reserve Board for the right to subscribe to the stock of the Federal reserve bank organized or to be organized within the Federal reserve district where the applicant is located. The organization committee or the Federal Reserve Board, under such rules and regulations as it may prescribe, subject to the provisions of this section, may permit the applying bank to become a stockholder in the Federal reserve bank of the district in which the applying bank is located. Whenever the organization committee or the Federal Reserve Board shall permit the applying bank to become a stockholder in the Federal reserve bank of the district, stock shall be issued and paid for under the rules and regulations in this Act provided for national banks which become stockholders in Federal reserve banks.

The organization committee or the Federal Reserve Board shall establish by-laws for the general government of its conduct in acting upon applications made by the State banks and banking associations and trust companies for stock ownership in Federal reserve banks. Such by-laws shall require applying banks not organized under Federal law to comply with the reserve and capital requirements and to submit to the examination and regulations prescribed by the organization committee or by the Federal Reserve Board. No applying bank shall be admitted to membership in a Federal reserve bank unless it possesses a paid-up unimpaired capital sufficient to entitle it to become a national banking association in the place where it is situated, under the provisions of the national banking Act.

Any bank becoming a member of a Federal reserve bank under the provisions of this section shall, in addition to the regulations and restrictions hereinbefore provided, be required to conform to the provisions of law imposed on the national banks respecting the limitation of liability which may be incurred by any person, firm, or corporation to such banks, the prohibition against making purchase of or loans on stock of such banks, and the withdrawal or impairment of capital, or the payment of unearned dividends, and to such rules and regulations as the Federal Reserve Board may, in pursuance thereof, prescribe.

Such banks, and the officers, agents, and employees thereof, shall also be subject to the provisions of and to the penalties prescribed by sections fifty-one hundred and ninety-eight, fifty-two hundred, fifty-two hundred and one, and fifty-two hundred and eight, and fifty-two hundred and nine of the Revised Statutes. The member banks shall also be required to make reports of the conditions and of the payments of dividends to the comptroller, as provided in sections fifty-two hundred and eleven and fifty-two hundred and twelve of the Revised Statutes, and shall be subject to the penalties prescribed by section fifty-two hundred and thirteen for the failure to make such report.

If at any time it shall appear to the Federal Reserve Board that a member bank has failed to comply with the provisions of this section or. the regulations of the Federal Reserve Board, it shall be within the power of the said board, after hearing, to require such bank to surrender its stock in the Federal reserve bank; upon such surrender the Federal reserve bank shall pay the cash-paid subscriptions to the said stock with interest at the rate of one-half of one per centum per month, computed from the last dividend, if earned, not to exceed the book value thereof, less any liability to said Federal reserve bank, except the subscription liability not previously called, which shall be canceled, and said Federal reserve bank shall, upon notice from the Federal Reserve Board, be required to suspend said bank from further privileges of membership, and shall within thirty days of such notice cancel and retire its stock and make payment therefor in the manner herein provided. The Federal Reserve Board may restore membership upon due proof of compliance with the conditions imposed by this section.

FEDERAL RESERVE BOARD

SEC. 10. A Federal Reserve Board is hereby created which shall consist of seven members, including the Secretary of the Treasury and the Comptroller of the Currency, who shall be members ex officio, and five members appointed by the President of the United States, by and with the advice and consent of the Senate. In selecting the five appointive members of the Federal Reserve Board, not more than one of whom shall be selected from any one Federal reserve district, the President shall have due regard to a fair representation of the different commercial, industrial and geographical divisions of the country. The five members of the Federal Reserve Board appointed by the President and confirmed as aforesaid shall devote their entire time to the business of the Federal Reserve Board and shall each receive an annual salary of $12,000, payable monthly together with actual necessary traveling. expenses, and the Comptroller of the Currency, as ex officio member of the Federal Reserve Board, shall, in addition to the salary now paid him as Comptroller of the Currency, receive the sum of $7,000 annually for his services as a member of said Board.

The members of said board, the Secretary of the Treasury, the Assistant Secretaries of the Treasury, and the Comptroller of the Currency shall be ineligible during the time they are in office and for two years thereafter to hold any office, position, or employment in any member bank. Of the five members thus appointed by the President at least two shall be persons experienced in banking or finance. One shall be designated by the President to serve for two, one for four, one for six, one for eight, and one for ten years, and thereafter each member so appointed shall serve for a term of ten years unless sooner removed for cause by the President. Of the five persons thus appointed, one shall be designated by the President as governor and one as vice governor of the Federal Reserve Board. The governor of the Federal Reserve Board, subject to its supervision, shall be the active executive officer. The Secretary of the Treasury may assign offices in the Department of the Treasury for the use of the Federal Reserve Board. Each member of the Federal Reserve Board shall within fifteen days after notice of appointment make and subscribe to the oath of office.

The Federal Reserve Board shall have power to levy semiannually upon the Federal reserve banks, in proportion to their capital stock and surplus, an assessment sufficient to pay its estimated expenses and the salaries of its members and employees for the half year succeeding the levying of such assessment, together with any deficit carried forward from the preceding half year.

The first meeting of the Federal Reserve Board shall be held in Washington, District of Columbia, as soon as may be after the passage of this Act, at a date to be fixed by the Reserve Bank Organization Committee. The Secretary of the Treasury shall be ex officio chairman of the Federal Reserve Board. No member of the Federal Reserve Board shall be an officer or director of any bank, banking institution, trust company, or Federal reserve bank nor hold stock in any bank, banking institution, or trust company; and before entering upon his duties as a member of the Federal Reserve Board he shall certify under oath to the Secretary of the Treasury that he has complied with this requirement. Whenever a vacancy shall occur, other than by expiration of term, among the five members of the Federal Reserve Board appointed by the President, as above provided, a successor shall be appointed by the President, with the advice and consent of the Senate, to fill such vacancy, and when appointed he shall hold office for the unexpired term of the member whose place he is selected to fill.

The President shall have power to fill all vacancies that may happen on the Federal Reserve Board during the recess of the Senate, by granting commissions which shall expire thirty days after the next session of the Senate convenes.

Nothing in this Act contained shall be construed as taking away any powers heretofore vested by law in the Secretary of the Treasury which relate to the supervision, management, and control of the Treasury Department and bureaus under such department, and wherever any power vested by this Act in the Federal Reserve Board or the Federal reserve agent appears to conflict with the powers of the Secretary of the Treasury, such powers shall be exercised subject to the supervision and control of the Secretary.

The Federal Reserve Board shall annually make a full report of its operations to the Speaker of the House of Representatives, who shall cause the same to be printed for the information of the Congress.

Section three hundred and twenty-four of the Revised Statutes of the United States shall be amended so as to read as follows: There shall be in the Department of the Treasury a bureau charged with the execution of all laws passed by Congress relating to the issue and regulation of national currency secured by United States bonds and, under the general supervision of the Federal Reserve Board, of all Federal reserve notes, the chief officer of which bureau shall be called the Comptroller of the Currency and shall perform his duties under the general directions of the Secretary of the Treasury.

SEC. 11. The Federal Reserve Board shall be authorized and empowered:

(a) To examine at its discretion the accounts, books and affairs of each Federal reserve bank and of each member bank and to require such statements and reports as it may deem necessary. The said board shall publish once each week a statement showing the condition of each Federal reserve bank and a consolidated statement for all Federal reserve banks. Such statements shall show in detail the assets and liabilities of the Federal reserve banks, single and combined, and shall furnish full information regarding the character of the money held as reserve and the amount, nature and maturities of the paper and other investments owned or held by Federal reserve banks.

(b) To permit, or, on the affirmative vote of at least five members of the Reserve Board to require Federal reserve banks to rediscount the discounted paper of other Federal reserve banks at rates of interest to be fixed by the Federal Reserve Board.

(c) To suspend for a period not exceeding thirty days, and from time to time to renew such suspension for periods not exceeding fifteen days, any reserve requirement specified in this Act: *Provided,* That it shall establish a graduated tax upon the amounts by which the reserve requirements of this Act may be permitted to fall below the level hereinafter specified: *And provided further,* That when the gold reserve held against Federal reserve notes falls below forty per centum, the Federal Reserve Board shall establish a graduated tax of not more than one per centum per annum upon such deficiency until the reserves fall to thirty-two and one-half per centum, and when said reserve falls below thirty-two and one-half per centum, a tax at the rate increasingly of not less than one and one-half per centum per annum upon each two and one-half per centum or fraction thereof that such reserve falls below thirty-two and one-half per centum. The tax shall be paid by the reserve bank, but the reserve bank shall add an amount equal to said tax to the rates of interest and discount fixed by the Federal Reserve Board.

(d) To supervise and regulate through the bureau under the charge of

. the Comptroller of the Currency the issue and retirement of Federal reserve notes, and to prescribe rules and regulations under which such notes may be delivered by the Comptroller to the Federal reserve agents applying therefor.

(e) To add to the number of cities classified as reserve and central reserve cities under existing law in which national banking associations are subject to the reserve requirements set forth in section twenty of this Act; or to reclassify existing reserve and central reserve cities or to terminate their designation as such.

(f) To suspend or remove any officer or director of any Federal reserve bank, the cause of such removal to be forthwith communicated in writing by the Federal Reserve Board to the removed officer or director and to said bank.

(g) To require the writing off of doubtful or worthless assets upon the books and balance sheets of Federal reserve banks.

(h) To suspend, for the violation of any of the provisions of this Act, the operations of any Federal reserve bank, to take possession thereof, administer the same during the period of suspension, and, when deemed advisable, to liquidate or reorganize such bank.

(i) To require bonds of Federal reserve agents, to make regulations for the safeguarding of all collateral, bonds, Federal reserve notes, money or property of any kind deposited in the hands of such agents, and said board shall perform the duties, functions, or services specified in this Act, and make all rules and regulations necessary to enable said board effectively to perform the same.

(j) To exercise general supervision over said Federal reserve banks.

(k) To grant by special permit to national banks applying therefor, when not in contravention of State or local law, the right to act as trustee, executor, administrator, or registrar of stocks and bonds under such rules and regulations as the said board may prescribe.

(l) To employ such attorneys, experts, assistants, clerks, or other employees as may be deemed necessary to conduct the business of the board. All salaries and fees shall be fixed in advance by said board and shall be paid in the same manner as the salaries of the members of said board. All such attorneys, experts, assistants, clerks, and other employees shall be appointed without regard to the provisions of the Act of January sixteenth, eighteen hundred and eighty-three (volume twenty-two, United States Statutes at Large, page four hundred and three), and amendments thereto, or any rule or regulation made in pursuance thereof: *Provided,* That nothing herein shall prevent the President from placing said employees in the classified service.

FEDERAL ADVISORY COUNCIL

SEC. 12. There is hereby created a Federal Advisory Council, which shall consist of as many members as there are Federal reserve districts. Each

Federal reserve bank by its board of directors shall annually select from its own Federal reserve district one member of said council, who shall receive such compensation and allowances as may be fixed by his board of directors subject to the approval of the Federal Reserve Board. The meetings of said advisory council shall be held at Washington, District of Columbia, at least four times each year, and oftener if called by the Federal Reserve Board. The council may in addition to the meetings above provided for hold such other meetings in Washington, District of Columbia, or elsewhere, as it may deem necessary, may select its own officers and adopt its own methods of procedure, and a majority of its members shall constitute a quorum for the transaction of business. Vacancies in the council shall be filled by the respective reserve banks, and members selected to fill vacancies, shall serve for the unexpired term.

The Federal Advisory Council shall have power, by itself or through its officers, (1) to confer directly with the Federal Reserve Board on general business conditions; (2) to make oral or written representations concerning matters within the jurisdiction of said board; (3) to call for information and to make recommendations in regard to discount rates, rediscount business, note issues, reserve conditions in the various districts, the purchase and sale of gold or securities by reserve banks, open-market operations by said banks, and the general affairs of the reserve banking system.

POWERS OF FEDERAL RESERVE BANKS

SEC. 13. Any Federal reserve bank may receive from any of its member banks, and from the United States, deposits of current funds in lawful money, national-bank notes, Federal reserve notes, or checks and drafts upon solvent member banks, payable upon presentation; or, solely for exchange purposes, may receive from other Federal reserve banks deposits of current funds in lawful money, national-bank notes, or checks and drafts upon solvent member or other Federal reserve banks, payable upon presentation.

Upon the indorsement of any of its member banks, with a waiver of demand, notice and protest by such bank, any Federal reserve bank may discount notes, drafts, and bills of exchange arising out of actual commercial transactions; that is, notes, drafts, and bills of exchange issued or drawn for agricultural, industrial, or commercial purposes, or the proceeds of which have been used, or are to be used, for such purposes, the Federal Reserve Board to have the right to determine or define the character of the paper thus eligible for discount, within the meaning of this Act. Nothing in this Act contained shall be construed to prohibit such notes, drafts, and bills of exchange, secured by staple agricultural products, or other goods, wares, or merchandise from being eligible for such discount; but such definition shall not include notes, drafts, or bills covering merely investments or issued or drawn for the purpose of carrying or trading in stocks, bonds, or other investment securities, except bonds and notes of the Government of the United States. Notes, drafts, and bills admitted to discount under the terms of this paragraph must have a maturity at the time of discount of not more than ninety days: *Provided,* That notes, drafts, and bills drawn or issued for agricultural purposes or based on live stock and having a maturity not exceeding six months may be discounted in an amount to be limited to a percentage of the capital of the Federal reserve bank, to be ascertained and fixed by the Federal Reserve Board.

Any Federal reserve bank may discount acceptances which are based on the importation or exportation of goods and which have a maturity at time of discount of not more than three months, and indorsed by at least one member bank. The amount of acceptances so discounted shall at no time exceed one-half the paid-up capital stock and surplus of the bank for which the rediscounts are made.

The aggregate of such notes and bills bearing the signature or indorsement of any one person, company, firm, or corporation rediscounted for any one bank shall at no time exceed ten per centum of the unimpaired capital and surplus of said bank; but this restriction shall not apply to the discount of bills of exchange drawn in good faith against actually existing values.

Any member bank may accept drafts or bills of exchange drawn upon it and growing out of transactions involving the importation or exportation of goods having not more than six months sight to run; but no bank shall accept such bills to an amount equal at any time in the aggregate to more than one-half its paid-up capital stock and surplus.

Section fifty-two hundred and two of the Revised Statutes of the United States is hereby amended so as to read as follows: No national banking association shall at any time be indebted, or in any way liable, to an amount exceeding the amount of its capital stock at such time actually paid in and remaining undiminished by losses or otherwise, except on account of demands of the nature following:

First. Notes of circulation.

Second. Moneys deposited with or collected by the association.

Third. Bills of exchange or drafts drawn against money actually on deposit to the credit of the association, or due thereto.

Fourth. Liabilities to the stockholders of the association for dividends and reserve profits.

Fifth. Liabilities incurred under the provisions of the Federal Reserve Act.

The rediscount by any Federal reserve bank of any bills receivable and of domestic and foreign bills of exchange, and of acceptances authorized by this Act, shall be subject to such restrictions, limitations, and regulations as may be imposed by the Federal Reserve Board.

Open-Market Operations

Sec. 14. Any Federal reserve bank may, under rules and regulations prescribed by the Federal Reserve Board, purchase and sell in the open market, at home or abroad, either from or to domestic or foreign banks, firms, corporations, or individuals, cable transfers and bankers' acceptances and bills of exchange of the kinds and maturities by this Act made eligible for rediscount, with or without the indorsement of a member bank.

Every Federal reserve bank shall have power:

(a) To deal in gold coin and bullion at home or abroad, to make loans thereon, exchange Federal reserve notes for gold, gold coin, or gold certificates, and to contract for loans of gold coin or bullion, giving therefor, when necessary, acceptable security, including the hypothecation of United States bonds or other securities which Federal reserve banks are authorized to hold;

(b) To buy and sell, at home or abroad, bonds and notes of the United States, and bills, notes, revenue bonds, and warrants with a maturity from date of purchase of not exceeding six months, issued in anticipation of the collection of taxes or in anticipation of the receipt of assured revenues by any State, county, district, political subdivision, or municipality in the continental United States, including irrigation, drainage and reclamation districts, such purchases to be made in accordance with rules and regulations prescribed by the Federal Reserve Board;

(c) To purchase from member banks and to sell, with or without its indorsement, bills of exchange arising out of commercial transactions, as hereinbefore defined;

(d) To establish from time to time, subject to review and determination of the Federal Reserve Board, rates of discount to be charged by the Federal reserve bank for each class of paper, which shall be fixed with a view of accommodating commerce and business;

(e) To establish accounts with other Federal reserve banks for exchange purposes and, with the consent of the Federal Reserve Board, to open and maintain banking accounts in foreign countries, appoint correspondents, and establish agencies in such countries wheresoever it may deem best for the purpose of purchasing, selling, and collecting bills of exchange, and to buy and sell with or without its indorsement, through such correspondents or agencies, bills of exchange arising out of actual commercial transactions which have not more than ninety days to run and which bear the signature of two or more responsible parties.

Government Deposits

Sec. 15. The moneys held in the general fund of the Treasury, except the five per centum fund for the redemption of outstanding national-bank notes and the funds provided in this Act for the redemption of Federal reserve notes may, upon the direction of the Secretary of the Treasury, be deposited in Federal reserve banks, which banks, when required by the Secretary of the Treasury, shall act as fiscal agents of the United States; and the revenues of the Government or any part thereof may be deposited in such banks, and disbursements may be made by checks drawn against such deposits.

No public funds of the Philippine Islands, or of the postal savings, or any Government funds, shall be deposited in the continental United States in any bank not belonging to the system established by this Act: *Provided, however,* That nothing in this Act shall be construed to deny the right of the Secretary of the Treasury to use member banks as depositories.

NOTE ISSUES

SEC. 16. Federal reserve notes, to be issued at the discretion of the Federal Reserve Board for the purpose of making advances to Federal reserve banks through the Federal reserve agents as hereinafter set forth and for no other purpose, are hereby authorized. The said notes shall be obligations of the United States and shall be receivable by all national and member banks and Federal reserve banks and for all taxes, customs, and other public dues. They shall be redeemed in gold on demand at the Treasury Department of the United States, in the city of Washington, District of Columbia, or in gold or lawful money at any Federal reserve bank.

Any Federal reserve bank may make application to the local Federal reserve agent for such amount of the Federal reserve notes hereinbefore provided for as it may require. Such application shall be accompanied with a tender to the local Federal reserve agent of collateral in amount equal to the sum of the Federal reserve notes thus applied for and issued pursuant to such application. The collateral security thus offered shall be notes and bills, accepted for rediscount under the provisions of section thirteen of this Act, and the Federal reserve agent shall each day notify the Federal Reserve Board of all issues and withdrawals of Federal reserve notes to and by the Federal reserve bank to which he is accredited. The said Federal Reserve Board may at any time call upon a Federal reserve bank for additional security to protect the Federal reserve notes issued to it.

Every Federal reserve bank shall maintain reserves in gold or lawful money of not less than thirty-five per centum against its deposits and reserves in gold of not less than forty per centum against its Federal reserve notes in actual circulation, and not offset by gold or lawful money deposited with the Federal reserve agent. Notes so paid out shall bear upon their faces a distinctive letter and serial number, which shall be assigned by the Federal Reserve Board to each Federal reserve bank. Whenever Federal reserve notes issued through one Federal reserve bank shall be received by another Federal reserve bank they shall be promptly returned for credit or redemption to the Federal reserve bank through which they were originally issued. No Federal reserve bank shall pay out notes issued through another under penalty of a tax of ten per centum upon the face value of notes so paid out. Notes presented for redemption at the Treasury of the United States shall be paid out of the redemption fund and returned to the Federal reserve banks through which they were originally issued, and thereupon such Federal reserve bank shall, upon demand of the Secretary of the Treasury, reimburse such redemption fund in lawful money or, if such Federal reserve notes have been redeemed by the Treasurer in gold or gold certificates, then such funds shall be reimbursed to the extent deemed necessary by the Secretary of the Treasury in gold or gold certificates, and such Federal reserve bank shall, so long as any of its Federal reserve notes remain outstanding, maintain with the Treasurer in gold an amount sufficient in the judgment of the Secretary to provide for all redemptions to be made by the Treasurer. Federal reserve notes received by the Treasury, otherwise than for redemption, may be exchanged for gold out of the redemption fund hereinafter provided and returned to the reserve bank through which they were originally issued, or they may be returned to such bank for the credit of the United States. Federal reserve notes unfit for circulation shall be returned by the Federal reserve agents to the Comptroller of the Currency for cancellation and destruction.

The Federal Reserve Board shall require each Federal reserve bank to maintain on deposit in the Treasury of the United States a sum in gold sufficient in the judgment of the Secretary of the Treasury for the redemption of the Federal reserve notes issued to such bank, but in no event less than five per centum; but such deposit of gold shall be counted and included as part of the forty per centum reserve hereinbefore required. The board shall have the right, acting through the Federal reserve agent, to grant in whole or in part or to reject entirely the application of any Federal reserve bank for Federal reserve notes; but to the extent that such application may be granted the Federal Reserve Board shall, through its local Federal reserve agent, supply Federal reserve notes to the bank so applying, and such bank shall be charged with the amount of such notes and shall pay such rate of interest on said amount as may be established by the Federal Reserve Board, and the amount of such Federal reserve notes so issued to any such bank shall, upon delivery, together with such notes of such Federal reserve bank as may be issued under section eighteen of this Act upon security of United States two per centum Government bonds, become a first and paramount lien on all the assets of such bank.

Any Federal reserve bank may at any time reduce its liability for outstanding Federal reserve notes by depositing, with the Federal reserve agent, its Federal reserve notes, gold, gold certificates, or lawful money of the United States. Federal reserve notes so deposited shall not be reissued, except upon compliance with the conditions of an original issue.

The Federal reserve agent shall hold such gold, gold certificates, or lawful money available exclusively for exchange for the outstanding Federal reserve notes when offered by the reserve bank of which he is a director. Upon the request of the Secretary of the Treasury the Federal Reserve Board shall require the Federal reserve agent to transmit so much of said gold to the Treasury of the United States as may be required for the exclusive purpose of the redemption of such notes.

Any Federal reserve bank may at its discretion withdraw collateral deposited with the local Federal reserve agent for the protection of its Federal reserve notes deposited with it and shall at the same time substitute therefor other like collateral of equal amount with the approval of the Federal reserve agent under regulations to be prescribed by the Federal Reserve Board.

In order to furnish suitable notes for circulation as Federal reserve notes, the Comptroller of the Currency shall, under the direction of the Secretary of the Treasury, cause plates and dies to be engraved in the best manner to guard against counterfeits and fraudulent alterations, and shall have printed therefrom and numbered such quantities of such notes of the denominations of $5, $10, $20, $50, $100, as may be required to supply the Federal reserve banks. Such notes shall be in form and tenor as directed by the Secretary of the Treasury under the provisions of this Act and shall bear the distinctive numbers of the several Federal reserve banks through which they are issued.

When such notes have been prepared, they shall be deposited in the Treasury, or in the subtreasury or mint of the United States, nearest the place of business of each Federal reserve bank and shall be held for the use of such bank, subject to the order of the Comptroller of the Currency for their delivery, as provided by this Act.

The plates and dies to be procured by the Comptroller of the Currency for the printing of such circulating notes shall remain under his control and direction, and the expenses necessarily incurred in executing the, laws relating to the procuring of such notes, and all other expenses incidental to their issue and retirement, shall be paid by the Federal reserve banks, and the Federal Reserve Board shall include in its estimate of expenses levied against the Federal reserve banks a sufficient amount to cover the expenses herein provided for.

The examination of plates, dies, bed pieces, and so forth, and regulations relating to such examination of plates, dies, and so forth, of national-bank notes provided for in section fifty-one hundred and seventy-four Revised Statutes, is hereby extended to include notes herein provided for.

Any appropriation heretofore made out of the general funds of the Treasury for engraving plates and dies, the purchase of distinctive paper, or to cover any other expense in connection with the printing of national-bank notes or notes provided for by the Act of May thirtieth, nineteen hundred and eight, and any distinctive paper that may be on hand at the time of the passage of this Act may be used in the discretion of the Secretary for the purposes of this Act, and should the appropriations heretofore made be insufficient to meet the requirements of this Act in addition to circulating notes provided for by existing law, the Secretary is hereby authorized to use so much of any funds in the Treasury not otherwise appropriated for the purpose of furnishing the notes aforesaid: *Provided, however,* That nothing in this section contained shall be construed as exempting national banks or Federal reserve banks from their liability to reimburse the United States for any expenses incurred in printing and issuing circulating notes.

Every Federal reserve bank shall receive on deposit at par from member banks or from Federal reserve banks checks and drafts drawn upon any of its depositors, and when remitted by a Federal reserve bank, checks and drafts drawn by any depositor in any other Federal reserve bank or member bank upon funds to the credit of said depositor in said reserve bank or member bank. Nothing herein contained shall be construed as prohibiting a member bank from charging its actual expense incurred in collecting and remitting funds, or for exchange sold to its patrons. The Federal Reserve Board shall, by rule, fix the charges to be collected by the member banks from its patrons whose checks are cleared through the Federal reserve bank and the charge which may be imposed for the service of clearing or collection rendered by the Federal reserve bank.

The Federal Reserve Board shall make and promulgate from time to time regulations governing the transfer of funds and charges therefor among Federal reserve banks and their branches, and may at its discretion exercise the functions of a clearing house for such Federal reserve banks, or may designate a Federal reserve bank to exercise such functions, and may also require each bank to exercise the functions of a clearing house for its member banks.

SEC. 17. So much of the provisions of section fifty-one hundred and fifty-nine of the Revised Statutes of the United States, and section four of the Act of June twentieth, eighteen hundred and seventy-four, and section eight of the Act of July twelfth, eighteen hundred and eighty-two, and of any other provisions of existing statutes as require that before any national banking associations, shall be authorized to commence banking business it shall transfer and deliver to the Treasurer of the United States a stated amount of United States registered bonds is hereby repealed.

REFUNDING BONDS

SEC. 18. After two years from the passage of this Act, and at any time during a period of twenty years thereafter, any member bank desiring to retire the whole or any part of its circulating notes, may file with the Treasurer of the United States an application to sell for its account, at par and accrued interest, United States bonds securing circulation to be retired.

The Treasurer shall, at the end of each quarterly period, furnish the

Federal Reserve Board with a list of such applications, and the Federal Reserve Board may, in its discretion, require the Federal reserve banks to purchase such bonds from the banks whose applications have been filed with the Treasurer at least ten days before the end of any quarterly period at which the Federal Reserve'Board may direct the purchase to be made: *Provided,* That Federal reserve banks shall not be permitted to purchase an amount to exceed $25,000,000 of such bonds in any one year, and which amount shall include bonds acquired under section four of this Act by the Federal reserve bank.

Provided further, That the Federal Reserve Board shall allot to each Federal reserve bank such proportion of such bonds as the capital and surplus of such bank shall bear to the aggregate capital and surplus of all the Federal reserve banks.

Upon notice from the Treasurer of the amount of bonds so sold for its account, each member bank shall duly assign and transfer, in writing, such bonds to the Federal reserve banks purchasing the same, and such Federal reserve bank shall, thereupon, deposit lawful money with the Treasurer of the United States for the purchase price of such bonds, and the Treasurer shall pay to the member bank selling such bonds any balance due after deducting a sufficient sum to redeem its outstanding notes secured by such bonds, which notes shall be canceled and permanently retired when redeemed.

The Federal reserve banks purchasing such bonds shall be permitted to take out an amount of circulating notes equal to the par value of such bonds.

Upon the deposit with the Treasurer of the United States of bonds so purchased, or any bonds with the circulating privilege acquired under section four of this Act, any Federal reserve bank making such deposit in the manner provided by existing law, shall be entitled to receive from the Comptroller of the Currency circulating notes in blank, registered, and countersigned as provided by law, equal in amount to the par value of the bonds so deposited. Such notes shall be the obligations of the Federal reserve bank procuring the same, and shall be in form prescribed by the Secretary of the Treasury, and to the same tenor and effect as national-bank notes now provided by law. They shall be issued and redeemed under the same terms and conditions as national-bank notes except that they shall not be limited to the amount of the capital stock of the Federal reserve bank issuing them.

Upon application of any Federal reserve bank, approved by the Federal Reserve Board, the Secretary of the Treasury may issue, in exchange for United States two per centum gold bonds bearing the circulation privilege, but against which no circulation is outstanding, one-year gold notes of the United States without the circulation privilege, to an amount not to exceed one-half of the two per centum bonds so tendered for exchange, and thirty-year three per centum gold bonds without the circulation privilege for the remainder of the two per centum bonds so tendered: *Provided,* That at the time of such exchange the Federal reserve bank obtaining such one-year gold notes shall enter into an obligation with the Secretary of the Treasury binding itself to purchase from the United States for gold at the maturity of such one-year notes, an amount equal to those delivered in exchange for such bonds, if so requested by the Secretary, and at each maturity of one-year notes so purchased by such Federal reserve bank, to purchase from the United States such an amount of one-year notes as the Secretary may tender to such bank, not to exceed the amount issued to such bank in the first instance, in exchange for the two per centum United States gold bonds; said obligation to purchase at maturity such notes shall continue in force for a period not to exceed thirty years.

For the purpose of making the exchange herein provided for, the Secretary of the Treasury is authorized to issue at par Treasury notes in coupon or registered form as he may prescribe in denominations of one hundred dollars, or any multiple thereof, bearing interest at the rate of three per centum per annum, payable quarterly, such Treasury notes to be payable not more than one year from the date of their issue in gold coin of the present standard value, and to be exempt as to principal and interest from the payment of all taxes and duties of the United States except as provided by this Act, as well as from taxes in any form by or under State, municipal, or local authorities. And for the same purpose, the Secretary is authorized and empowered to issue United States gold bonds at par, bearing three per centum interest payable thirty years from date of issue, such bonds to be of the same general tenor and effect and to be issued under the same general terms and conditions as the United States three per centum bonds without the circulation privilege now issued and outstanding.

Upon application of any Federal reserve bank, approved by the Federal Reserve Board, the Secretary may issue at par such three per centum bonds in exchange for the one-year gold notes herein provided for.

BANK RESERVES

SEC. 19. Demand deposits within the meaning of this Act shall comprise all deposits payable within thirty days, and time deposits shall comprise all deposits payable after thirty days, and all savings accounts and certificates of deposit which are subject to not less than thirty days' notice before payment.

When the Secretary of the Treasury shall have officially announced, in such manner as he may elect, the establishment of a Federal reserve bank in any district, every subscribing member bank shall establish and maintain reserves as follows:

(a) A bank not in a reserve or central reserve city as now or hereafter defined shall hold and maintain reserves equal to twelve per centum of the aggregate amount of its demand deposits and five per centum of its time deposits, as follows:

In its vaults for a period of thirty-six months after said date five-twelfths thereof and permanently thereafter four-twelfths.

In the Federal reserve bank of its district, for a period of twelve months after said date, two-twelfths, and for each succeeding six months an additional one-twelfth, until five-twelfths have been so deposited, which shall be the amount permanently required.

For a period of thirty-six months after said date the balance of the reserves may be held in its own vaults, or in the Federal reserve bank, or in national banks in reserve or central reserve cities as now defined by law.

After said thirty-six months' period said reserves, other than those hereinbefore required to be held in the vaults of the member bank and in the Federal reserve bank, shall be held in the vaults of the member bank or in the Federal reserve bank, or in both, at the option of the member bank.

(b) A bank in a reserve city, as now or hereafter defined, shall hold and maintain reserves equal to fifteen per centum of the aggregate amount of its demand deposits and five per centum of its time deposits, as follows:

In its vaults for a period of thirty-six months after said date six-fifteenths thereof, and permanently thereafter five-fifteenths.

In the Federal reserve bank of its district for a period of twelve months after the date aforesaid at least three-fifteenths, and for each succeeding six months an additional one-fifteenth, until six-fifteenths have been so deposited, which shall be the amount permanently required.

For a period of thirty-six months after said date the balance of the reserves may be held in its own vaults, or in the Federal reserve bank, or in national banks in reserve or central reserve cities as now defined by law.

After said thirty-six months' period all of said reserves, except those hereinbefore required to be held permanently in the vaults of the member bank and in the Federal reserve bank, shall be held in its vaults or in the Federal reserve bank, or in both, at the option of the member bank.

(c) A bank in a central reserve city, as now or hereafter defined, shall hold and maintain a reserve equal to eighteen per centum of the aggregate amount of its demand deposits and five per centum of its time deposits, as follows:

In its vaults six-eighteenths thereof.

In the Federal reserve bank seven-eighteenths.

The balance of said reserves shall be held in its own vaults or in the Federal reserve bank, at its option.

Any Federal reserve bank may receive from the member banks as reserves, not exceeding one-half of each installment, eligible paper as described in section fourteen properly indorsed and acceptable to the said reserve bank.

If a State bank or trust company is required by the law of its State to keep its reserves either in its own vaults or with another State bank or trust company, such reserve deposits so kept in such State bank or trust company shall be construed, within the meaning of this section, as if they were reserve deposits in a national bank in a reserve or central reserve city for a period of three years after the Secretary of the Treasury shall have officially announced the establishment of a Federal reserve bank in the district in which such State bank or trust company is situate. Except as thus provided, no member bank shall keep on deposit with any nonmember bank a sum in excess of ten per centum of its own paid-up capital and surplus. No member bank shall act as the medium or agent of a nonmember bank in applying for or receiving discounts from a Federal reserve bank under the provisions of this Act except by permission of the Federal Reserve Board.

' The reserve carried by a member bank with a Federal reserve bank may, under the regulations and subject to such penalties as may be prescribed by the Federal Reserve Board, be checked against and withdrawn by such member bank for the purpose of meeting existing liabilities: *Provided, however*, That no bank shall at any time make new loans or shall pay any dividends unless and until the total reserve required by law is fully restored.

In estimating the reserves required by this Act, the net balance of amounts due to and from other banks shall be taken as the basis for ascertaining the deposits against which reserves shall be determined. Balances in reserve banks due to member banks shall, to the extent herein provided, be counted as reserves.

National banks located in Alaska or outside the continental United States may remain nonmember banks, and shall in that event maintain reserves and comply with all the conditions now provided by law regulating them; or said banks, except in the Philippine Islands, may, with the consent of the Reserve Board, become member banks of any one of the reserve districts, and shall, in that event, take stock, maintain reserves, and be subject to all the other provisions of this Act.

SEC. 20. So much of sections two and three of the Act of June twentieth, eighteen hundred and seventy-four, entitled "An Act fixing the amount of United States notes, providing for a redistribution of the national-bank currency, and for other purposes," as provides that the fund deposited by any national banking association with the Treasurer of the United States for the redemption of its notes shall be counted as a part of its lawful reserve as provided in the Act aforesaid, is hereby repealed. And from and after the passage of this Act such fund of five per centum shall in no case be counted by any national banking association as a part of its lawful reserve.

BANK EXAMINATIONS

SEC. 21. Section fifty-two hundred and forty, United States Revised Statutes, is amended to read as follows:

The Comptroller of the Currency, with the approval of the Secretary of the Treasury, shall appoint examiners who shall examine every member bank at least twice in each calendar year and oftener if considered necessary: *Provided, however,* That the Federal Reserve Board may authorize examination by the State authorities to be accepted in the case of State banks and trust companies and may at any time direct the holding of a special examination of State banks or trust companies that are stockholders in any Federal reserve bank. The examiner making the examination of any national bank, or of any other member bank, shall have power to make a thorough examination of all the affairs of the bank and in doing so he shall have power to administer oaths and to examine any of the officers and agents thereof under oath and shall make a full and detailed report of the condition of said bank to the Comptroller of the Currency.

The Federal Reserve Board, upon the recommendation of the Comptroller of the Currency, shall fix the salaries of all bank examiners and make report thereof to Congress. The expense of the examinations herein provided for shall be assessed by the Comptroller of the Currency upon the banks examined in proportion to assets or resources held by the banks upon the dates of examination of the various banks.

In addition to the examinations made and conducted by the Comptroller of the Currency, every Federal reserve bank may, with the approval of the Federal reserve agent or the Federal Reserve Board, provide for special examination of member banks within its district. The expense of such examinations shall be borne by the bank examined. Such examinations shall be so conducted as to inform the Federal reserve bank of the condition of its member banks and of the lines of credit which are being extended by them. Every Federal reserve bank shall at all times furnish to the Federal Reserve Board such information as may be demanded concerning the condition of any member bank within the district of the said Federal reserve bank.

No bank shall be subject to any visitatorial powers other than such as are authorized by law, or vested in the courts of justice or such as shall be or shall have been exercised or directed by Congress, or by either House thereof or by any committee of Congress or of either House duly authorized.

The Federal Reserve Board shall, at least once each year, order an examination of each Federal reserve bank, and upon joint application of ten member banks the Federal Reserve Board shall order a special examination and report of the condition of any Federal reserve bank.

Sec. 22. No member bank or any officer, director, or employee thereof shall hereafter make any loan or grant any gratuity to any bank examiner. Any bank officer, director, or employee violating this provision shall be deemed guilty of a misdemeanor and shall be imprisoned not exceeding one year or fined not more than $5,000, or both; and may be fined a further sum equal to the money so loaned or gratuity given. Any examiner accepting a loan or gratuity from any bank examined by him or from an officer, director, or employee thereof shall be deemed guilty of a misdemeanor and shall be imprisoned not exceeding one year or fined not more than $5,000, or both; and may be fined a further sum equal to the money so loaned or gratuity given; and shall forever thereafter be disqualified from holding office as a national-bank examiner. No national-bank examiner shall perform any other service for compensation while holding such office for any bank or officer, director, or employee thereof.

Other than the usual salary or director's fee paid to any officer, director, or employee of a member bank and other than a reasonable fee paid by said bank to such officer, director, or employee for services rendered to such bank, no officer, director, employee, or attorney of a member bank shall be a beneficiary of or receive, directly or indirectly, any fee, commission, gift, or other consideration for or in connection with any transaction or business of the bank. No examiner, public or private, shall disclose the names of borrowers or the collateral for loans of a member bank to other than the proper officers of such bank without first having obtained the express permission in writing from the Comptroller of the Currency, or from the board of directors of such bank, except when ordered to do so by a court of competent jurisdiction, or by direction of the Congress of the United States, or of either House thereof, or any committee of Congress or of either House duly authorized. Any person violating any provision of this section shall be punished by a fine of not exceeding $5,000 or by imprisonment not exceeding one year, or both.

Except as provided in existing laws, this provision shall not take effect until sixty days after the passage of this Act.

SEC. 23. The stockholders of every national banking association shall be held individually responsible for all contracts, debts, and engagements of such association, each to the amount of his stock therein, at the par value thereof in addition to the amount invested in such stock. The stockholders in any national banking association who shall have transferred their shares or registered the transfer thereof within sixty days next before the date of the failure of such association to meet its obligations, or with knowledge of such impending failure, shall be liable to the same extent as if they had made no such transfer, to the extent that the subsequent transferee fails to meet such liability; but this provision shall not be construed to affect in any way any recourse which such shareholders might otherwise have against those in whose names such shares are registered at the time of such failure.

LOANS ON FARM LANDS

SEC. 24. Any national banking association not situated in a central reserve city may make loans secured by improved and unencumbered farm land, situated within its Federal reserve district, but no such loan shall be made for a longer time than five years, nor for an amount exceeding fifty per centum of the actual value of the property offered as security. Any such bank may make such loans in an aggregate sum equal to twenty-five per centum of its capital and surplus or to one-third of its time deposits and such banks may continue hereafter as heretofore to receive time deposits and to pay interest on the same.

The Federal Reserve Board shall have power from time to time to add to the list of cities in which national banks shall not be permitted to make loans secured upon real estate in the manner described in this section.

FOREIGN BRANCHES

SEC. 25. Any national banking association possessing a capital and surplus of $1,000,000 or more may file application with the Federal Reserve Board, upon such conditions and under such regulations as may be prescribed by the said board, for the purpose of securing authority to establish branches in foreign countries or dependencies of the United States for the furtherance of the foreign commerce of the United States, and to act, if required to do so, as fiscal agents of the United States. Such application shall specify, in addition to the name and capital of the banking association filing it, the place or places where the banking operations proposed are to be carried on, and the amount of capital set aside for the conduct of its foreign business. The Federal Reserve Board shall have power to approve or to reject such application if, in its judgment, the amount of capital proposed to be set aside for the conduct of foreign business is inadequate, or if for other reasons the granting of such application is deemed inexpedient.

Every national banking association which shall receive authority to establish foreign branches shall be required at all times to furnish information concerning the condition of such branches to the Comptroller of the Currency upon demand, and the Federal Reserve Board may order special examinations of the said foreign branches at such time or times as it may deem best. Every such national banking association shall conduct the accounts of each foreign branch independently of the accounts of other foreign branches established by it and of its home office, and shall at the end of each fiscal period transfer to its general ledger the profit or loss accruing at each branch as a separate item.

SEC. 26. All provisions of law inconsistent with or superseded by any of the provisions of this Act are to that extent and to that extent only hereby repealed: *Provided*, Nothing in this Act contained shall be construed to repeal the parity provision or provisions contained in an Act approved March fourteenth, nineteen hundred, entitled "An Act to define and fix the standard of value, to maintain the parity of all forms of money issued or coined by the United States, to refund the public debt, and for other purposes," and the Secretary of the Treasury may for the purpose of maintaining such parity and to strengthen the gold reserve, borrow gold on the security of United States bonds authorized by section two of the Act last referred to or for one-year gold notes bearing interest at a rate of not to exceed three per centum per annum, or sell the same if necessary to obtain gold. When the funds of the Treasury on hand justify, he may purchase and retire such outstanding bonds and notes.

SEC. 27. The provisions of ·the Act of May thirtieth, nineteen hundred
and eight, authorizing national currency associations, the issue of additional
national-bank circulation, and creating a National Monetary Commission,
which expires by limitation under the terms of such Act on the thirtieth day
of June, nineteen hundred and fourteen, are hereby extended to June thirtieth, nineteen hundred and fifteen, and sections fifty-one hundred and fifty-
three, fifty-one hundred and seventy-two, fifty-one hundred and ninety-one,
and fifty-two hundred and fourteen of the Revised Statutes of the United
States, which were amended by the Act of May thirtieth, nineteen hundred
and eight, are hereby reenacted to read as such sections read prior to May
thirtieth, nineteen hundred and eight, subject to such amendments or modifications as are prescribed in this Act: *Provided, however,* That section
nine of the Act first referred to ¹n this section is hereby amended so as to
change the tax rates fixed in said Act by making the portion applicable
thereto read as follows:

National banking associations having circulating notes secured otherwise than by bonds of the United States, shall pay for the first three months
a tax at the rate of three per centum per annum upon the average amount
of such of their notes in circulation as are based upon the deposit of such
securities, and afterwards an additional tax rate of one-half of one per
centum per annum for each month until a tax of six per centum per annum
is reached, and thereafter such tax of six per centum per annum upon the
average amount of such notes.

SEC. 28. Section fifty-one hundred and forty-three of the Revised Statutes is hereby amended and reenacted to read as follows: Any association
formed under this title may, by the vote of shareholders owning two-thirds
of its capital stock, reduce its capital to any sum not below the amount required by this title to authorize the formation of associations; but no such
reduction shall be allowable which will reduce the capital of the association
below the amount required for its outstanding circulation, nor shall any
reduction be made until the amount of the proposed reduction has been reported to the Comptroller of the Currency and such reduction has been
approved by the said Comptroller of the Currency and by the Federal Reserve Board, or by the organization committee pending the organization of
the Federal Reserve Board.

SEC. 29. If any clause, sentence, paragraph, or part of this Act shall for
any reason be adjudged by any court of competent jurisdiction to be invalid,
such judgment shall not affect, impair, or invalidate the remainder of this
Act, but shall be confined in its operation to the clause, sentence, paragraph,
or part thereof directly involved in the controversy in which such judgment
shall have been rendered.

SEC. 30. The right to amend, alter, or repeal this Act is hereby expressly
reserved.

Approved, December 23, 1913.

Commercial banks named by the Organization Committee to execute the organization certificate for each Federal Reserve bank. Names of officers signing the certificate given if available.

District No. 1—Boston
National Shawmut Bank, Boston
First National Bank, Concord, N.H.
First Bridgeport National Bank, Bridgeport, Conn.
National Bank of Commerce, Providence, R.I.
Casco National Bank, Portland, Me.

District No. 2—New York
National Park Bank, New York Richard Delafield, President
First National Bank of Syracuse, N.Y.; A.W. Hudson, Vice President
National Commercial Bank, Albany, N.Y.; James H. Perkins, President
Marine National Bank, Buffalo, N.Y. L.H. Gethoefer, Vice President
Irving National Bank, New York Rollin P. Grant, President

District No. 3—Philadelphia
Philadelphia National Bank, Philadelphia, Pa.
Essex County National Bank, Newark, N.J.
First National Bank, Jersey City, N.J.
Union National Bank, Wilmington, Del.
Bank of North America, Philadelphia, Pa.

District No. 4—Cleveland
First National Bank, Cleveland, Ohio John Sherman, President; C.C. Farnsworth, Cashier
First National Bank, Cincinnati T.J. Davis, Vice President; Robert McEvilly, Cashier
New First National Bank, Columbus, Ohio; Charles R. Mayers, President; Mr. Shields, Cashier
Bank of Pittsburgh National Association, Pittsburgh, Pa.; Harison Nesbit, President; Alexander Dunbar, Cashier
Phoenix & Third National Bank, Lexington, Ky.; W.A. McDowell, Vice President; W.L. Threlkeld, Cashier

District No. 5—Richmond
Merchants—Mechanics National Bank, Baltimore, Md.; William Ingle, Vice President; John B. Dunn, Cashier
First National Bank, Roanoke, Va. H.S. Trout, President; J. Tyler Meadows, Cashier
Citizens National Bank, Charleston, W. Va.; W.A. McCorkle, President; J.N. Carnes, Cashier
Palmetto National Bank, Columbia, S. Carolina; J.J. Seibels, Vice President; J. Pope Matthews, Cashier
Murchison National Bank, Wilmington, N.C.; H.C. MacQueen, President; C.S. Granger, Cashier

District No. 6—Atlanta
First National Bank, Chattanooga, Tenn.
First National Bank, Jackson, Miss.
Hibernia National Bank, New Orleans, La.
Exchange National Bank, Tampa, Fla.
First National Bank, Montgomery, Ala.

District No. 7—Chicago
Continental & Commercial Bank, Chicago; George M. Reynolds, President

First National Bank, Sioux City,
Iowa; John McHugh, President
National City Bank, Indianapolis,
Ind.; James M. McIntosh, President
First & Old Detroit National Bank,
Detroit; Wm. J. Gray, President
Wisconsin National Bank, Milwaukee, Wis.; L.G. Bournique, President

District No. 8 — St. Louis
German National Bank, Little Rock
Ark.
Ayers National Bank, Jacksonville,
Ill.
Second National Bank, New Albany,
Ind.
First National Bank, Memphis, Tenn.
National Bank of Kentucky, Louisville, Ky.

District No. 9 — Minneapolis
Capital National Bank, St. Paul,
Minn.
First National Bank, Grand Forks,
N. Dak.
First National Bank, Lead, S. Dak.
Merchants National Bank, Billings,
Mont.
Commercial National Bank,
Oshkosh, Wis.

District No. 10 — Kansas City
Denver National Bank, Denver,
Colo.; J.C. Mitchell, President
Central National Bank, Lincoln,
Nebr.; P.L. Hall, President
United States National Bank,
Omaha, Nebr.; V.B. Caldwell,

Vice President
First National Bank, Muskogee,
Okla.; Asa E. Ramsay, Vice President
Rawlins National Bank, Rawlins,
Wyo.; William Daley, President

District No. 11 — Dallas
Durant National Bank, Durant,
Okla; Jas. R. McKinney, Vice
President; B.A. McKinney, Cashier
First National Bank, El Paso, Tex.
J.G. McNary, Vice President;
E.W. Keyser, Cashier
Union National Bank, Houston, Tex.
T.C. Dunn, Vice President; DeWitt
C. Dunn, Cashier
Frost National Bank, San Antonio,
Tex.; T.C. Frost, President; Ned
McIlhenny, Cashier
First National Bank, Shreveport, La.
Andrew Querbes, President; W.J.
Bayersdorffer, Cashier

District No. 12 — San Francisco
Phoenix National Bank, Phoenix,
Ariz.; H.J. McClung, President;
H.D. Marshall, Cashier
First National Bank, San Francisco,
Calif.; R. Spreckels, President;
J.K. Moffitt, Cashier
First National Bank, Portland, Ore.
Henry L. Corbett, Vice President;
J.W. Newkirk, Cashier
Deseret National Bank, Salt Lake
City, Utah; John C. Cutler, President; H.S. Young, Cashier
National Bank of Commerce, Seattle,
Wash.; M.F. Backus, President;
G.F. Clark, Cashier

Governors and Directors of Federal Reserve Banks at Opening of Banks — 1914

The following is a list of the governors, directors, chairmen, Federal reserve agents, deputy chairmen, and deputy reserve agents of the Federal reserve banks.

Boston — District No. 1
Alfred L. Aiken, *Governor*
Class C — Frederic H. Curtiss, Boston, Federal reserve agent and chairman of

board of directors; Walter S. Hackney, Providence, R.I., deputy federal reserve agent and vice chairman of board of directors; Allen Hollis, Concord, N.H., director.

Class A — Thomas P. Beal, Boston, Mass., Group No. 1; C.G. Sanford, Bridgeport, Conn., Group No. 2; A.M. Heard, Manchester, N.H., Group No. 3.

Class B — Charles A. Morse, Boston, Mass., Group No. 1; E.R. Morse, Proctor, Vt., Group No. 2; Charles G. Washburn, Worcester, Mass., Group No. 3.

Member Federal Advisory Council, Daniel G. Wing, Boston.

New York — District No. 2
Benjamin Strong, Jr., *Governor*

Class C — Pierre Jay, New York, N.Y., Federal reserve agent and chairman of board of directors; Charles Starek, New York, N.Y., deputy Federal reserve agent and vice chairman of board of directors; George Foster Peabody, Lake George, N.Y., director.

Class A — William Woodward, New York, N.Y., Group No. 1; Robert H. Treman, Ithaca, N.Y., Group No. 2; Franklin D. Locke, Buffalo, N.Y., Group No. 3.

Class B — H.R. Towne, New York, N.Y., Group No. 1; William B. Thompson, Yonkers, N.Y., Group No. 2; Leslie R. Palmer, Croton-on-Hudson, N.Y., Group No. 3.

Member Federal Advisory Council, J.P. Morgan, New York City.

Philadelphia — District No. 3
Charles J. Rhoads, *Governor*

Class C — Richard L. Austin, Philadelphia, Federal reserve agent and chairman of board of directors; George M. La Monte, deputy Federal reserve agent and vice chairman of board of directors, Bound Brook, N.J.; George W. Norris, Philadelphia, director.

Class A — Charles J. Rhoads, Philadelphia, Pa., Group No. 1; W.H. Peck, Scranton, Pa., Group No. 2; M.J. Murphy, Scranton, Pa., Group No. 3.

Class B — Alba B. Johnson, Philadelphia, Pa., Group No. 1; Edwin S. Stuart, Philadelphia, Pa., Group No. 2; George W.F. Gaunt, Mullica Hill, N.J., Group No. 3.

Member Federal Advisory Council, Levi L. Rue, Philadelphia.

Cleveland — District No. 4
E.R. Fancher, *Governor*

Class C — D.C. Wills, Bellevue, Pa., Federal reserve agent and chairman of board of directors; Lyman H. Treadway, Cleveland, Ohio, deputy Federal reserve agent and vice chairman of board of directors; H.P. Wolfe, Columbus, Ohio, director.

Class A — Robert Wardrop, Pittsburgh, Pa., Group No. 1; W.S. Rowe, Cincinnati, Ohio, Group No. 2; S.B. Rankin, South Charleston, Ohio, Group No. 3.

Class B — Thomas A. Combs, Lexington, Ky., Group No. 1; C.H. Bagley, Corry, Pa., Group No. 2; A.B. Patrick, Salyersville, Ky., Group No. 3.

Member Federal Advisory Council, W.S. Rowe, Cincinnati.

Richmond — District No. 5
George J. Seay, *Governor*

Class C — William Ingle, Baltimore, Federal reserve agent and chairman of board of directors; James A. Moncure, Richmond, deputy Federal reserve agent and vice chairman of board of directors; M.F.H. Gouverneur, Wilmington, N.C., director.

Class A — Waldo Newcomer, Baltimore, Md., Group No. 1; John F. Bruton, Wilson, N.C., Group No. 2; Edwin Mann, Bluefield, W.Va., Group No. 3.

Class B — George J. Seay, Richmond, Va., Group No. 1; D.R. Coker, Hartsville, S.C., Group No. 2; J.F. Oyster, Washington, D.C., Group No. 3.

Member Federal Advisory Council, Geo. J. Seay, Richmond.

Atlanta — District No. 6
Joseph A. McCord, *Governor*

Class C — M.B. Wellborn, Anniston, Ala., Federal reserve agent and chairman of board of directors; Edward T. Brown, Atlanta, Ga., deputy Federal reserve agent and vice chairman of board of directors; W.H. Kettig, Birmingham, Ala., director.

Class A — L.P. Hillyer, Macon, Ga., Group No. 1; F.W. Foote, Hattiesburg, Miss., Group No. 2; W.H. Toole, Winder, Ga., Group No. 3.

Class B — P.H. Saunders, New Orleans, La., Group No. 1; J.A. McCrary, Decatur, Ga., Group No. 2; W.H. Hartford, Nashville, Tenn., Group No. 3.

Member Federal Advisory Council, Chas. A. Lyerly, Chattanooga.

Chicago — District No. 7
James B. McDougal, *Governor*

Class C — C.H. Bosworth, Chicago, Ill., Federal reserve agent and chairman of board of directors; W.L. McLallen, Columbia City, Ind., deputy Federal reserve agent and vice chairman of board of directors; Edwin T. Meredith, Des Moines, Iowa, director.

Class A — George M. Reynolds, Chicago, Ill., Group No. 1; J.B. Forgan, Chicago, Ill., Group No. 2; E.L. Johnson, Waterloo, Iowa, Group No. 3.

Class B — Henry B. Joy, Detroit, Mich., Group No. 1; M.B. Hutchison, Ottumwa, Iowa, Group No. 2; A.H. Vogel, Milwaukee, Wis., Group No. 3.

Member Federal Advisory Council, J.B. Forgan, Chicago.

St. Louis — District No. 8
Rolla Wells, *Governor*

Class C — William McC. Martin, St. Louis, Federal reserve agent and chairman of board of directors; Walter W. Smith, St. Louis, deputy Federal reserve agent and vice chairman of board of directors; John Boehne, Evansville, Ind., director.

Class A — Walker Hill, St. Louis, Mo., Group No. 1; F.O. Watts, St. Louis, Mo., Group No. 2; Oscar Fenley, Louisville, Ky., Group No. 3.

Class B — Murray Carlton, St. Louis, Mo., Group No. 1; W.B. Plunkett, Little Rock, Ark., Group No. 2; LeRoy Percy, Greenville, Miss., Group No. 3.

Member Federal Advisory Council, Rolla Wells, St. Louis.

Minneapolis — District No. 9
Theodore Wold, *Governor*

Class C — John H. Rich, Red Wing, Minn., Federal reserve agent and chairman of board of directors; P.M. Kerst, St. Paul, deputy Federal reserve agent and vice chairman of board of directors; John W. Black, Houghton, Mich., director.

Class A — E.W. Decker, Minneapolis, Minn., Group No. 1; L.B. Hanna, Fargo, N. Dak., Group No. 2; J.C. Bassett, Aberdeen, S. Dak., Group No. 3.

Class B — F.R. Bigelow, St. Paul, Minn., Group No. 1; F.P. Hixon, La Crosse, Wis., Group No. 2; Norman B. Holter, Helena, Mont., Group No. 3.

Member Federal Advisory Council, C.T. Jaffray, Minneapolis.

Kansas City—District No. 10
Charles M. Sawyer, *Governor*

Class C—J.Z. Miller, Jr., Kansas City, Mo., Federal reserve agent and chairman of board of directors; A.E. Ramsey, Muskogee, Okla., deputy Federal reserve agent and vice chairman of board of directors; R.H. Malone, Denver, Colo., director.

Class A—Gordon Jones, Denver, Colo., Group No. 1; W.J. Bailey, Atchison, Kans., Group No. 2; C.E. Burnham, Norfolk, Nebr., Group No. 3.

Class B—M.L. McClure, Kansas City, Mo., Group No. 1; T.C. Byrne, Omaha, Nebr., Group No. 2; L.A. Wilson, El Reno, Okla., Group No. 3.

Member Federal Advisory Council, E.F. Swinney, Kansas City.

Dallas—District No. 11
Oscar Wells, *Governor*

Class C—E.O. Tenison, Dallas, Tex., Federal reserve agent and chairman of board of directors; W.F. McCaleb, San Antonio, Tex., deputy Federal reserve agent and vice chairman of board of directors; Felix Martinez, El Paso, Tex., director.

Class A—Oscar Wells, Houston, Tex., Group No. 1; E.K. Smith, Shreveport, La., Group No. 2; B.A. McKinney, Durant, Okla., Group No. 3.

Class B—Marion Sansom, Fort Worth, Tex., Group No. 1; Frank Kell, Wichita Falls, Tex., Group No. 2; J.J. Culbertson, Paris, Tex., Group No. 3.

Member Federal Advisory Council, J. Howard Ardrey, Dallas.

San Francisco—District No. 12
Archibald Kains, *Governor*

Class C—John Perrin, Pasadena, Cal., Federal reserve agent and chairman of board of directors; Claud Gatch, San Francisco, Cal., deputy Federal reserve agent and vice chairman of board of directors; Charles E. Peabody, Seattle, Wash., director.

Class A—C.K. McIntosh, San Francisco, Cal., Group No. 1; James K. Lynch, San Francisco, Cal., Group No. 2; Alden Anderson, Sacramento, Cal., Group No. 3.

Class B—A.B.C. Dohrman, San Francisco, Cal., Group No. 1; J.A. McGregor, San Francisco, Cal., Group No. 2; Elmer H. Cox, Madera, Cal., Group No. 3.

Member Federal Advisory Council, Archibald Kains, San Francisco.

Source: Annual Report of the Comptroller of the Currency, 1914.

Design of Federal Reserve Notes Issued in 1914 (From the 1914 Annual Report of the Comptroller of the Currency)

An order for $250,000,000 of Federal Reserve notes has been placed with the Bureau of Engraving and Printing, deliveries of which will be available as required by the Reserve banks.

The inscription on the face of the Federal Reserve notes reads: Federal Reserve Note. The United States of America will pay to the bearer on demand ____ dollars. Authorized by the Federal Reserve Act of December 23, 1913.

The corporate title of each bank is shown as "Federal reserve bank of ____ ____."

The note bears the facsimile signatures of the Secretary of the Treasury and Treasurer of the United States.

The legend on the bank of the notes reads as follows:

This note is receivable by all national and member banks and Federal Reserve banks and for all taxes, customs, and other public dues. It is redeemable in gold on demand at the Treasury Department of the United States in the City of Washington, District of Columbia, or in gold or lawful money at any Federal Reserve bank.

The notes are in denominations of 5s, 10s, 20s, 50s, and 100s, and each note is of new and original design.

The five-dollar bills contain on the left-hand side of their back an engraving of the landing of Columbus and on the opposite side of the back the landing of the Pilgrim Fathers on Plymouth Rock.

The back of the ten-dollar bill represents a typical manufacturing and agricultural scene, the picture on the left-hand side showing a harvesting scene and a modern harvester, while on the right there is a picture of a modern factory in operation.

The engraving on the back of the twenty-dollar bill represents transportation on land and water and in the air; the picture on the left being a modern railroad train, and automobile, and an aeroplane, and that on the right an ocean liner in New York Harbor with the New York skyline and the Statue of Liberty in the background.

The engraving on the back of the fifty-dollar bill is symbolical of the Panama Canal, the center piece being a picture of a woman; on one side a trans–Atlantic steamer is shown and on the other side a battleship, the idea being to represent America presiding over the Panama Canal, the oceans representing the Atlantic and the Pacific.

An allegorical picture covers the entire back of the hundred-dollar bill. There is a central group representing America with Peace and Plenty on either side. A figure on the left-hand end of the note represents Labor bearing the harvest and the figure on the other end represents Mercury distributing the harvest.

By contrast Federal Reserve notes in 1989 had the following portraits and designs.

	Face of note	*Back side of note*
$1	Washington	Great Seal of the United States
$2	Jefferson	The Signing of the Declaration of Independence
$5	Lincoln	Lincoln Memorial
$10	Hamilton	U.S. Treasury Building
$20	Jackson	White House
$50	Grant	U.S. Capitol
$100	Franklin	Independence Hall

Federal Reserve Banks and Branches
(date in parentheses is date of organization of branch)

No. 1. Boston (no branches).
No. 2. New York. Buffalo, NY (May 15, 1919).
No. 3. Philadelphia (no branches).
No. 4. Cleveland. Cincinnati, OH (January 10, 1918); Pittsburgh, PA (March 16, 1918).
No. 5. Richmond. Baltimore, MD (March 1, 1918); Charlotte, NC (December 1, 1927).
No. 6. Atlanta. New Orleans, LA (September 10, 1915); Birmingham, AL (August 1, 1918); Jacksonville, FL (August 5, 1918); Nashville, TN (October 21, 1919); Miami, FL (April 1, 1975).
No. 7. Chicago. Detroit, MI (March 18, 1918).
No. 8. St. Louis. Louisville, KY (December 3, 1919); Memphis, TN (September 3, 1918); Little Rock, AR (January 6, 1919).
No. 9. Minneapolis. Helena, MT (February 1, 1921).
No. 10. Kansas City. Omaha, NE (September 14, 1917); Denver, CO (January 14, 1918); Oklahoma City, OK (August 20, 1920).
No. 11. Dallas. El Paso, TX (June 17, 1917); Houston, TX (August 4, 1919); San Antonio, TX (July 5, 1927).
No. 12. San Francisco. Seattle, WA (September 19, 1917); Portland, OR (October 1, 1917); Spokane, WA (July 26, 1917 — closed October 1938); Los Angeles, CA (January 2, 1920).

Source: Moore, Carl H., and Russell, Alvin E. *Money — Its Origin, Development and Modern Use,* 1987.

Boundaries of Federal Reserve Districts and Their Branch Territories

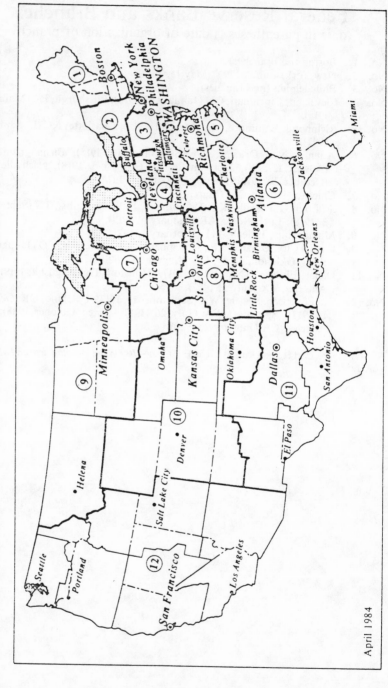

April 1984

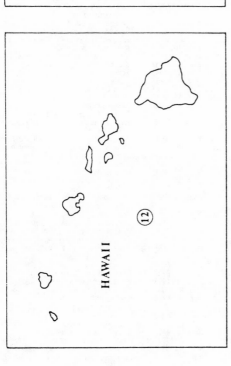

LEGEND

— Boundaries of Federal Reserve Districts

— Boundaries of Federal Reserve Branch Territories

⊛ Board of Governors of the Federal Reserve System

◉ Federal Reserve Bank Cities

● Federal Reserve Branch Cities

· Federal Reserve Bank Facility

Membership of the Board of Governors of the Federal Reserve System, 1913–89

APPOINTIVE MEMBERS[1]

Name	Federal Reserve District	Date of initial oath of office	Other dates and information relating to membership[2]
Charles S. Hamlin	Boston	Aug. 10, 1914	Reappointed in 1916 and 1926. Served until Feb. 3, 1936.[3]
Paul M. Warburg	New York	do	Term expired Aug. 9, 1918.
Frederic A. Delano	Chicago	do	Resigned July 21, 1918.
W.P.G. Harding	Atlanta	do	Term expired Aug. 9, 1922.
Adolph C. Miller	San Francisco	do	Reappointed in 1924. Reappointed in 1934 from the Richmond District. Served until Feb. 3, 1936.[3]
Albert Strauss	New York	Oct. 26, 1918	Resigned Mar. 15, 1920.
Henry A. Moehlenpah	Chicago	Nov. 10, 1919	Term expired Aug. 9, 1920.
Edmund Platt	New York	June 8, 1920	Reappointed in 1928. Resigned Sept. 14, 1930.
David C. Wills	Cleveland	Sept. 29, 1920	Term expired Mar. 4, 1921.
John R. Mitchell	Minneapolis	May 12, 1921	Resigned May 12, 1923.
Milo D. Campbell	Chicago	Mar. 14, 1923	Died Mar. 22, 1923.
Daniel R. Crissinger	Cleveland	May 1, 1923	Resigned Sept. 15, 1927.
George R. James	St. Louis	May 14, 1923	Reappointed in 1931. Served until Feb. 3, 1936.[4]
Edward H. Cunningham	Chicago	do	Died Nov. 28, 1930.
Roy A. Young	Minneapolis	Oct. 4, 1927	Resigned Aug. 31, 1930.
Eugene Meyer	New York	Sept. 16, 1930	Resigned May 10, 1933.
Wayland W. Magee	Kansas City	May 18, 1931	Term expired Jan. 24, 1933.
Eugene R. Black	Atlanta	May 19, 1933	Resigned Aug. 15, 1934.
M.S. Szymczak	Chicago	June 14, 1933	Reappointed in 1936 and 1948. Resigned May 31, 1961.
J.J. Thomas	Kansas City	do	Served until Feb. 10, 1936.[3]
Marriner S. Eccles	San Francisco	Nov. 15, 1934	Reappointed in 1936, 1940, and 1944. Resigned July 14, 1951.
Joseph A. Broderick	New York	Feb. 3, 1936	Resigned Sept. 30, 1937.
John K. McKee	Cleveland	do	Served until Apr. 4, 1946.[3]
Ronald Ransom	Atlanta	do	Reappointed in 1942. Died Dec. 2, 1947.
Ralph W. Morrison	Dallas	Feb. 10, 1936	Resigned July 9, 1936.
Chester C. Davis	Richmond	June 25, 1936	Reappointed in 1940. Resigned Apr. 15, 1941.
Ernest G. Draper	New York	Mar. 30, 1938	Served until Sept. 1, 1950.[3]
Rudolph M. Evans	Richmond	Mar. 14, 1942	Served until Aug. 13, 1954.[3]
James K. Vardaman, Jr.	St. Louis	Apr. 4, 1946	Resigned Nov. 30, 1958.
Lawrence Clayton	Boston	Feb. 14, 1947	Died Dec. 4, 1949.
Thomas B. McCabe	Philadelphia	Apr. 15, 1948	Resigned Mar. 31, 1951.
Edward L. Norton	Atlanta	Sept. 1, 1950	Resigned Jan. 31, 1952.
Oliver S. Powell	Minneapolis	do	Resigned June 30, 1952.
Wm. McC. Martin, Jr.	New York	April 2, 1951	Reappointed in 1956. Term expired Jan. 31, 1970.
A.L. Mills, Jr.	San Francisco	Feb. 18, 1952	Reappointed in 1958. Resigned Feb. 28, 1965.
J.L. Robertson	Kansas City	do	Reappointed in 1964. Resigned Apr. 30, 1973.
C. Canby Balderston	Philadelphia	Aug. 12, 1954	Served through Feb. 28, 1966.
Paul E. Miller	Minneapolis	Aug. 13, 1954	Died Oct. 21, 1954.
Chas. N. Shepardson	Dallas	Mar. 17, 1955	Retired Apr. 30, 1967.
G.H. King, Jr.	Atlanta	Mar. 25, 1959	Reappointed in 1960. Resigned Sept. 18, 1963.
George W. Mitchell	Chicago	Aug. 31, 1961	Reappointed in 1962. Served until Feb. 13, 1976.[3]
J. Dewey Daane	Richmond	Nov. 29, 1963	Served until Mar. 8, 1974.[3]
Sherman J. Maisel	San Francisco	Apr. 30, 1965	Served through May 31, 1972.
Andrew F. Brimmer	Philadelphia	Mar. 9, 1966	Resigned Aug. 31, 1974.
William W. Sherrill	Dallas	May 1, 1967	Reappointed in 1968. Resigned Nov. 15, 1971.
Arthur F. Burns	New York	Jan. 31, 1970	Term began Feb. 1, 1970. Resigned Mar. 31, 1978.
John E. Sheehan	St. Louis	Jan. 4, 1972	Resigned June 1, 1975.
Jeffrey M. Bucher	San Francisco	June 5, 1972	Resigned Jan. 2, 1976.
Robert C. Holland	Kansas City	June 11, 1973	Resigned May 15, 1976.
Henry C. Wallich	Boston	Mar. 8, 1974	Resigned Dec. 15, 1986.
Philip E. Coldwell	Dallas	Oct. 29, 1974	Served through Feb. 29, 1980.
Philip C. Jackson, Jr.	Atlanta	July 14, 1975	Resigned Nov. 17, 1978.
J. Charles Partee	Richmond	Jan. 5, 1976	Served until Feb. 7, 1986.[3]
Stephen S. Gardner	Philadelphia	Feb. 13, 1976	Died Nov. 19, 1978.
David M. Lilly	Minneapolis	June 1, 1976	Resigned Feb. 24, 1978.
G. William Miller	San Francisco	Mar. 8, 1978	Resigned Aug. 6, 1979.
Nancy H. Teeters	Chicago	Sept. 18, 1978	Served through June 27, 1984.
Emmett J. Rice	New York	June 20, 1979	Resigned Dec. 31, 1986.

Name	Federal Reserve District	Date of initial oath of office	Other dates and information relating to membership[2]
Frederick H. Schultz	Atlanta	July 27, 1979	Served through Feb. 11, 1982.
Paul A. Volcker	Philadelphia	Aug. 6, 1979	Resigned August 11, 1987.
Lyle E. Gramley	Kansas City	May 28, 1980	Resigned Sept. 1, 1985.
Preston Martin	San Francisco	Mar. 31, 1982	Resigned April 30, 1986.
Martha R. Seger	Chicago	July 2, 1984	
Wayne D. Angell	Kansas City	Feb. 7, 1986	
Manuel H. Johnson	Richmond	Feb. 7, 1986	
H. Robert Heller	San Francisco	Aug. 19, 1986	
Edward W. Kelley, Jr.	Dallas	May 26, 1987	
Alan Greenspan	New York	Aug. 11, 1987	

Chairmen[4]

Charles S. Hamlin	Aug. 10, 1914–Aug. 9, 1916
W.P.G. Harding	Aug. 10, 1916–Aug. 9, 1922
Daniel R. Crissinger	May 1, 1923–Sept. 15, 1927
Roy A. Young	Oct. 4, 1927–Aug. 31, 1930
Eugene Meyer	Sept. 16, 1930–May 10, 1933
Eugene R. Black	May 19, 1933–Aug. 15, 1934
Marriner S. Eccles	Nov. 15, 1934–Jan. 31, 1948
Thomas B. McCabe	Apr. 15, 1948–Mar. 31, 1951
Wm. McC. Martin, Jr.	Apr. 2, 1951–Jan. 31, 1970
Arthur F. Burns	Feb. 1, 1970–Jan. 31, 1978
G. William Miller	Mar. 8, 1978–Aug. 6, 1979
Paul A. Volcker	Aug. 6, 1979–Aug. 11, 1987
Alan Greenspan	Aug. 11, 1987–

Vice Chairmen[4]

Frederic A. Delano	Aug. 10, 1914–Aug. 9, 1916
Paul M. Warburg	Aug. 10, 1916–Aug. 9, 1918
Albert Strauss	Oct. 26, 1918–Mar. 15, 1920
Edmund Platt	July 23, 1920–Sept. 14, 1930
J.J. Thomas	Aug. 21, 1934–Feb. 10, 1936
Ronald Ransom	Aug. 6, 1936–Dec. 2, 1947
C. Canby Balderston	Mar. 11, 1955–Feb. 28, 1966
J.L. Robertson	Mar. 1, 1966–Apr. 30, 1973
George W. Mitchell	May 1, 1973–Feb. 13, 1976
Stephen S. Gardner	Feb. 13, 1976–Nov. 19, 1978
Frederick H. Schultz	July 27, 1979–Feb. 11, 1982
Preston Martin	Mar. 31, 1982–Mar. 31, 1986
Manuel H. Johnson	Aug. 22, 1986–

EX-OFFICIO MEMBERS[1]

Secretaries of the Treasury

W.G. McAdoo	Dec. 23, 1913–Dec. 15, 1918
Carter Glass	Dec. 16, 1918–Feb. 1, 1920
David F. Houston	Feb. 2, 1920–Mar. 3, 1921
Andrew W. Mellon	Mar. 4, 1921–Feb. 12, 1932
Ogden L. Mills	Feb. 12, 1932–Mar. 4, 1933
William H. Woodin	Mar. 4, 1933–Dec. 31, 1933
Henry Morgenthau, Jr.	Jan. 1, 1934–Feb. 1, 1936

Comptrollers of the Currency

John Skelton Williams	Feb. 2, 1914–Mar. 2, 1921
Daniel R. Crissinger	Mar. 17, 1921–Apr. 30, 1923
Henry M. Dawes	May 1, 1923–Dec. 17, 1924
Joseph W. McIntosh	Dec. 20, 1924–Nov. 20, 1928
J.W. Pole	Nov. 21, 1928–Sept. 20, 1932
J.F.T. O'Connor	May 11, 1933–Feb. 1, 1936

1. Under the provisions of the original Federal Reserve Act, the Federal Reserve Board was composed of seven members, including five appointive members, the Secretary of the Treasury, who was ex-officio chairman of the Board, and the Comptroller of the Currency. The original term of office was ten years, and the five original appointive members had terms of two, four, six, eight, and ten years respectively. In 1922 the number of appointive members was increased to six, and in 1933 the term of office was increased to twelve years. The Banking Act of 1935, approved Aug. 23, 1935, changed the name of the Federal Reserve Board to the Board of Governors of the Federal Reserve System and provided that the Board should be composed of seven appointive members; that the

Secretary of the Treasury and the Comptroller of the Currency should continue to serve as members until Feb. 1, 1936, or until their successors were appointed and had qualified; and that thereafter the terms of members should be fourteen years and that the designation of Chairman and Vice Chairman of the Board should be for a term of four years.
2. Date after words "Resigned" and "Retired" denotes final day of service.
3. Successor took office on this date.
4. Chairman and Vice Chairman were designated Governor and Vice Governor before Aug. 23, 1935.

Source: Board of Governors, Washington, D.C.

Federal Reserve Board of Governors

Alan Greenspan, *Chairman*
Manuel H. Johnson, *Vice Chairman*
Martha R. Seger
Wayne D. Angell

H. Robert Heller
Edward W. Kelley, Jr.
John P. LaWare

Official Staff

Office of Board Members
Joseph R. Coyne, *Assistant to the Board*
Donald J. Winn, *Assistant to the Board*
Bob Stahly Moore, *Special Assistant to the Board*

Legal Division
Michael Bradfield, *General Counsel*
J. Virgil Mattingly, Jr., *Deputy General Counsel*
Richard M. Ashton, *Associate General Counsel*
Oliver Ireland, *Associate General Counsel*
Ricki R. Tigert, *Associate General Counsel*
Scott G. Alvarez, *Assistant General Counsel*
MaryEllen A. Brown, *Assistant to the General Counsel*

Office of the Secretary
William W. Wiles, *Secretary*
Jennifer J. Johnson, *Associate Secretary*
Barbara R. Lowrey, *Associate Secretary*

Division of Consumer and Community Affairs
Griffith L. Garwood, *Director*
Glenn E. Loney, *Assistant Director*
Ellen Maland, *Assistant Director*
Dolores S. Smith, *Assistant Director*

Division of Banking Supervision and Regulation
William Taylor, *Staff Director*
Don E. Kline, *Associate Director*
Frederick M. Struble, *Associate Director*

William A. Ryback, *Deputy Associate Director*
Stephen C. Schemering, *Deputy Associate Director*
Richard Spillenkothen, *Deputy Associate Director*
Herbert A. Biern, *Assistant Director*
Joe M. Cleaver, *Assistant Director*
Roger T. Cole, *Assistant Director*
James I. Garner, *Assistant Director*
James D. Goetzinger, *Assistant Director*
Michael G. Martinson, *Assistant Director*
Robert S. Plotkin, *Assistant Director*
Sidney M. Sussan, *Assistant Director*
Laura M. Homer, *Securities Credit Officer*

Division of International Finance
Edwin M. Truman, *Staff Director*
Larry J. Promisel, *Senior Associate Director*
Charles J. Siegman, *Senior Associate Director*
David H. Howard, *Deputy Associate Director*
Robert F. Gemmill, *Staff Adviser*
Donald B. Adams, *Assistant Director*
Peter Hooper III, *Assistant Director*
Karen H. Johnson, *Assistant Director*
Ralph W. Smith, Jr., *Assistant Director*

Division of Research and Statistics
Michael J. Prell, *Director*
Edward C. Ettin, *Deputy Director*
Thomas D. Simpson, *Associate Director*
Lawrence Slifman, *Associate Director*
Martha Bethea, *Deputy Associate Director*

Peter A. Tinsley, *Deputy Associate Director*
Myron L. Kwast, *Assistant Director*
Susan J. Lepper, *Assistant Director*
Martha S. Scanlon, *Assistant Director*
David J. Stockton, *Assistant Director*
Joyce K. Zickler, *Assistant Director*
Levon H. Garabedian, *Assistant Director (Administration)*

Division of Monetary Affairs
Donald L. Kohn, *Director*
David E. Lindsey, *Deputy Director*
Brian F. Madigan, *Assistant Director*
Richard D. Porter, *Assistant Director*
Normand R.V. Bernard, *Special Assistant to the Board*

Office of the Inspector General
Brent L. Bowen, *Inspector General*

**Office of Staff Director
for Management**
S. David Frost, *Staff Director*
Edward T. Mulrenin, *Assistant Staff Director*
Portia W. Thompson, *Equal Employment Opportunity Programs Officer*

**Division of Human
Resources Management**
David L. Shannon, *Director*
John R. Weis, *Associate Director*
Anthony V. DiGioia, *Assistant Director*
Joseph H. Hayes, Jr., *Assistant Director*
Fred Horowitz, *Assistant Director*

Office of the Controller
George E. Livingston, *Controller*
Stephen J. Clark, *Assistant Controller (Programs and Budgets)*
Darrell R. Pauley, *Assistant Controller (Finance)*

Division of Support Services
Robert E. Frazier, *Director*
George M. Lopez, *Assistant Director*
David L. Williams, *Assistant Director*

**Office of the Executive Director for
Information Resources Management**
Allen E. Beutel, *Executive Director*
Stephen R. Malphrus, *Deputy Executive Director*

**Division of Hardware
and Software Systems**
Bruce M. Beardsley, *Director*
Thomas C. Judd, *Assistant Director*
Elizabeth B. Riggs, *Assistant Director*
Robert J. Zemel, *Assistant Director*

Division of Applications Development and Statistical Services
William R. Jones, *Director*

**Office of Staff Director for
Federal Reserve Bank Activities**
Theodore E. Allison, *Staff Director*

**Division of Federal
Reserve Bank Operations**
Clyde H. Farnsworth, Jr., *Director*
David L. Robinson, *Associate Director*
C. William Schleicher, Jr., *Associate Director*
Bruce J. Summers, *Associate Director*
Charles W. Bennett, *Assistant Director*
Jack Dennis, Jr., *Assistant Director*
Earl G. Hamilton, *Assistant Director*
John H. Parrish, *Assistant Director*
Louise L. Roseman, *Assistant Director*
Florence M. Young, *Adviser*

Source: Federal Reserve Bulletin, March 1989.

Federal Open Market Committee

Members
Alan Greenspan, *Chairman*
E. Gerald Corrigan, *Vice Chairman*
Wayne D. Angell
Roger Guffey
H. Robert Heller
Manuel H. Johnson
Silas Keehn
Edward W. Kelley, Jr.
John P. LaWare
Thomas C. Melzer
Martha R. Seger
Richard F. Syron

Alternate Members
Edward G. Boehne
Robert H. Boykin
W. Lee Hoskins
James H. Oltman
Gary H. Stern

Staff
Donald L. Kohn, *Secretary and Economist*
Normand R.V. Bernard, *Assistant Secretary*
Michael Bradfield, *General Counsel*

Ernest T. Patrikis, *Deputy General Counsel*
Michael J. Prell, *Economist*
Edwin M. Truman, *Economist*
John H. Beebe, *Associate Economist*
J. Alfred Broaddus, Jr., *Associate Economist*
John M. Davis, *Associate Economist*
Richard G. Davis, *Associate Economist*
David E. Lindsey, *Associate Economist*
Charles J. Siegman, *Associate Economist*
Thomas D. Simpson, *Associate Economist*
Lawrence Slifman, *Associate Economist*
Sheila L. Tschinkel, *Associate Economist*
Peter D. Sternlight, *Manager for Domestic Operations, System Open Market Account*
Sam Y. Cross, *Manager for Foreign Operations, System Open Market Account*

Advisory Councils

Federal Advisory Council
Donald N. Brandin, *President*
Samuel A. McCullough, *Vice President*
J. Terrence Murray, First District
Willard C. Butcher, Second District
Samuel A. McCullough, Third District
Thomas H. O'Brien, Fourth District
Frederick Deane, Jr., Fifth District
Kenneth L. Roberts, Sixth District
B. Kenneth West, Seventh District
Donald N. Brandin, Eighth District
Lloyd P. Johnson, Ninth District
Jordan L. Haines, Tenth District
James E. Burt, III, Eleventh District
Paul Hazen, Twelfth District
Herbert V. Prochnow, *Secretary*
William J. Korsvik, *Associate Secretary*

Consumer Advisory Council
Judith N. Brown, Edina, Minnesota, *Chairman*
William E. Odom, Dearborn, Michigan, *Vice Chairman*
Naomi G. Albanese, Greensboro, North Carolina
George H. Braasch, Chicago, Illinois
Betty Tom Chu, Arcadia, California
Cliff E. Cook, Tacoma, Washington
Jerry D. Craft, Atlanta, Georgia
Donald C. Day, Boston, Massachusetts
R.B. (Joe) Dean, Jr., Columbia, South Carolina
Richard B. Doby, Denver, Colorado
William C. Dunkelberg, Philadelphia, Pennsylvania
Richard H. Fink, Washington, D.C.
James Fletcher, Chicago, Illinois

Stephen Gardner, Dallas, Texas
Elena G. Hanggi, Little Rock, Arkansas
James Head, Berkeley, California
Robert A. Hess, Washington, D.C.
Ramon E. Johnson, Salt Lake City, Utah
Barbara Kaufman, San Francisco, California
A.J. (Jack) King, Kalispell, Montana
Michelle S. Meier, Washington, D.C.
Richard L.D. Morse, Manhattan, Kansas
Linda K. Page, Columbus, Ohio
Sandra Phillips, Pittsburgh, Pennsylvania
Vincent P. Quayle, Baltimore, Maryland
Clifford N. Rosenthal, New York, New York
Alan M. Spurgin, New York, New York
Ralph E. Spurgin, Columbus, Ohio
David P. Ward, Peapack, New Jersey

Lawrence Winthrop, Portland, Oregon

Thrift Institutions Advisory Council
Gerald M. Czarnecki, Honolulu, Hawaii, *President*
Donald B. Shackelford, Columbus, Ohio, *Vice President*
Charlotte Chamberlain, Glendale, California
Robert S. Duncan, Hattiesburg, Mississippi
Adam A. Jahns, Chicago, Illinois
H.C. Klein, Jacksonville, Arkansas
Philip E. Lamb, Springfield, Massachusetts
Joe C. Morris, Overland Park, Kansas
Joseph W. Mosmiller, Baltimore, Maryland
Louis H. Pepper, Seattle, Washington
Marion O. Sandler, Oakland, California
Charles B. Stuzin, Miami, Florida

Source: Federal Reserve Bulletin, March 1989.

Principal Officers at Federal Reserve Banks; Governor and Chairman of the Board of Directors and Federal Reserve Agent — 1914-1935; President and First Vice President — 1936-1989

Governor was principal operating officer and Federal Reserve Agent was liaison officer with the Federal Reserve Board and responsible for note issue, holding of collateral against notes and deposits and reporting annually to the board on conditions in the district. First Vice President is primary operation officer. President is major participant in monetary policy decisions. Partial years not indicated.

Boston

Years of Service	Governor	Ch. & Fed. Res. Agent
1914-16	Alfred L. Aiken	Frederic H. Curtis
1917-21	Charles A. Morss	" "
1922-29	W.P.G. Harding	" "
1930-35	R.A. Young	" "

	President	*First Vice President*
1936–41	R.A. Young	W.W. Paddock
1942–43	W.W. Paddock	William Willett
1944–47	Lawrence F. Whittemore	" "
1948–50	J.A. Erickson	" "
1951–55	" "	Alfred C. Neal
1956–60		E.O. Latham
1961–67	George H. Ellis	" "
1968–72	Frank E. Morris	" "
1973–83	" "	James A. McIntosh
1984–88	" "	Robert W. Eisenmenger
1989–	Richard F. Syron	" "

New York

	Governor	*Ch. & Fed. Res. Agent*
1914–25	Benjamin Strong, Jr.	Pierre Jay
1926–27	" "	Gates W. McGarrah
1928–29	George L. Harrison	" "
1930–35	" "	J.H. Case

	President	*First Vice President*
1936–40	George L. Harrison	Allen Sprowl
1941–51	Allen Sprowl	L.A. Rounds
1952–55	" "	William F. Treiber
1956–72	Alfred Hayes	" "
1973–74	" "	Richard E. Debs
1975–75	Paul Volcker	" "
1976–79	" "	T.M. Timlen, Jr.
1980–80	Vacant	" "
1981–84	Anthony M. Solomon	" "
1985–88	E. Gerald Corrigan	" "
1987–88	" "	" "
1989–	" "	James H. Oltman

Philadelphia

	Governor	*Ch. & Fed. Res. Agent*
1914–17	Charles H. Rhodes	Richard L. Austin
1918–19	E.P. Passmore	" "
1920–35	George W. Norris	" "

	President	*First Vice President*
1936–40	John S. Sinclair	Frank J. Drinnen
1941–45	Alfred H. Williams	" "
1946–57	" "	W.J. Davis
1958–69	Karl R. Bopp	Robert N. Hilkert
1970–70	David Eastburn	David C. Melnicoff
1971–76	" "	Mark H. Wiles
1977–80	" "	Richard L. Smoot
1981–86	Edward G. Bohne	" "
1987–	" "	William H. Stone, Jr.

Cleveland

	Governor	Ch. & Fed. Res. Agent
1914–19	E.R. Fancher	D.C. Wells
1920–20	" "	Lewis B. Williams
1921–24	" "	D.C. Wells
1925–32	" "	George DeCamp
1933–33	" "	Lewis B. Williams
1934–34	" "	E.S. Burke, Jr.
1935–35	Mathew J. Fleming	" "
	President	First Vice President
1936–42	" "	F.J. Zurlinden
1943–43	" "	Reuben B. Hays
1944–44	Ray M. Gidney	" "
1945–52	" "	William H. Fletcher
1953–53	" "	Donald S. Thompson
1954–62	W.D. Fulton	" "
1963–63	W. Braddock Hickman	" "
1964–65	" "	Edward A. Fink
1966–69	" "	Walter H. McDonald
1970–70	Vacant	" "
1971–81	Willis J. Winn	" "
1982–86	Karen N. Horn	William H. Hendricks
1987–	W. Lee Hoskins	" "

Richmond

	Governor	Ch. & Fed. Res. Agent
1914–14	George J. Seay	William Ingle
1915–22	" "	Caldwell Hardy
1923–34	" "	William W. Hoxton
1935–35	" "	Vacant
	President	First Vice President
1936–53	Hugh Leach	J.S. Walden, Jr.
1954–60	" "	Edward A. Wayne
1961–67	Edward A. Wayne	Aubrey N. Heflin
1968–72	Aubrey N. Heflin	Robert P. Black
1973–73	Robert P. Black	Vacant
1974–80	" "	George C. Rankin
1981–	" "	Jimmie R. Monohollon

Atlanta

	Governor	Ch. & Fed. Res. Agent
1914–18	Joseph A. McCord	M.B. Wellborn
1919–23	M.B. Wellborn	Joseph A. McCord
1924–26	" "	Oscar Newton
1927–32	E.R. Black	" "
1933–33	W.S. Johns (acting)	" "
1934–34	Vacant	" "
1935–35	Oscar Newton	Vacant

	President	*First Vice President*
1936–38	" "	Robert S. Parker
1939–40	Robert S. Parker	W.S. McLarin, Jr.
1941–45	W.S. McLarin, Jr.	Malcolm Bryan
1946–50	" "	Lewis M. Clark
1951–59	Malcolm Bryan	" "
1960–64	" "	Harold T. Patterson
1965–67	Harold T. Patterson	Monroe Kimbrel
1968–68	Monroe Kimbrel	Robert E. Moody, Jr.
1969–79	" "	Kyle K. Fossum
1980–80	" "	Robert P. Forrestal
1981–82	William F. Ford	" "
1983–83	Robert P. Forrestal	Vacant
1984–	" "	Jack Guynn

Chicago

	Governor	*Ch. & Fed. Res. Agent*
1914–14	James B. McDougal	C.H. Bosworth
1915–30	" "	William A. Heath
1931–33	" "	E.M. Stevens
1934–35	G.J. Schaller	" "

	President	*First Vice President*
1936–41	G.J. Schaller	H.D. Preston
1942–44	C.S. Young	" "
1945–48	" "	Charles B. Dunn
1949–49	" "	Vacant
1950–55	" "	E.C. Harris
1956–58	Carl E. Allen	" "
1959–61	" "	Charles J. Scanlon
1962–69	Charles S. Scanlon	Hugh J. Helmer
1970–73	Robert P. Mayo	Earnest T. Baughman
1974–74	" "	Vacant
1975–81	" "	Daniel M. Doyle
1982–	Silas Keehn	" "

St. Louis

	Governor	*Ch. & Fed. Res. Agent*
1914–17	Rolla Wells	William McChes. Martin
1918–27	David C. Biggs	" "
1928–29	William McChes. Martin	Rolla Wells
1930–35	" "	J.S. Wood

	President	*First Vice President*
1936–37	William McChes. Martin	O.M. Atterberry
1938–39	" "	F. Guy Hitt
1940–50	Chester C. Davis	" "
1951–52	Delos C. Johns	O.M. Atterberry
1953–56	" "	Frederick L. Deming
1957–58	" "	Guy S. Freutel
1959–61	" "	Darryl Francis
1962–65	Harry A. Shuford	" "

1966–70	Darryl Francis	Dale M. Lewis
1971–75	" "	Eugene A. Leonard
1976–76	Lawrence K. Roos	" "
1977–82	" "	Donald Moriarty, Jr.
1983–84	Theodore H. Roberts	Joseph P. Garbarini
1985–86	Thomas C. Meltzer	" "
1987–	" "	James R. Bowen

Minneapolis

	Governor	*Ch. & Fed. Res. Agent*
1914–18	Theodore Wold	John H. Rich
1919–23	R.A. Young	" "
1924–26	" "	J.R. Mitchell
1927–32	W.B. Geery	" "
1933–35	" "	J.N. Peyton

	President	*First Vice President*
1936–50	J.N. Peyton	O.S. Powell
1951–51	" "	O.W. Mills
1952–56	O.S. Powell	" "
1957–63	Frederick L. Deming	" "
1964–64	" "	M.H. Strothman, Jr.
1965–70	Hugh D. Galusha, Jr.	" "
1971–73	Bruce K. MacLaury	" "
1974–77	" "	Clement A. Van Nice
1978–80	Mark H. Willes	Thomas E. Gainor
1981–84	E. Gerald Corrigan	" "
1985–	Gary H. Stern	" "

Kansas City

1914–14	Charles M. Sawyer	J.Z. Miller, Jr.
1915–17	J.Z. Miller, Jr.	Charles M. Sawyer
1918–21	" "	Asa E. Ramsey
1922–22	W.J. Bailey	" "
1923–31	" "	M.L. McClure
1932–33	George H. Hamilton	" "
1934–35	" "	Vacant

	President	*First Vice President*
1936–40	George H. Hamilton	C.A. Worthington
1941–60	H.G. Leedy	Henry O. Koppang
1961–65	George H. Clay	" "
1966–75	" "	John T. Boysen
1976–76	Roger Guffey	" "
1977–	" "	Henry R. Czerwinski

Dallas

	Governor	*Ch. & Fed. Res. Agent*
1914–14	Oscar Wells	E.O. Tennison

1915–20	R.L. Van Zant	W.F. Ramsey
1921–21	B.A. McKinney	" "
1922–22	" "	W.B. Newsom
1923–24	" "	Lynn P. Talley
1925–30	Lynn P. Talley	C.C. Walsh
1931–35	B.A. McKinney	" "

	President	*First Vice President*
1936–38	B.A. McKinney	Randall R. Gilbert
1939–43	Randall R. Gilbert	E.B. Stroud
1944–53	" "	W.D. Gentry
1954–58	Watrous H. Irons	" "
1959–61	" "	Harry A. Shuford
1962–67	" "	Phillip E. Coldwell
1968–73	Phillip E. Coldwell	Tom W. Plant
1974–75	Earnest T. Baughman	" "
1976–80	" "	Robert H. Boykin
1981–	Robert H. Boykin	William H. Wallace

San Francisco

	Governor	*Ch. & Fed. Res. Agent*
1914–16	Archibald Kains	John Perrin
1917–18	James K. Lynch	" "
1919–25	John V. Calkins	" "
1926–33	" "	Isaac B. Newton
1934–35	" "	Vacant

	President	*First Vice President*
1936–45	William A. Day	Ira Clerk
1946–46	C.E. Earhart	Vacant
1947–55	" "	H.N. Mangels
1956–60	H.N. Mangels	Eliot Swan
1961–66	Eliot Swan	H. Edward Hemmings
1967–71	" "	A.B. Merritt
1972–72	John S. Balles	" "
1973–82	" "	John B. Williams
1983–85	" "	Richard T. Griffith
1986–	Robert T. Perry	Carl E. Powell

Source: Annual Reports of the Federal Reserve Board and the Board of Governors, 1915–1989.

Principal Officers
at Federal Reserve Banks and Branches

(As of March 1989)

FEDERAL RESERVE BANK branch, or *facility* Zip	Chairman Deputy Chairman	President First Vice President	Vice President in charge of branch
BOSTON*............... 02106	George N. Hatsopoulos Richard N. Cooper	Richard F. Syron Robert W. Eisenmenger	
NEW YORK*.......... 10045	Cyrus R. Vance Ellen V. Futter	E. Gerald Corrigan James H. Oltman	
Buffalo.................. 14240	Mary Ann Lambertsen		John T. Keane
PHILADELPHIA......... 19105	Peter A. Benoliel Gunnar E. Sarsten	Edward G. Boehne William H. Stone, Jr.	
CLEVELAND*............ 44101	Charles W. Parry John R. Miller	W. Lee Hoskins William H. Hendricks	
Cincinnati.............. 45201	Owen B. Butler		Charles A. Cerino[1]
Pittsburgh.............. 15230	James E. Haas		Harold J. Swart[1]
RICHMOND*............. 23219	Hanne Merriman Leroy T. Canoles, Jr.	Robert P. Black Jimmie R. Monhollon	
Baltimore................. 21203	Thomas R. Shelton		Robert D. McTeer, Jr.[1]
Charlotte................ 28230	William E. Masters		Albert D. Tinkelenberg[1]
Culpeper Communications and Records Center 22701			John G. Stoides[1]
ATLANTA................. 30303	Bradley Currey, Jr. Larry L. Prince	Robert P. Forrestal Jack Guynn	Delmar Harrison[1]
Birmingham............. 35283	Nelda P. Stephenson		Fred R. Herr[1]
Jacksonville............. 32231	Winnie F. Taylor		James D. Hawkins[1]
Miami...................... 33152	Jose L. Saumat		James Curry III
Nashville................. 37203	Patsy R. Williams		Donald E. Nelson
New Orleans............. 70161	James A. Hefner		Robert J. Musso
CHICAGO*................ 60690	Robert J. Day Marcus Alexis	Silas Keehn Daniel M. Doyle	
Detroit.................... 48231	Richard T. Lindgren		Roby L. Sloan[1]
ST. LOUIS................. 63166	Robert L. Virgil, Jr. H. Edwin Trusheim	Thomas C. Melzer James R. Bowen	
Little Rock.............. 72203	L. Dickson Flake		John F. Breen[1]
Louisville................ 40232	Thomas A. Alvey		Howard Wells
Memphis.................. 38101	Seymour B. Johnson		Ray Laurence
MINNEAPOLIS........... 55480	Michael W. Wright John A. Rollwagen	Gary H. Stern Thomas E. Gainor	
Helena.................... 59601	Warren H. Ross		Robert F. McNellis
KANSAS CITY............ 64198	Fred W. Lyons, Jr. Burton A. Dole, Jr.	Roger Guffey Henry R. Czerwinski	
Denver.................... 80217	James C. Wilson		Kent M. Scott
Oklahoma City......... 73125	Patience S. Latting		David J. France
Omaha.................... 68102	Kenneth L. Morrison		Harold L. Shewmaker
DALLAS.................... 75222	Bobby R. Inman Hugh G. Robinson	Robert H. Boykin William H. Wallace	Tony J. Salvaggio[1]
El Paso................... 79999	Diana S. Natalicio		Sammie C. Clay
Houston.................. 77252	Andrew L. Jefferson, Jr.		Robert Smith, III[1]
San Antonio............. 78295	Lawrence E. Jenkins		Thomas H. Robertson
SAN FRANCISCO........ 94120	Robert F. Erburu Carolyn S. Chambers	Robert T. Parry Carl E. Powell	John F. Hoover[1]
Los Angeles............. 90051	Yvonne B. Burke		Thomas C. Warren[2]
Portland.................. 97208	Paul E. Bragdon		Angelo S. Carella[1]
Salt Lake City........... 84125	Don M. Wheeler		E. Ronald Liggett[1]
Seattle.................... 98124	Carol A. Nygren		Gerald R. Kelly[1]

*Additional offices of these Banks are located at Lewiston, Maine 04240; Windsor Locks, Connecticut 06096; Cranford, New Jersey 07016; Jericho, New York 11753; Utica at Oriskany, New York 13424; Columbus, Ohio 43216; Columbia, South Carolina 29210; Charleston, West Virginia 25311; Des Moines, Iowa 50306; Indianapolis, Indiana 46204; and Milwaukee, Wisconsin 53202.

1. Senior Vice President.
2. Executive Vice President.

Number of Officers and Employees, Federal Reserve Banks for Selected Years

(Figures in parentheses are officers)
(Data are for end of year)

Bank	1915	1920	1930	1940	1950	1960	1970	1980	1988
Boston	(4)	(13)	(10)	(10)	(19)	(25)	(34)	(49)	(52)
	20	776	714	720	1,257	1,348	1,433	1,608	1,673
New York	(6)	(36)	(36)	(40)	(49)	(63)	(94)	(133)	(159)
	73	2,936	2,415	2,520	3,611	3,924	4,788	4,412	3,927
Philadelphia	(3)	(10)	(11)	(12)	(17)	(30)	(40)	(46)	(56)
	45	841	696	793	1,097	1,057	1,051	1,205	1,269
Cleveland	(4)	(20)	(21)	(19)	(30)	(38)	(34)	(37)	(57)
	31	969	891	956	1,688	1,567	1,361	1,546	1,457
Richmond	(4)	(18)	(19)	(18)	(26)	(37)	(50)	(66)	(82)
	30	667	558	674	1,216	1,391	1,873	2,125	2,025
Atlanta	(6)	(23)	(33)	(23)	(30)	(35)	(48)	(69)	(72)
	41	446	423	750	960	1,388	1,768	2,391	2,358
Chicago	(4)	(36)	(32)	(22)	(37)	(39)	(52)	(73)	(89)
	50	1,731	1,334	1,849	2,656	3,003	3,054	3,199	2,571
St. Louis	(4)	(21)	(22)	(20)	(28)	(36)	(48)	(44)	(61)
	39	851	518	695	1,121	1,157	1,396	1,411	1,313
Minneapolis	(3)	(10)	(14)	(14)	(23)	(26)	(31)	(39)	(45)
	19	459	279	441	689	709	811	1,015	1,166
Kansas City	(3)	(22)	(22)	(20)	(28)	(32)	(43)	(53)	(64)
	40	863	599	692	1,064	1,126	1,406	1,699	1,726
Dallas	(4)	(19)	(21)	(16)	(26)	(31)	(35)	(36)	(60)
	31	613	414	647	935	995	1,123	1,405	1,627
San Francisco	(5)	(31)	(30)	(27)	(34)	(39)	(50)	(77)	(103)
	22	1,132	768	903	1,699	2,216	2,015	2,192	2,548
Total	(50)	(259)	(271)	(230)	(335)	(432)	(558)	(716)	(890)
	441	12,286	9,609	11,640	17,993	19,931	22,079	24,208	23,660

Totals include officers and part time employees.
Source: Annual Reports of Board of Governors, Federal Reserve System.

Number Employees at Board of Governors

1915:58. 1920:367. 1930:206. 1945:455. 1960:631. 1970:901. 1979:1,572. 1988:1,573.

Source: Board of Governors of Federal Reserve System.

Sample of Directive to Manager
of the Trading Desk at the New York Fed
from the Federal Open Market Committee

A summary of economic and financial conditions as viewed by the Committee precedes this directive in the published record.

Meeting held October 5-6, 1981

Domestic Policy Directive

The following domestic policy directive was issued to the Federal Reserve Bank of New York:

The information reviewed at this meeting suggests that real GNP declined slightly further in the third quarter and prices on the average continued to rise at the somewhat lower rate that emerged in the second quarter. In July and August the nominal value of total retail sales was essentially unchanged from the June level, and unit sales of domestic automobiles weakened in September. Industrial production declined slightly in August and apparently slackened further in September, while nonfarm payroll employment changed little in both months. The unemployment rate rose to 7.5 percent in September about equal to its average in the first half of 1981. Housing starts fell in August to the lowest level in several years. Over the first nine months of the year, the rise in the index of average hourly earnings was somewhat less rapid than during 1980.

The weighted average value of the dollar against major foreign currencies declined sharply through mid-September from its peak in early August and on balance has changed little since then. In August the U.S. foreign trade deficit widened substantially from the low rate in July; for July and August combined, the deficit was considerably larger than the second-quarter rate.

M-1B, adjusted for the estimated effects of shifts into NOW accounts, increased little over the period from June to September, while M-2 grew at a relatively strong pace. The level of adjusted M-1B in September was well below the lower end of the Committee's range for growth over the year from the fourth quarter of 1980 to the fourth quarter of 1981; the level of M-2 was at the upper end of its range for the year. In frequently volatile markets, short-term interest rates have declined on balance since mid-August while long-term rates have risen considerably further. On September 21 the Board of Governors announced a reduction in the surcharge from 4 to 3 percentage points on frequent borrowings of large depository institutions.

The Federal Open Market Committee seeks to foster monetary and financial conditions that will help to reduce inflation, promote sustained economic growth, and contribute to a sustainable pattern of international transactions. At its meeting in July, the Committee agreed that these objectives would be furthered by reaffirming the monetary growth ranges for the period from the fourth quarter of 1980 to the fourth quarter of 1981 that it had set at the February meeting. These ranges included growth of 3½ to 6 percent for M-1B, abstracting from the impact of flows into NOW accounts on a national basis, and growth of 6 to 9 percent and 6½ to 9½ percent for M-2 and M-3 respectively. The Committee recognized that the short fall in M-1B growth in the first half of the year partly reflected a shift in public preference toward other highly liquid assets and that growth in the broader aggregates had been running at about or somewhat above the upper ends of their ranges. In light of its desire to maintain moderate growth in money over the balance of the year, the Committee expected that growth for M-1B for the year would be near the lower end of its ranges. At the same time, the growth in the broader aggregates might be high in their ranges. The associate range for bank credit was 6 to 9 percent. The Committee also tentatively agreed that for the period from the fourth quarter of 1981 to the fourth quarter of 1982 growth of M-1, M-2, and M-3 within the ranges of 2½ to 5½ percent, 6 to 9 percent and 6½ to 9½ percent would be appropriate. These ranges will be considered as warranted to take account of developing experience with public preference for NOW and similar accounts as well as changing economic and financial conditions.

In the short run, the Committee seeks behavior of reserve aggregates consistent with growth of M-1B from September to December at an annual rate of 7 percent after allowance for the impact of NOW accounts and with growth of M-2 at an annual rate around 10 percent or slightly higher, recognizing that the behavior of M-2 will be affected by recent regulatory and legislative changes, particularly the public's response to the availability of the all savers certificate. The Chairman may call for Committee consultation if it appears to the Manager for Domestic Operations that pursuit of the monetary objectives and related reserve paths during the period before the next meeting is likely to be associated with a federal funds rate persistently outside a range of 12 to 17 percent.

Votes for this action: Messrs. Volcker, Solomon, Boehne, Boykin, Corrigan, Gramley, Keehn, Partee, Rice, Schultz, and Mrs. Teeters. Vote against this action: Mr. Wallich.

(There followed Mr. Wallich's reason for dissenting.)

Discount Rate at Federal Reserve Bank of New York
November 16, 1914–July 1, 1989

Data at the New York bank are used as typical for the System although rates sometimes varied temporarily between banks.

Date of Change	Effective Rate-%	Date of Change	Effective Rate-%	Date of Change	Effective Rate-%
1914		**1918**		September 22	5
November 16	6	April 6	4	November 3	4½
December 18	5½	**1919**		**1922**	
December 23	5	November 3	4¾	June 22	4
1915		**1920**		**1923**	
February 3	4½	January 23	6	February 23	4½
February 18	4	June 1	7	**1924**	
1916		**1921**		May 1	4
September 26	3	May 5	6½	June 12	3½
1917		June 16	6	**1925**	
December 21	3½	July 21	5½	February 27	3½

Date of Change	Effective Rate-%	Date of Change	Effective Rate-%	Date of Change	Effective Rate-%
1926		**1955**		**1973**	
January 8	4	April 15	1¾	January 15	5
April 23	3½	August 5	2	February 26	5½
August 13	4	September 9	2¼	May 4	5¾
1927		November 18	2½	May 11	6
August 5	3½	**1956**		June 11	6½
1928		April 13	2¾	July 2	7
February 3	4	August 24	3	August 14	7½
May 18	4½	**1957**		**1974**	
July 13	5	August 23	3½	April 28	8
1929		**1958**		December 9	7¾
August 9	6	January 22	2¾	**1975**	
November 1	5	March 7	2¼	January 10	7¼
November 15	4½	April 18	1¾	February 5	6¾
1930		September 12	2	March 10	6¼
February 7	4	November 7	2½	May 16	6
March 14	3½	**1959**		**1976**	
May 2	3	March 6	3	January 19	5½
June 20	2½	May 29	3½	November 22	5¼
December 24	2	September 11	4	**1977**	
1931		**1960**		August 31	5¾
May 8	1½	June 10	3½	October 26	6
October 9	2½	August 12	3	**1978**	
October 16	3½	**1963**		January 9	6½
1932		July 17	3½	May 11	7
February 26	3	**1964**		July 3	7¼
June 24	2½	November 24	4	August 21	7¾
1933		**1965**		September 22	8
March 3	3½	December 6	4½	October 16	8½
April 7	3	**1967**		November 1	9½
May 26	2½	April 7	4	**1979**	
October 20	2	November 20	4½	July 20	10
1934		**1968**		October 8	12
February 2	1½	March 22	5	**1980**	
Next change		April 19	5½	February 15	13
1937		August 30	5¼	May 30	12
August 27	1	December 18	5½	June 13	11
Next change		**1969**		July 28	10
1948		April 4	6	September 26	11
January 12	1¼	**1970**		November 17	12
August 13	1½	November 13	5¾	December 5	13
1950		December 4	5½	**1981**	
August 21	1¾	**1971**		May 5	14
1953		January 8	5¼	November 2	13
January 16	2	January 22	5	December 4	12
1954		July 16	5	**1982**	
February 5	1¾	November 19	4¾	July 20	11½
April 16	1½	December 17	4½	August 2	11

Date of Change	Effective Rate-%	Date of Change	Effective Rate-%	Date of Change	Effective Rate-%
August 16	10½	December 24	8	August 25	5½
August 27	10	**1985**		**1987**	
October 12	9½	May 20	7½	September 4	6
November 22	9	**1986**		**1988**	
December 15	8½	March 7	7	August 9	6½
1984		April 21	6½	**1989**	
April 9	9	July 11	6	February 24	7
November 21	8½				

Note: No change in the following years: 1935, 1936, 1939 to 1947, 1949, 1951, 1952, 1961, 1962, 1966, 1972 and 1983.

Source: Banking and Monetary Statistics, 1914–1941, and 1941–1970; Annual Statistical Digest, 1970–1979; Federal Reserve Bulletin, 1971–1989. Washington, D.C., Board of Governors.

United States Government Marketable Securities (Debt) and Related Data
(as of end of fiscal year)

Year	Amount in Millions	Percent held by FRS	Held by FRS as % of GNP	Year	Amount in Millions	Percent held by FRS	Held by FRS as % of GNP
1915	$ 970	1.6	—	1937	$ 33,054	7.8	2.8
1916	972	5.7	.11	1938	32,344	7.9	3.0
1917	2,713	4.5	.20	1939	33,965	7.3	2.7
1918	11,636	2.0	.31	1940	34,436	6.3	2.2
1919	24,280	1.2	.36	1941	37,713	6.0	1.8
1920	23,234	1.2	.31	1942	50,600	11.0	3.5
1921	23,043	1.0	.34	1943	95,300	11.7	5.8
1922	22,032	2.0	.59	1944	140,400	13.3	8.9
1923	21,670	—	.16	1945	181,300	13.1	11.2
1924	20,568	2.6	.64	1946	189,600	12.5	11.4
1925	19,730	1.9	.40	1947	168,700	13.0	9.5
1926	18,820	1.7	.32	1948	160,300	14.6	8.9
1927	17,583	3.5	.65	1949	155,100	12.0	7.1
1928	16,711	1.4	.24	1950	155,300	13.1	7.1
1929	16,019	3.2	.50	1951	137,900	17.0	7.1
1930	15,158	4.8	.81	1952	140,400	17.4	7.0
1931	16,229	5.0	1.1	1953	147,300	17.4	7.0
1932	18,852	8.8	3.1	1954	150,400	16.6	6.8
1933	21,834	11.1	3.6	1955	155,200	15.9	6.2
1934	26,084	9.3	3.7	1956	155,000	16.0	5.9
1935	26,950	9.0	3.4	1957	155,700	15.4	5.4
1936	31,102	7.8	3.0	1958	166,700	15.8	5.9

Year	Amount in Millions	Percent held by FRS	Held by FRS as % of GNP	Year	Amount in Millions	Percent held by FRS	Held by FRS as % of GNP
1959	$178,000	15.2	5.6	1974	$ 266,575	30.2	5.6
1960	183,800	14.8	5.4	1975	315,606	27.5	5.6
1961	187,100	15.6	5.6	1976	392,581	23.8	5.4
1962	196,100	15.6	5.5	1977	431,149	23.4	5.3
1963	203,500	16.6	5.7	1978	477,699	22.9	5.1
1964	209,000	17.8	5.9	1979	499,343	23.5	4.0
1965	212,500	19.2	6.0	1980	594,506	20.4	4.4
1966	211,800	21.0	5.8	1981	683,209	19.2	4.3
1967	210,700	23.2	6.2	1982	824,422	16.9	4.4
1968	226,600	23.2	6.1	1983	1,024,000	14.8	4.5
1969	226,100	25.4	6.2	1984	1,247,400	12.9	4.3
1970	232,600	26.5	6.3	1985	1,437,700	12.6	4.5
1971	245,473	28.6	6.5	1986	1,619,000	13.1	5.0
1972	257,202	27.2	5.9	1987	1,724,700	12.9	4.9
1973	262,971	29.9	5.9	1988	1,802,900	13.4	5.0

— Less than one percent.

Source: Banking and Monetary Statistics, 1914–1941. Annual Statistical Digest, 1941–1970. Federal Reserve Bulletin, March 1989. Washington, D.C.: Board of Governors. *Historical Statistics of the United States, Colonial Times to 1970.* Washington, D.C.: U.S. Dept. of Commerce.

Commercial Bank Suspensions

Year	No. banks	Year	No. banks	Year	No. banks	Year	No. banks
1892	80	1910	58	1928	498	1946	0
1893	491	1911	85	1929	659	1947	1
1894	83	1912	78	1930	1,350	1948	0
1895	110	1913	103	1931	2,293	1949	4
1896	141	1914	149	1932	1,453	1950	1
1897	139	1915	152	1933	4,000	1951	3
1898	63	1916	52	1934	57	1952	3
1899	32	1917	49	1935	34	1953	4
1900	35	1918	47	1936	44	1954	3
1901	65	1919	62	1937	59	1955	4
1902	54	1920	167	1938	54	1956	3
1903	52	1921	505	1939	42	1957	3
1904	125	1922	366	1940	22	1958	9
1905	80	1923	646	1941	8	1959	3
1906	53	1924	775	1942	8	1960	2
1907	90	1925	618	1943	4	1961	8
1908	153	1926	979	1944	1	1962	2
1909	78	1927	669	1945	0	1963	2

Year	No. banks	Year	No. banks	Year	No. banks	Year	No. banks
1964	8	1971	4	1977	7	1983	48
1965	7	1972	2	1978	1	1984	79
1966	1	1973	3	1979	6	1985	120
1967	4	1974	3	1980	10	1986	145
1968	0	1975	3	1981	10	1987	184
1969	4	1976	5	1982	42	1988	200
1970	1						

Source: Historical Statistics of the United States, Colonial Times to 1970. Statistical Abstract, 1984. U.S. Dept. of Commerce. *Annual Statistical Digest, 1970–79.* Board of Governors, Washington, D.C.: Federal Deposit Insurance Corporation Office, Dallas, Texas.

Number Commercial Banks in United States, Total Assets, Number Member of Federal Reserve System, Percent of Total Assets Held by Member Banks, Number Nonpar Banks and Number Uninsured Banks, 1915–1988

Year	Number comm'l banks	Total assets all banks (in mil.)	Number member* banks	Percent assets held by MB banks	Number nonpar banks	Number Uninsured banks
1915	27,390	$24,106	7,614	49	n.a.	n.a.
1916	27,739	28,217	7,605	50	n.a.	n.a.
1917	28,298	32,802	7,652	52	n.a.	n.a.
1918	28,856	36,352	8,212	67	10,247	n.a.
1919	29,147	42,462	8,821	70	3,996	n.a.
1920	30,291	47,509	9,398	71	1,755	n.a.
1921	30,456	43,669	9,745	71	2,263	n.a.
1922	30,120	44,106	9,892	72	2,288	n.a.
1923	29,829	47,332	9,856	71	2,896	n.a.
1924	28,988	50,136	9,650	71	3,647	n.a.
1925	28,442	54,401	9,538	72	3,970	n.a.
1926	27,742	56,781	9,275	72	3,913	n.a.
1927	26,650	58,973	9,099	72	3,910	n.a.
1928	25,798	61,563	8,929	73	3,911	n.a.
1929	24,970	62,442	8,707	73	3,754	n.a.
1930	23,679	64,125	8,315	74	3,437	n.a.
1931	21,654	59,017	7,782	76	3,207	n.a.
1932	18,734	46,304	6,980	77	3,046	n.a.
1933	14,207	40,511	5,606	82	2,695	n.a.
1934	15,348	44,978	6,375	83	2,643	1,476
1935	15,488	48,905	6,410	83	2,694	1,532
1936	15,329	55,572	6,400	84	2,732	1,307
1937	15,094	56,907	6,338	83	2,743	1,247

Year	Number comm'l banks	Total assets all banks (in mil.)	Number member* banks	Percent assets held by MB banks	Number nonpar banks	Number Uninsured banks
1938	14,867	56,185	6,338	84	2,722	1,179
1939	15,210	61,422	6,330	85	2,719	1,135
1940	14,534	67,804	6,398	85	2,715	1,093
1941	14,434	75,356	6,553	86	2,731	1,051
1942	14,353	80,276	6,644	87	2,710	988
1943	14,197	104,322	6,700	87	2,529	934
1944	14,138	125,031	6,770	87	2,445	909
1945	14,126	146,245	6,837	86	2,133	885
1946	14,152	153,507	6,884	86	2,086	860
1947	14,182	146,974	6,925	85	2,041	836
1948	14,189	149,799	6,922	85	2,011	814
1949	14,151	149,705	6,900	85	1,873	769
1950	14,146	156,914	6,882	85	1,853	738
1951	14,107	165,503	6,856	86	1,829	697
1952	14,069	177,417	6,812	85	1,820	658
1953	14,005	181,427	6,762	85	1,801	610
1954	13,936	190,581	6,718	85	1,787	578
1955	13,780	199,244	6,607	85	1,785	534
1956	13,719	206,846	6,495	85	1,734	490
1957	13,658	209,601	6,441	84	1,741	447
1958	13,574	229,182	6,353	85	1,719	430
1959	13,492	234,782	6,276	84	1,690	395
1960	13,503	243,274	6,214	84	1,672	356
1961	13,474	254,627	6,139	84	1,636	338
1962	13,434	277,211	6,068	84	1,617	323
1963	13,494	312,773	6,056	83	1,594	298
1964	13,682	346,921	6,179	83	1,547	281
1965	13,805	377,264	6,234	83	1,492	270
1966	13,821	403,368	6,193	83	1,449	262
1967	13,762	451,012	6,107	83	1,375	229
1968	13,743	500,657	6,038	82	932	224
1969	13,694	530,665	5,937	82	792	221
1970	13,690	577,000	5,768	81	501	203
1971	13,784	640,255	5,728	80	262	185
1972	13,928	739,033	5,705	79	179	181
1973	14,172	835,224	5,737	79	147	206*
1974	14,457	919,552	5,782	78	87	237
1975	14,632	964,200	5,750	76	73	257
1976	14,673	1,030,700	5,760	75	54	274
1977	14,705	1,166,000	5,669	74	40	307
1978	14,712	1,303,900	5,564	69	23	333
1979	14,708	1,480,300	5,425	70	7	357
1980	14,836	1,530,000	5,422	74	1	414
1981	14,882	1,678,800	5,474	74	none	481
1982	14,963	1,863,300	5,619	75	none	526
1983	14,796	2,113,000	5,806	72	none	327

Year	Number comm'l banks	Total assets all banks (in mil.)	Number member* banks	Percent assets held by MB banks	Number nonpar banks	Number Uninsured banks
1984	15,126	2,097,800	5,983	***	none	630
1985	15,068	2,284,800	6,050	***	none	651
1986	14,848	2,572,800	5,992	70	none	639
1987	14,100	2,563,509	5,753	75	none	378
1988	13,274	3,030,800	5,472	**	none	136

*Member of Federal Reserve System
**Data not available
***Data unreliable because of change in reporting

Note: Data for years after 1980 may be inconsistent with other data as information was taken from different sources. For example, variations in number of uninsured banks appear erratic and may be the result of using different classifications of depository institutions.

Source: Historical Statistics of the United States, Colonial Times to 1970; Annual Reports of the Board of Governors, *Federal Reserve Bulletin* and Board of Governors, Washington, D.C.; *Statistical Abstract of the United States,* 104th Edition, U.S. Dept. of Commerce, Washington, D.C.

Gold: World Production and Gold Stocks Held by United States, 1914–1986 (1914 to 1934 priced at $20.67 per fine ounce; 1934–1986 at $35 per fine ounce) (In Millions of Dollars)

Year	World Production	U.S. Stock	Year	World Production	U.S. Stock
1914	$ 448	$ 1,207	1929	$ 397	$ 3,900
1915	472	1,207	1930	432	4,225
1916	455	2,202	1931	461	4,052
1917	421	2,523	1932	498	4,045
1918	384	2,658	1933	525	4,012
1919	358	2,518	1934	958	8,238*
1920	334	2,451	1935	1,050	10,125
1921	331	3,221	1936	1,153	11,258
1922	320	3,505	1937	1,229	12,760
1923	369	3,834	1938	1,320	14,512
1924	385	4,090	1939	1,384	17,644
1925	384	3,985	1940	1,437	20,995
1926	395	4,083	1941	1,412	22,737
1927	394	3,977	1942	1,261	22,739
1928	390	3,746	1943	1,008	21,981

Year	World Production	U.S. Stock	Year	World Production	U.S. Stock
1944	$ 915	$20,631	1966	$1,630	$13,235
1945	920	20,083	1967	1,601	12,065
1946	968	20,706	1968	1,631	10,892
1947	1,013	22,868	1969	1,631	11,859
1948	1,049	24,399	1970	1,663	11,072
1949	1,084	24,563	1971	1,627	11,100
1950	1,143	22,820	1972	1,570	11,100
1951	1,172	22,873	1973	1,200	11,100
1952	1,201	23,252	1974	1,398	11,600
1953	1,180	22,091	1975	1,350	11,600
1954	1,229	21,793	1976	1,366	11,600
1955	1,271	21,753	1977	1,362	11,700
1956	1,344	22,058	1978	1,365	11,600
1957	1,386	22,857	1979	1,358	11,100
1958	1,421	20,582	1980	1,361	11,200
1959	1,498	19,507	1981	1,444	11,200
1960	1,306	17,804	1982	1,509	11,100
1961	1,375	16,947	1983	1,575	11,100
1962	1,441	16,057	1984	1,627	11,100
1963	1,570	15,596	1985	1,704	11,100
1964	1,569	15,471	1986	1,783	11,100
1965	1,619	13,806			

*New price.

Source: *Minerals Yearbook,* U.S. Dept. of the Interior, Bureau of Mines; *Banking and Monetary Statistics, 1914-1941; Banking and Monetary Statistics, 1941-1970,* and Annual Reports of Board of Governors, 1971-1988.

United States Government Debt
As of End of Fiscal year
(In billions of dollars)

Year	Gross Debt	Year	Gross Debt	Year	Gross Debt
1916	$ 1.2	1929	$ 16.9	1942	72.4
1917	3.0	1930	16.2	1943	136.7
1918	12.2	1931	16.8	1944	201.0
1919	25.4	1932	19.5	1945	258.7
1920	24.3	1933	22.5	1946	269.4
1921	24.0	1934	27.0	1947	256.6
1922	23.0	1935	28.7	1948	251.1
1923	22.4	1936	33.8	1949	251.7
1924	21.3	1937	36.4	1950	256.1
1925	20.5	1938	37.2	1951	253.9
1926	19.6	1939	40.4	1952	257.8
1927	18.5	1940	43.0	1953	264.8
1928	17.6	1941	49.0	1954	269.8

Year	Gross Debt	Year	Gross Debt	Year	Gross Debt
1955	$ 272.8	1966	$ 316.1	1977	700.0
1956	271.0	1967	322.9	1978	772.7
1957	269.5	1968	369.8	1979	827.6
1958	275.7	1969	367.1	1980	914.3
1959	282.7	1970	382.6	1981	1,003.9
1960	284.1	1971	413.6	1982	1,147.0
1961	286.4	1972	435.3	1983	1,381.9
1962	295.4	1973	462.4	1984	1,576.7
1963	302.7	1974	481.7	1985	1,827.5
1964	308.1	1975	554.7	1986	2,111.0
1965	313.8	1976	635.8	1987	2,336.0

Source: *Banking and Monetary Statistics, 1914–1941* and *1941–1970; Annual Statistical Digest, 1970–1979; Federal Reserve Bulletins*, 1979–1989. Washington, D.C.: Board of Governors.

Description of Federal Reserve Districts, 1917

Below are furnished descriptions of the 12 Federal Reserve districts, accompanied by estimates of the population of each district, recently prepared by the Bureau of the Census for use of investigators at work on the Liberty Loan. No detailed description of Federal Reserve districts has been issued since the Organization Committee completed its work in 1986.

District No. 1 — Boston (6,963,987)

Connecticut (except Fairfield County) (975,434). Maine (777,340). Massachusetts (3,775,973). New Hampshire (444,429). Rhode Island (625,865). Vermont (364,946).

District No. 2 — New York (13,111,816)

Connecticut (county of Fairfield) (289,939). New Jersey (counties of Monmouth, Middlesex, Hunterdon, Somerset, Union, Essex, Passaic, Hudson, Bergen, Morris, Sussex, and Warren) (2,361,695). New York (10,460,182).

District No. 3 — Philadelphia (6,632,611)

Delaware (215,160). New Jersey (except counties enumerated under District No. 2) (652,499). Pennsylvania (eastern part) (counties of Adams, Bedford, Berks, Blair, Bradford, Bucks, Cambria, Cameron, Carbon, Center, Chester, Clearfield, Clinton, Columbia, Cumberland, Dauphin, Delaware, Elk, Franklin, Fulton, Huntingdon, Juniata, Lackawanna, Lancaster, Lebanon, Lehigh, Luzerne, Lycoming, McKean, Mifflin, Monroe, Montgomery, Montour, Northampton, Northumberland, Perry, Philadelphia, Pike, Potter, Schuylkill, Snyder, Sullivan, Susquehanna, Tioga, Union, Wayne, Wyoming, and York) (5,764,952).

District No. 4 — Cleveland (9,314,762)

Kentucky (eastern part) (counties of Bath, Bell, Boone, Bourbon, Boyd, Bracken, Breathitt, Campbell, Carter, Clark, Clay, Elliott, Estill, Fayette, Fleming, Floyd, Garrard, Grant, Greenup, Harlan, Harrison, Jackson, Jessamine, Johnson, Kenton, Knott, Knox, Laurel, Lawrence, Lee, Leslie, Letcher, Lewis, Lincoln,

McCreary, Madison, Magoffin, Martin, Mason, Menifee, Montgomery, Morgan, Nicholas, Owsley, Pendleton, Perry, Pike, Powell, Pulaski, Robertson, Rockcastle, Rowan, Scott, Whitley, Wolfe, and Woodford) (1,039,880). Ohio (5,212,085). Pennsylvania (western part) (counties of Alleghany, Armstrong, Beaver, Butler, Clarion, Crawford, Erie, Fayette, Forest, Greene, Indiana, Jefferson, Lawrence, Mercer, Somerset, Venango, Warren, Washington, and Westmoreland) (2,895,090). West Virginia (northern part) (counties of Brooke, Hancock, Marshall, Ohio, Tyler, and Wetzel) (167,707).

District No. 5 — Richmond (9,278,461)

District of Columbia (369,282). Maryland (1,373,673). North Carolina (2,434,381). South Carolina (1,643,205). Virginia (2,213,025). West Virginia (all counties except Brooke, Hancock, Marshall, Ohio, Tyler, and Wetzel) (1,244,895).

District No. 6 — Atlanta (10,055,640)

Alabama (2,363,939). Florida (916,185). Georgia (2,895,841). Louisiana (southern part) (parishes of Acadia, Allen, Ascension, Assumption, Avoyelles, Calcasieu, Cameron, East Baton Rouge, East Feliciana, Evangeline, Iberville, Iberia, Jefferson, Jefferson Davis, Lafayette, Lafourche, Livingston, Orleans, Plaquemines, Pointe Coupee, Rapides, St. Bernard, St. Charles, St. Helena, St. James, St. John the Baptist, St. Landry, St. Martin, St. Mary, St. Tammany, Tangipahoa, Terrebonne, Vermilion, Vernon, Washington, West Baton Rouge, and West Feliciana) (1,260,490). Mississippi (southern part) (counties of Adams, Amite, Claiborne, Clarke, Copiah, Covington, Forrest, Franklin, George, Greene, Hancock, Harrison, Hinds, Issaquena, Jackson, Jasper, Jefferson, Jefferson Davis, Jones, Kemper, Lamar, Lauderdale, Lawrence, Leake, Lincoln, Madison, Marion, Neshoba, Newton, Pearl River, Perry, Pike, Rankin, Scott, Sharkey, Simpson, Smith, Walthall, Warren, Wayne, Wilkinson, and Yazoo) (996,935). Tennessee (eastern part) (counties of Anderson, Bedford, Bledsoe, Blount, Bradley, Campbell, Cannon, Carter, Cheatham, Claiborne, Clay, Cocke, Coffee, Cumberland, Davidson, Dekalb, Dickson, Fentress, Franklin, Giles, Grainger, Greene, Grundy, Hamblen, Hamilton, Hancock, Hawkins, Hickman, Houston, Humphreys, Jackson, James, Jefferson, Johnson, Knox, Lawrence, Lewis, Lincoln, Loudon, McMinn, Macon, Marion, Marshall, Maury, Meigs, Monroe, Montgomery, Moore, Morgan, Overton, Perry, Pickett, Polk, Putnam, Rhea, Roane, Robertson, Rutherford, Scott, Sequatchie, Sevier, Smith, Stewart, Sullivan, Sumner, Trousdale, Unicoi, Union, Van Buren, Warren, Washington, Wayne, White, Williamson, and Wilson) (1,622,250).

District No. 7 — Chicago (14,154,175)

Illinois (northern part) (counties of Boone, Bureau, Carroll, Cass, Champaign, Christian, Clark, Coles, Cook, Cumberland, Dekalb, Dewitt, Douglas, Dupage, Edgar, Ford, Fulton, Grundy, Hancock, Henderson, Henry, Iroquois, Jo Daviess, Kane, Kankakee, Kendall, Knox, Lake, La Salle, Lee, Livingston, Logan, McDonough, McHenry, McLean, Macon, Marshall, Mason, Menard, Mercer, Moultrie, Ogle, Peoria, Platt, Putnam, Rock Island, Sangamon, Schuyler, Shelby, Stark, Stephenson, Tazewell, Vermilion, Warren, Whiteside, Will, Winnebago, and Woodford) (4,977,386). Indiana (northern part) (counties of Adams, Allen, Bartholomew, Benton, Blackford, Boone, Brown, Carroll, Cass, Clay, Clinton,

Dearborn, Decatur, Dekalb, Delaware, Elkhart, Fayette, Fountain, Franklin, Fulton, Grant, Hamilton, Hancock, Hendricks, Henry, Howard, Huntington, Jasper, Jay, Jennings, Johnson, Kosciusko, Lagrange, Lake, Laporte, Madison, Marion, Marshall, Miami, Monroe, Montgomery, Morgan, Newton, Noble, Ohio, Owen, Parke, Porter, Pulaski, Putnam, Randolph, Ripley, Rush, St. Joseph, Shelby, Starke, Steuben, Tippecanoe, Tipton, Union, Vermilion, Vigo, Wabash, Warren, Wayne, Wells, White, and Whitley) (2,227,340). Iowa (2,224,771). Michigan (southern part) (counties of Alcona, Allegan, Alpena, Antrim, Arenac, Barry, Bay, Benzie, Berrien, Branch, Calhoun, Cass, Charlevoix, Cheboygan, Claire, Clinton, Crawford, Eaton, Emmet, Genesee, Gladwin, Grand Traverse, Gratiot, Hillsdale, Huron, Ingham, Ionia, Iosco, Isabella, Jackson, Kalamazoo, Kalkaska, Kent, Lake, Lapeer, Leelanau, Lenawee, Livingston, Macomb, Manistee, Mason, Mecosta, Midland, Missaukee, Monroe, Montcalm, Montmorency, Muskegon, Newaygo, Oakland, Oceana, Ogenaw, Osceola, Oscoda, Otsego, Ottawa, Presque Isle, Roscommon, Saginaw, St. Clair, St. Joseph, Sanilac, Shiawasee, Tuscola, Van Buren, Washtenaw, Wayne, and Wexford) (2,721,733). Wisconsin (southern part) (counties of Adams, Brown, Calumet, Clark, Columbia, Crawford, Dane, Dodge, Door, Fond du Lac, Grant, Green, Green Lake, Iowa, Jackson, Jefferson, Juneau, Kenosha, Kewaunee, Lafayette, Langlade, Manitowoc, Marathon, Marinette, Marquette, Milwaukee, Monroe, Oconto, Outagamie, Ozaukee, Portage, Racine, Richland, Rock, Sauk, Shawano, Sheboygan, Vernon, Walworth, Washington, Waukesha, Waupaca, Waushara, Winnebago, and Wood) (2,002,945).

District No. 8 – St. Louis (9,291,698)

Arkansas (1,766,343). Illinois (southern part) counties of Adams, Alexander, Bond, Brown, Calhoun, Clay, Clinton, Crawford, Edwards, Effingham, Fayette, Franklin, Gallatin, Greene, Hamilton, Hardin, Jackson, Jasper, Jefferson, Jersey, Johnson, Lawrence, Macoupin, Madison, Marion, Massac, Monroe, Montgomery, Morgan, Perry, Pike, Pope, Pulaski, Randolph, Richland, St. Clair, Saline, Scott, Union, Wabash, Washington, Wayne, White, and Williamson) (1,257,609). Indiana (southern part) (counties of Clark, Crawford, Daviess, Dubois, Floyd, Gibson, Greene, Harrison, Jackson, Jefferson, Knox, Lawrence, Martin, Orange, Perry, Pike, Posey, Scott, Sullivan, Spencer, Switzerland, Vanderburg, Warrick, and Washington) (608,152). Kentucky (western part) (counties of Adair, Allen, Anderson, Ballard, Barren, Boyle, Breckenridge, Bullitt, Butler, Caldwell, Calloway, Carlisle, Carroll, Casey, Christian, Clinton, Crittenden, Cumberland, Daviess, Edmonson, Franklin, Fulton, Gallatin, Graves, Grayson, Greene, Hancock, Hardin, Hart, Henderson, Henry, Hickman, Hopkins, Jefferson, Larue, Livingston, Logan, Lyon, McCracken, McLean, Marion, Marshall, Meade, Mercer, Metcalfe, Monroe, Muhlenberg, Nelson, Ohio, Oldham, Owen, Russell, Shelby, Simpson, Spencer, Taylor, Todd, Trigg, Trimble, Union, Warren, Washington, Wayne, and Webster) (1,354,213). Mississippi (northern part) (counties of Alcorn, Attala, Benton, Bolivar, Calhoun, Carroll, Chickasaw, Choctaw, Clay, Coahoma, De Soto, Grenada, Holmes, Itawamba, Lafayette, Lee, Leflore, Lowndes, Marshall, Monroe, Montgomery, Noxubee, Oktibbeha, Panola, Pontotoc, Prentiss, Quitman, Sunflower, Tallahatchie, Tato, Tippah, Tishomingo, Tunica, Union, Washington, Webster, Winston, and Yalobusha) (979,635). Missouri (eastern part) (includes all counties except those included in District No. 10) (2,643,367). Tennessee (western part) (counties of Benton, Carroll, Chester, Crockett, Decatur, Dyer, Fayette, Gibson, Hardeman, Hardin,

Haywood, Henderson, Henry, Lake, Lauderdale, McNairy, Madison, Obion, Shelby, Tipton, and Weakley) (682,379).

District No. 9 — Minneapolis (5,164,426)

Michigan (northern part) (counties of Alger, Baraga, Chippewa, Delta, Dickinson, Gogebic, Houghton, Iron, Keweenaw, Luce, Mackinac, Marquette, Menominee, Ontonagon, and Schoolcraft) (372,533). Minnesota (2,312,445). Montana (472,935). North Dakota (765,319). South Dakota (716,972). Wisconsin (northern part) (counties of Ashland, Barron, Bayfield, Buffalo, Burnett, Chippewa, Douglas, Dunn, Eau Claire, Florence, Forest, Iron, La Crosse, Lincoln, Oneida, Pepin, Pierce, Polk, Price, Rusk, St. Croix, Sawyer, Taylor, Trempealeau, Vilas, and Washburn) (524,222).

District No. 10 — Kansas City (7,404,443)

Colorado (988,320). Kansas (1,851,870). Missouri (western part) (counties of Andrew, Atchison, Barton, Bates, Buchanan, Cass, Clay, Clinton, Dekalb, Gentry, Holt, Jackson, Jasper, McDonald, Newton, Nodaway, Platte, Vernon, and Worth) (786,228). Nebraska (1,284,126). New Mexico (northern part) (counties of Colfax, McKinley, Mora, Rio Arriba, Sandoval, San Juan, San Miguel, Santa Fe, Taos, and Union) (196,440). Oklahoma (all except southeastern part) (counties of Adair, Alfalfa, Beaver, Blaine, Beckham, Caddo, Canadian, Carter, Comanche, Cotton, Custer, Cherokee, Cimarron, Cleveland, Craig, Creek, Delaware, Dewey, Ellis, Garfield, Garvin, Grant, Grady, Greer, Harper, Harmon, Haskell, Hughes, Jackson, Jefferson, Kay, Kingfisher, Kiowa, Latimer, Le Flore, Lincoln, Logan, Love, McClain, McIntosh, Major, Mayes, Muskogee, Murray, Noble, Nowata, Okfuskee, Oklahoma, Okmulgee, Osage, Ottawa, Pawnee, Payne, Pottawatomie, Pittsburg, Pontotoc, Rogers, Roger Mills, Seminole, Sequoyah, Stephens, Texas, Tulsa, Tillman, Washita, Wagoner, Washington, Woods, and Woodward) (2,112,489). Wyoming (184,970).

District No. 11 — Dallas (5,637,290)

Arizona (southeastern part) (counties of Cochise, Pima, Graham, Santa Cruz, and Greenlee) (120,828). Louisiana (northern part) (parishes of Bienville, Bossier, Beauregard, Caddo, Caldwell, Catahoula, Claiborne, Concordia, De Sota, East Carroll, Franklin, Grant, Jackson, La Salle, Lincoln, Madison, Morehouse, Natchitoches, Ouachita, Red River, Richland, Sabine, Tensas, Union, Webster, West Carroll, and Winn) (596,464). New Mexico (southern part) (counties of Bernalillo, Chaves, Curry, Dona Ana, Eddy, Grant, Guadalupe, Lincoln, Luna, Otero, Quay, Roosevelt, Sierra, Socorro, Torrance, and Valencia) (227,209). Oklahoma (southeastern part) (counties of Atoka, Bryan, Choctaw, Coal, Johnston, McCurtain, Marshall, and Pushmataha) (177,366). Texas (4,515,423).

District No. 12 — San Francisco (6,631,164)

Arizona (northwestern part) (counties of Apache, Coconino, Gila, Maricopa, Mohave, Navajo, Pinal, Yavapai, and Yuma) (142,960). California (3,029,032). Idaho (445,176). Nevada (110,738). Oregon (861,992). Utah (443,866). Washington (1,597,400).

Source: Federal Reserve Bulletin, September 1917.

Appendixes

Income and Expenses of

Dollars

Period, or Federal Reserve Bank	Current income	Net expenses	Net additions or deductions (−)	Assessments by Board of Governors	
				Board expenditures	Costs of currency
All Banks					
1914–15	2,173,252	2,018,282	5,875	302,304	. . .
1916	5,217,998	2,081,722	−193,001	192,277	. . .
1917	16,128,339	4,921,932	−1,386,545	237,795	. . .
1918	67,584,417	10,576,892	−3,908,574	382,641	. . .
1919	102,380,583	18,744,815	−4,673,446	594,818	. . .
1920	181,296,711	27,548,505	−3,743,907	709,525	. . .
1921	122,865,866	33,722,409	−6,314,796	741,436	. . .
1922	50,498,699	28,836,504	−4,441,914	722,545	. . .
1923	50,708,566	29,061,539	−8,233,107	702,634	. . .
1924	38,340,449	27,767,886	−6,191,143	663,240	. . .
1925	41,800,706	26,818,664	−4,823,477	709,499	. . .
1926	47,599,595	24,914,037	−3,637,668	721,724	1,714,421
1927	43,024,484	24,894,487	−2,456,792	779,116	1,844,840
1928	64,052,860	25,401,233 ʼ	−5,026,029	697,677	805,900
1929	70,955,496	25,810,067	−4,861,642	781,644	3,099,402
1930	36,424,044	25,357,611	−93,136	809,585	2,175,530
1931	29,701,279	24,842,964	311,451	718,554	1,479,146
1932	50,018,817	24,456,755	−1,413,192	728,810	1,105,816
1933	49,487,318	25,917,847	−12,307,074	800,160	2,504,830
1934	48,902,813	26,843,653	−4,430,008	1,372,022	1,025,721
1935	42,751,959	28,694,965	−1,736,758	1,405,898	1,476,580
1936	37,900,639	26,016,338	485,817	1,679,566	2,178,119
1937	41,233,135	25,294,835	−1,631,274	1,748,380	1,757,399
1938	36,261,428	25,556,949	2,232,134	1,724,924	1,629,735
1939	38,500,665	25,668,907	2,389,555	1,621,464	1,356,484
1940	43,537,805	25,950,946	11,487,697	1,704,011	1,510,520
1941	41,380,095	28,535,547	720,636	1,839,541	2,588,062
1942	52,662,704	32,051,226	−1,568,208	1,746,326	4,826,492
1943	69,305,715	35,793,816	23,768,282	2,415,630	5,336,118
1944	104,391,829	39,659,496	3,221,880	2,296,357	7,220,068
1945	142,209,546	41,666,453	−830,007	2,340,509	4,710,309
1946	150,385,033	50,493,246	−625,991	2,259,784	4,482,077
1947	158,655,566	58,191,428	1,973,001	2,639,667	4,561,880
1948	304,160,818	64,280,271	−34,317,947	3,243,670	5,186,247
1949	316,536,930	67,930,860	−12,122,274	3,242,500	6,304,316
1950	275,838,994	69,822,227	36,294,117	3,433,700	7,315,844
1951	394,656,072	83,792,676	−2,127,889	4,095,497	7,580,913
1952	456,060,260	92,051,063	1,583,988	4,121,602	8,521,426
1953	513,037,237	98,493,153	−1,058,993	4,099,800	10,922,067
1954	438,486,040	99,068,436	−133,641	4,174,600	6,489,895
1955	412,487,931	101,158,921	−265,456	4,194,100	4,707,002
1956	595,649,092	110,239,520	−23,436	5,339,800	5,603,176
1957	763,347,530	117,931,908	−7,140,914	7,507,900	6,374,195
1958	742,068,150	125,831,215	124,175	5,917,200	5,973,240
1959	886,226,116	131,848,023	98,247,253	6,470,600	6,384,083
1960	1,103,385,257	139,893,564	13,874,702	6,533,700	7,455,011
1961	941,648,170	148,253,719	3,481,628	6,265,100	6,755,756
1962	1,048,508,335	161,451,206	−55,779	6,654,900	8,030,028
1963	1,151,120,060	169,637,656	614,835	7,572,800	10,062,901
1964	1,343,747,303	171,511,018	725,948	8,655,200	17,229,671
1965	1,559,484,027	172,110,934	1,021,614	8,576,396	23,602,856
1966	1,908,499,896	178,212,045	996,230	9,021,600	20,167,481
1967	2,190,403,752	190,561,166	2,093,876	10,769,596	18,790,084
1968	2,764,445,943	207,677,768	8,519,996	14,198,198	20,474,404
1969	3,373,360,559	237,827,579	−557,553	15,020,084	22,125,657

Federal Reserve Banks, 1914–1988

Dividends paid	Payments to U.S. Treasury			Transferred to surplus (section 13b)	Transferred to surplus (section 7)
	Franchise tax	Under section 13b	Interest on Federal Reserve notes		
217,463	. . .	. . .	. . .	. . .	. . .
1,742,775	. . .	. . .	. . .	. . .	. . .
6,804,186	1,134,234	. . .	. . .	. . .	1,134,234
5,540,684	. . .	. . .	. . .	. . .	48,334,341
5,011,832	2,703,894	. . .	. . .	. . .	70,651,778
5.654,018	60,724,742	. . .	. . .	. . .	82,916,014
6,119,673	59,974,466	. . .	. . .	. . .	15,993,086
6,307,035	10,850,605	. . .	. . .	. . .	−659,904
6.552.717	3.613.056	. . .	. . .	. . .	2,545,513
6,682,496	113,646	. . .	. . .	. . .	−3,077,962
6,915,958	59,300	. . .	. . .	. . .	2,473,808
7,329,169	818,150	. . .	. . .	. . .	8,464,426
7,754,539	249,591	. . .	. . .	. . .	5.044,119
8,458,463	2,584,659	. . .	. . .	. . .	21.078.899
9,583,911	4,283,231	. . .	. . .	. . .	22,535,597
10,268,598	17,308	. . .	. . .	. . .	−2,297,724
10,029,760	. . .	. . .	. . .	. . .	−7,057.694
9,282,244	2,011,418	. . .	. . .	. . .	11,020.582
8,874,262	. . .	. . .	. . .	. . .	−916,855
8,781,661	. . .	. . .	. . .	−60.323	6,510.071
8,504,974	. . .	297,667	. . .	27,695	607,422
7,829,581	. . .	227,448	. . .	102,880	352,524
7,940,966	. . .	176,625	. . .	67,304	2.616,352
8,019,137	. . .	119,524	. . .	−419,140	1,862,433
8,110,462	. . .	24,579	. . .	−425,653	4,533,977
8,214,971	. . .	82,152	. . .	−54,456	17,617.358
8,429,936	. . .	141,465	. . .	−4.333	570.513
8,669,076	. . .	197,672	. . .	49,602	3,554,101
8,911,342	. . .	244,726	. . .	135,003	40,327.237
9,500,126	. . .	226,717	. . .	201,150	48,409,795
10,182,851	. . .	247,659	. . .	262,133	81,969.625
10,962,160	. . .	67,054	. . .	27,708	81,467.013
11,523,047	. . .	35,605	75,283,818	86,772	8,366,350
11,919,809	. . .	. . .	166,690,356	. . .	18,522,518
12,329,373	. . .	. . .	193,145,837	. . .	21,461,770
13,082,992	. . .	. . .	196,628,858	. . .	21,849,490
13,864,750	. . .	. . .	254,873,588	. . .	28.320,759
14,681,788	. . .	. . .	291,934,634	. . .	46,333,735
15,558,377	. . .	. . .	342,567,985	. . .	40,336,862
16,442,236	. . .	. . .	276,289,457	. . .	35,887,775
17,711,937	. . .	. . .	251,740,721	. . .	32,709,794
18,904,897	. . .	. . .	401,555,581	. . .	53,982,682
20,080,527	. . .	. . .	542,708,405	. . .	61,603,682
21,197,452	. . .	. . .	524,058,650	. . .	59,214,569
22,721,687	. . .	. . .	910,649,768	. . .	−93,600,791
23,948,225	. . .	. . .	896,816,359	. . .	42,613,100
25.569,541	. . .	. . .	687,393,382	. . .	70,892,300
27,412,241	. . .	. . .	799,365,981	. . .	45,538,200
28,912,019	. . .	. . .	879,685,219	. . .	55,864,300
30,781,548	. . .	. . .	1,582,118,614	. . .	−465,822,800
32,351,602	. . .	. . .	1,296,810,053	. . .	27,053,800
33,696,336	. . .	. . .	1,649,455,164	. . .	18,943,500
35,027,312	. . .	. . .	1,907,498,270	. . .	29,851,200
36,959,336	. . .	. . .	2,463,628,983	. . .	30,027,250
39,236,599	. . .	. . .	3,019,160,638	. . .	39,432,450

Income and Expenses of

Period, or Federal Reserve Bank	Current income	Net expenses	Net additions or deductions (−)	Assessments by Board of Governors	
				Board expenditures	Costs of currency
1970	3,877,218,444	276,571,876	11,441,829	21,227,800	23,573,710
1971	3,723,369,921	319,608,270	94,266,075	32,634,002	24,942,528
1972	3,792,334,523	347,917,112	(49,615,790)	35,234,499	31,454,740
1973	5,016,769,328	416,879,377	(80,653,488)	44,411,700	33,826,299
1974	6,280,090,965	476,234,586	(78,487,237)	41,116,600	30,190,288
1975	6,257,936,784	514,358,633	(202,369,615)	33,577,201	37,130,081
1976	6,623,220,383	558,128,811	7,310,500	41,827,700	48,819,453
1977	6,891,317,498	568,851,419	(177,033,463)	47,366,100	55,008,163
1978	8,455,309,401	592,557,841	(633,123,486)	53,321,700	60,059,365
1979	10,310,148,406	625,168,261	(151,148,220)	50,529,700	68,391,270
1980	12,802,319,335	718,032,836	(115,385,855)	62,230,800	73,124,423
1981	15,508,349,653	814,190,392	(372,879,185)	63,162,700	82,924,013
1982	16,517,385,129	926,033,957	(68,833,150)	61,813,400	98,441,027
1983	16,068,362,117	1,023,678,474	(400,365,922)	71,551,000	152,135,488
1984	18,068,820,742	1,102,444,454	(412,943,156)	82,115,700	162,606,410
1985	18,131,982,786	1,127,744,490	1,301,624,294	77,377,700	173,738,745
1986	17,464,528,361	1,156,867,714	1,975,893,356	97,337,500	180,779,613
1987	17,633,011,623	1,146,910,699	1,796,593,917 [2]	81,869,800	170,674,979
1988	19,526,431,297	1,205,960,134	(516,910,320)	84,410,500	164,244,653
Total, 1914–88	**238,510,484,581**	**17,741,836,222**	**1,999,244,205**	**1,271,014,708**	**1,967,511,010**
Aggregate for each Bank, 1914–88					
Boston	12,005,096,843	1,174,105,749	55,134,542	45,779,286	114,917,920
New York	69,376,122,412	3,525,480,072	534,167,103	328,683,786	492,365,339
Philadelphia	9,836,833,130	935,307,310	86,170,618	62,160,518	90,575,610
Cleveland	16,280,828,013	1,198,233,303	67,205,461	98,122,690	124,358,035
Richmond	18,788,385,425	1,393,781,737	92,183,673	66,169,276	185,156,576
Atlanta	9,898,281,276	1,524,845,146	182,174,022	94,744,360	120,997,307
Chicago	34,738,042,867	2,334,955,874	226,221,946	180,357,672	275,191,342
St. Louis	8,187,287,027	948,898,211	45,150,118	39,683,972	75,231,451
Minneapolis	4,313,264,726	816,101,971	66,677,954	37,826,415	34,325,191
Kansas City	10,348,387,248	1,126,493,481	86,680,029	54,354,709	94,968,427
Dallas	13,763,880,880	1,012,280,569	209,610,258	82,922,773	116,662,362
San Francisco	30,974,074,736	1,800,655,287	347,868,477	180,179,251	242,761,450
Total	**238,510,484,582**	**17,741,836,222** [4]	**1,999,244,205**	**1,271,014,708**	**1,967,511,010**

1. Details may not add to totals because of rounding.
2. For 1987 and subsequent years, includes the cost of services provided to the Treasury by Federal Reserve Banks for which reimbursement was not received.
3. The $2,240,750,999 transferred to surplus was reduced by direct changes of $500,000 for charge-off on Bank premises (1927), $139,299,557 for contributions to

capital of the Federal Deposit Insurance Corporation (1934) and $3,657 net upon elimination of sec. 13b surplus (1958); and was increased by transfer of $11,131,013 from reserves for contingencies (1945), leaving a balance of $2,112,057,800 on Dec. 31, 1987.
4. See note 2, table 6.

Source: Annual Report, Board of Governors, 1988.

Federal Reserve Banks, 1914–1988 (cont.)

Dividends paid	Payments to U.S. Treasury			Transferred to surplus (section 13b)	Transferred to surplus (section 7)
	Franchise tax	Under section 13b	Interest on Federal Reserve notes		
41,136,551	. . .	. . .	3,493,570,636	. . .	32,579,700
43,488,074	. . .	. . .	3,356,559,873	. . .	40,403,250
46,183,719	. . .	. . .	3,231,267,663	. . .	50,661,000
49,139,682	. . .	. . .	4,340,680,482	. . .	51,178,300
52,579,643	. . .	. . .	5,549,999,411	. . .	51,483,200
54,609,555	. . .	. . .	5,382,064,098	. . .	33,827,600
57,351,487	. . .	. . .	5,870,463,382	. . .	53,940,050
60,182,278	. . .	. . .	5,937,148,425	. . .	45,727,650
63,280,312	. . .	. . .	7,005,779,497	. . .	47,268,200
67,193,615	. . .	. . .	9,278,576,140	. . .	69,141,200
70,354,516	. . .	. . .	11,706,369,955	. . .	56,820,950
74,573,806	. . .	. . .	14,023,722,907	. . .	76,896,650
79,352,304	. . .	. . .	15,204,590,947	. . .	78,320,350
85,151,835	. . .	. . .	14,228,816,297	. . .	106,663,100
92,620,451	. . .	. . .	16,054,094,674	. . .	161,995,900
103,028,905	. . .	. . .	17,796,464,292	. . .	155,252,950
109,587,968	. . .	. . .	17,803,894,710	. . .	91,954,150
117,499,115	. . .	. . .	17,738,879,542	. . .	173,771,400
125,616,018	. . .	. . .	17,364,318,571	. . .	64,971,100
2,160,030,490	**149,138,300**	**2,188,893**	**214,977,261,822**	**(3,657)**	**2,240,750,999** [3]
89,004,996	7,111,395	280,843	10,543,845,860	135,411	84,049,925
586,093,192	68,006,262	369,116	64,355,883,827	(433,412)	603,043,821
116,936,323	5,558,901	722,406	8,594,442,847	290,661	117,109,172
175,777,068	4,842,447	82,930	14,618,489,864	(9,906)	128,137,043
108,956,701	6,200,189	172,493	16,990,867,850	(71,517)	129,335,658
147,368,065	8,950,561	79,264	7,982,401,044	5,491	201,034,190
298,326,916	25,313,526	151,045	31,561,621,600	11,682	288,335,154
68,733,059	2,755,629	7,464	7,033,553,602	(26,515)	63,600,278
60,824,362	5,202,900	55,615	3,354,818,340	64,874	70,723,013
90,002,435	6,939,100	64,213	8,971,201,935	(8,674)	91,051,650
131,996,042	560,049	102,083	12,466,603,395	55,337	162,308,528
286,011,331	7,697,341	101,421	28,503,531,658	(17,089)	301,022,567
2,160,030,491	**149,138,300**	**2,188,893**	**214,977,261,822**	**(3,657)**	**2,240,750,999**

Statement of Condition of All and Each Federal Reserve Bank, 1914 (in millions of dollars)

Item	All Banks	Boston	New York	Philadelphia	Cleveland	Richmond	Atlanta
Assets							
Total Gold reserves	$ 229.069	$ 12.919	$82.235	$ 16.642	$ 17.674	$ 8.686	$3.133
Special Drawing Rights	not an item until 1970						
Cash–F.R. notes + coin	26.578	.935	16.864	2.626	1.017	.112	2.193
Discounts & Advances	10.593	.154	.279	.786	.506	2.022	1.079
U.S. Gov't Securities	.255	-----	.050	-----	-----	-----	-----
Cash items in process	------ none ------						
Bank Premises	------ none ------						
Other assets	11.349	.068	5.457	1.447	.318	.213	.970
Total assets	**$ 277.844**	**$14.076**	**$104.885**	**$ 21.501**	**$19.515**	**$ 11.035**	**$7.375**
Liabilities							
Own F.R. notes	$ 3.775	$ -----	$ -----	$ -----	$ .140	$ .780	$ .343
Deposits – member banks	256.018	12.457	101.563	19.415	17.344	9.161	6.155
– U.S. Treasurer	---------- none ----------						
Other deposits	---------- none ----------						
Deferred availability cash items	---------- none ----------						
Other liabilities							
Total Liabilities	**$ 259.793**	**$ 12.457**	**$ 101.563**	**$ 19.415**	**$17.484**	**$ 9.941**	**$ 6.589**
Paid in capital	$ 18.051	$ 1.619	$ 3.322	$ 2.086	$ 2.031	$ 1.094	$ .786
Surplus	---------- none ----------						
Other capital accts.	---------- none ----------						
Ratio: gold to note & deposit liability							

Item	Chicago	St. Louis	Minneapolis	Kansas City	Dallas	San Francisco
Assets						
Total Gold reserves	$ 37.776	$ 9.226	$ 9.904	$ 10.284	$ 6.292	$ 14.296
Special Drawing Rights		not an item until 1970				
Cash–F.R. notes + coin	.931	.869	.021	.534	.404	.072
Discounts & Advances	2.617	.288	1.104	.079	.927	.752
U.S. Gov't Securities	.205	----	----	----	----	----
Cash items in process			none			
Bank Premises			none			
Other assets	.880	.951	.271	.044	.652	.078
Total assets	$ 42.409	$ 11.334	$ 11.300	$ 10.941	$ 8.275	$ 15.198
Liabilities						
Own F.R. notes	$ 1.717	$ .039	$ ----	$ .072	$ .410	$ .183
Deposits – member banks	38.495	10.372	10.486	9.942	6.909	13.719
– U.S. Treasurer						
Other deposits						
Deferred availability cash items						
Other liabilities						
Total Liabilities	$ 40.212	$ 10.411	$ 10.486	$ 10.014	$ 7.319	$ 13.902
Paid in capital	$ 2.917	$ .923	$ .814	$ .927	$ .956	$ 1.296
Surplus			none			
Other capital accts.			none			
Ratio: gold to note & deposit liability	94%	89%	94%	103%	86%	103%

Source: Annual Report of Federal Reserve Board.

Item	All banks	Boston	New York	Philadelphia	Cleveland	Richmond	Atlanta
Assets							
Total Gold reserves	$ 2,075	$ 206	$ 475	$ 205	$ 282	$ 87	$ 88
Special Drawing Rights		not an item until 1970					
Cash–F.R. notes + coin	282	22	146	10	10	8	12
Discounts & Advances	2,948	194	985	185	229	121	136
U.S. Gov't Securities	287	22	61	32	25	13	17
Cash items in process	637	48	126	58	66	53	21
Bank Premises	17	3	4	1	2	1	1
Other assets	7	---	1	---	---	1	---
Total assets	$6,254	$ 495	$1,814	$ 492	$ 614	$ 283	$ 275
Liabilities							
Own F.R. notes	$3,553	$309	$906	$301	$372	$167	$189
Deposits – member banks	1,781	115	702	111	150	57	49
– U.S. Treasurer	57	5	11	1	5	3	4
Other deposits	23	1	12	1	---	---	---
Deferred availability cash items	519	42	93	51	55	40	20
Other liabilities	19	1	6	---	---	1	1
Total Liabilities	$5,952	$ 472	$1,731	$ 467	$ 583	$ 268	$ 263
Paid in capital	$ 100	$ 8	$ 26	$ 8	$ 11	$ 5	$ 4
Surplus	202	16	56	17	20	11	8
Other capital accts.	---	---	---	---	---	---	---
Ratio of gold reserves to F.R. note & deposit liability	38%	48%	29%	50%	54%	39%	38%

Item	Chicago	St. Louis	Minneapolis	Kansas City	Dallas	San Francisco
Assets						
Total Gold reserves	$ 299	$ 83	$ 47	$ 75	$ 42	$ 182
Special Drawing Rights	not an item until 1970					
Cash–F.R. notes + coin	24	11	1	7	9	9
Discounts & Advances	501	116	83	113	71	214
U.S. Gov't Securities	44	17	9	22	12	13
Cash items in process	80	35	21	51	39	40
Bank Premises	2	1	1	1	2	---
Other assets	1	---	---	---	---	1
Total assets	**$ 951**	**$ 263**	**$ 161**	**$ 269**	**$ 175**	**$ 461**
Liabilities						
Own F.R. notes	$584	$ 145	$ 87	$ 126	$ 87	$ 281
Deposits – member banks	250	67	44	74	47	114
– U.S. Treasurer	13	3	2	5	2	6
Other deposits	2	1	1	1	---	4
Deferred availability cash items	56	34	17	48	28	34
Other liabilities	4	1	---	2	---	---
Total Liabilities	**$908**	**$ 250**	**$ 151**	**$ 255**	**$165**	**$ 440**
Paid in capital	$14	$ 4	$ 3	$ 4	$ 4	$ 7
Surplus	29	8	7	9	6	14
Other capital accts.	---	---	---	---	---	---
Ratio: gold to note & deposit liability	38.4%	43.1%	37.4%	39.9%	35.4%	46.1%

Source: Annual Report of Federal Reserve Board.

Item	All banks	Boston	New York	Philadelphia	Cleveland	Richmond	Atlanta
Assets							
Total Gold reserves	$2,941	$211	$1,047	$247	$287	$120	$159
Special Drawing Rights			not an item until 1970				
Cash-F.R.notes + coin	242	7	29	5	8	7	7
Discounts & Advances	615	39	220	29	63	34	34
U.S.Gov't Securities	737	51	286	55	64	14	8
Cash items in process	585	66	183	52	54	38	13
Bank Premises	58	3	15	3	7	3	3
Other assets	22	---	9	---	1	1	5
Total assets	$5,200	$377	$1,790	$392	$483	$217	$228
Liabilities							
Own F.R.notes	$1,664	$132	$385	$154	$195	$101	$134
Deposits – member banks	2,471	151	1,062	143	186	61	61
– U.S.Treasurer	19	1	4	1	2	---	1
Other deposits	27	---	10	---	3	---	---
Deferred availability cash items	564	59	179	49	51	36	13
Other liabilities	12	---	2	---	1	1	2
Total Liabilities	$4,756	$343	$1,642	$347	$438	$199	$211
Paid in capital	$170	$12	$66	$17	$16	$6	$5
Surplus	275	21	81	27	29	12	11
Other capital accts.	---	---	---	---	---	---	---
Ratio of gold reserves to F.R.note & deposit liability	74%	75%	72%	83%	75%	74%	81%

Item	Chicago	St.Louis	Minneapolis	Kansas City	Dallas	San Francisco
Assets						
Total Gold reserves	$375	$114	$69	$100	$54	$299
Special Drawing Rights		not an item	until 1970			
Cash–F.R.notes + coin	14	6	3	4	5	8
Discounts & Advances	75	22	12	28	13	47
U.S.Gov't Securities	91	26	27	32	31	51
Cash items in process	69	22	10	32	17	29
Bank Premises	8	4	2	4	2	5
Other assets	– 1	4	1	----	---	1
Total assets	$ 633	$ 197	$ 124	$ 199	$122	$439
Liabilities						
Own F.R.notes	$139	$ 85	$54	$68	$32	$ 186
Deposits – member banks	361	70	48	88	58	183
– U.S.Treasurer	3	1	1	2	1	1
Other deposits	2	1	---	---	---	7
Deferred availability cash items	67	24	8	28	18	31
Other liabilities	2	1		---		1
Total Liabilities	$ 574	$ 182	$ 112	$ 186	$ 110	$ 408
Paid in capital	$ 20	$ 5	$ 3	$ 4	$ 4	$ 12
Surplus	40	11	7	9	9	18
Other capital accts.	------ none --------					
Ratio: gold to note & deposit liability	75%	74%	68%	64%	60%	81%

Source: Annual Report of Federal Reserve Board.

Item	All banks	Boston	New York	Philadelphia	Cleveland	Richmond	Atlanta
Assets							
Total Gold reserves	$19,761	$1,137	$9,758	$1,048	$1,332	$554	$385
Special Drawing Rights		not an item until 1970					
Cash-F.R. notes + coin	306	27	56	21	21	22	22
Discounts & Advances	10	1	2	3	1	1	---
U.S. Gov't Securities	2,184	157	645	183	219	116	84
Cash items in process	1,912	83	235	63	102	76	43
Bank Premises	40	3	10	5	5	3	2
Other assets	48	3	13	5	5	3	2
Total assets	$23,262	$1,411	$10,720	$1,326	$1,685	$775	$539
Liabilities							
Own F.R. notes	$5,931	$480	$1,576	$411	$541	$284	$196
Deposits – member banks	14,026	756	7,557	704	921	354	247
– U.S. Treasurer	368	6	132	14	16	13	13
Other deposits	1,732	63	1,126	103	77	38	33
Deferred availability cash items	833	80	201	60	96	71	38
Other liabilities	2	---	---	1	---	---	---
Total Liabilities	$22,893	$1,386	$10,592	$1,292	$1,651	$759	$526
Paid in capital	$139	$9	$51	$12	$14	$5	$5
Surplus	184	13	64	20	15	9	6
Other capital accts.	47	2	13	3	5	2	2
Ratio of gold reserves to F.R.note & deposit liability	98%	87%	87%	87%	86%	70%	79%

Item	Chicago	St. Louis	Minneapolis	Kansas City	Dallas	San Francisco
Assets						
Total Gold reserves	$ 2,901	$ 495	$ 311	$ 421	$ 281	$ 1,137
Special Drawing Rights	not an item until 1970					
Cash-F.R. notes + coin	40	19	8	18	15	36
Discounts & Advances	----	----	----	1	----	1
U.S. Gov't Securities	249	94	62	107	85	183
Cash items in process	127	53	20	36	30	46
Bank Premises	3	2	1	3	1	3
Other assets	5	2	1	2	2	4
Total assets	**$ 3,326**	**$665**	**$405**	**$588**	**$414**	**$1,408**
Liabilities						
Own F.R. notes	$ 1,262	$ 221	$ 159	$211	$ 98	$ 493
Deposits – member banks	1,711	327	174	280	240	754
– U.S. Treasurer	85	24	23	17	11	17
Other deposits	98	30	22	36	26	81
Deferred availability cash items	122	51	16	33	27	37
Other liabilities	------------- none -------------					
Total Liabilities	**$ 3,279**	**$ 654**	**$ 395**	**$ 577**	**$ 402**	**$ 1,381**
Paid in capital	$ 15	$ 4	$ 3	$ 4	$ 4	$ 12
Surplus	24	5	4	5	5	13
Other capital accts.	8	2	3	2	2	3
Ratio: gold to note & deposit liability	97%	82%	82%	78%	75%	85%

Source: Annual Report of Board of Governors, Federal Reserve System.

Item	All banks	Boston	New York	Philadelphia	Cleveland	Richmond	Atlanta
Assets							
Total Gold reserves	$21,458	$846	$6,584	$1,181	$1,544	$1,004	$930
Special Drawing Rights			not an item until 1970				
Cash-F.R. notes + coin	437	35	71	31	34	54	39
Discounts & Advances	70	----	62	4	----	1	---
U.S. Gov't Securities	20,778	1,429	4,883	1,378	1,921	1,339	1,110
Cash items in process	4,270	324	807	268	458	341	277
Bank Premises	40	1	8	3	5	3	2
Other assets	120	8	28	8	11	8	6
Total assets	$47,172	$2,643	$12,433	$2,874	$3,973	$2,750	$2,365
Liabilities							
F.R. note	$23,587	$1,424	$5,343	$1,666	$2,112	$1,616	$1,276
Deposits – member banks	17,681	784	5,665	822	1,324	751	740
–U.S. Treasurer	668	78	116	58	82	37	39
Other deposits	1,460	63	542	76	95	73	80
Deferred availability cash items	2,901	238	518	184	279	226	191
Other liabilities	6	1	2	----		1	----
Total Liabilities	$46,304	$2,588	$12,186	$2,807	$3,892	$2,704	$2,326
Paid in capital	225	12	73	16	22	10	9
Surplus	538	35	161	44	49	29	23
Other capital accts.	106	8	22	8	10	7	6
Ratio of gold reserves to F.R.note & deposit liability	49%	38%	63%	47%	44%	42%	47%

Item	Chicago	St. Louis	Minneapolis	Kansas City	Dallas	San Francisco
Assets						
Total Gold reserves	$ 4,260	$ 631	$ 388	$ 868	$ 648	$ 2,573
Special Drawing Rights		not an item until 1970		none		
Cash-F.R. notes + coin	51	25	12	18	21	48
Discounts & Advances			none			
U.S. Gov't Securities	3,143	1,138	642	962	941	1,893
Cash items in process	717	212	113	217	192	343
Bank Premises	5	4	1	3	1	6
Other assets	18	6	4	6	5	11
Total assets	$ 8,195	$ 2,016	$ 1,159	$ 2,074	$ 1,807	$ 4,874
Liabilities						
Own F.R. notes	$ 4,560	$ 1,097	$ 611	$ 920	$ 639	$ 2,322
Deposits – member banks	2,798	651	392	837	891	2,025
– U.S. Treasurer	102	25	23	44	24	41
Other deposits	132	64	27	65	75	167
Deferred availability cash items	483	144	83	173	145	237
Other liabilities	1	1	none			
Total Liabilities	$ 8,075	$1,982	$1,135	$ 2,040	$ 1,774	$ 4,794
Paid in capital	$ 29	$ 7	$ 5	$ 8	$ 10	$ 24
Surplus	77	21	14	20	18	47
Other capital accts.	14	6	4	6	5	8
Ratio: gold to note & deposit liability	56%	34%	37%	47%	42%	56%

Source: Annual Report of Board of Governors, Federal Reserve System.

Item	All banks	Boston	New York	Philadelphia	Cleveland	Richmond	Atlanta
Assets							
Total Gold reserves	$17,479	$895	$4,074	$1,122	$1,449	$1,116	$982
Special Drawing Rights		not an item	until 1970				
Cash–F.R. notes + coin	888	78	177	54	64	65	88
Discounts & Advances	107	1	76	4	1	1	2
U.S. Gov't Securities	27,384	1,450	7,131	1,545	2,318	1,708	1,480
Cash items in process	6,809	483	1,457	412	556	482	517
Bank Premises	108	4	9	4	9	6	11
Other assets	209	11	52	12	18	13	12
Total assets	$52,984	$2,922	$12,976	$3,153	$4,415	$3,391	$3,092
Liabilities							
Own F.R. notes	$28,449	$1,625	$6,663	$1,867	$2,575	$2,185	$1,614
Deposits – member banks	17,080	778	4,582	832	1,254	727	906
– U.S. Treasurer	4485	36	72	27	38	24	32
Other deposits	771	15	461	18	26	16	15
Deferred availability cash items	4,941	406	844	335	406	381	431
Other liabilities	32	2	10	2	3	2	1
Total Liabilities	$51,758	$2,862	$12,632	$3,081	$4,302	$3,335	$3,026
Paid in capital	$409	20	115	24	38	19	22
Surplus	817	40	229	48	75	37	44
Other capital accts.	----	----	----	----	----	----	----
Ratio: gold to note & deposit liability	37.4%	36.5%	34.6%	40.9%	37.2%	37.8%	37.9%

Item	Chicago	St. Louis	Minneapolis	Kansas City	Dallas	San Francisco
Assets						
Total Gold reserves	$2,979	$722	$370	$825	$764	$2,181
Special Drawing Rights	not an item until 1970			none		
Cash–F.R. notes + coin	104	45	28	36	40	109
Discounts & Advances	none					
U.S. Gov't Securities	4,621	1,098	628	1,167	1,088	3,172
Cash items in process	1,112	329	181	329	259	692
Bank Premises	— 22	7	5	5	14	12
Other assets	35	8	5	9	9	25
Total assets	**$8,873**	**$2,209**	**$1,217**	**$2,371**	**$2,174**	**$6,191**
Liabilities						
Own F.R. notes	$5,302	$1,232	$595	$1,153	$836	$2,775
Deposits – member banks	2,495	651	419	863	971	2,602
– U.S. Treasurer	63	27	23	30	54	59
Other deposits	43	54	7	13	15	88
Deferred availability cash items	791	203	144	259	227	514
Other liabilities	5	1	1	1	1	3
Total Liabilities	**$8,699**	**$2,168**	**$1,189**	**$2,319**	**$2,104**	**$6,041**
Paid in capital	$58	$14	$9	$17	$23	$50
Surplus	116	27	19	35	47	100
Other capital accts.	none					
Ratio: gold to note & deposit liability	38%	37%	36%	40%	41%	40%

Source: Annual Report of Board of Governors, Federal Reserve System.

Item	All banks	Boston	New York	Philadelphia	Cleveland	Richmond	Atlanta
Assets							
Total Gold reserves	$10,457	$591	$1,943	$721	$1,095	$1,044	$555
Special Drawing Rights	400	23	93	23	33	36	22
Cash-F.R. notes + coin	1,286	141	207	70	92	95	252
Discounts & Advances	335	----	104	---	---	----	----
Total U.S. Gov't Securities	62,141	3,040	15,845	3,261	4,848	4,627	3,229
Cash items in process	14,248	780	2,810	694	912	996	1,456
Bank Premises	128	2	8	3	12	11	17
Other assets	1,051	53	434	43	66	58	45
Total assets	**$90,046**	**$4,631**	**$21,444**	**$4,815**	**$7,058**	**$6,867**	**$5,576**
Liabilities							
F.R. Notes	$51,387	$2,919	$12,196	$2,934	$4,198	$4,604	$2,645
Deposits-member banks	24,040	875	6,162	1,163	1,813	1,807	1,606
- U.S. Treasurer	1,156	52	337	64	76	39	79
Other deposits	1,381	21	793	23	34	36	22
Deferred availibility cash items	10,098	669	1,439	529	764	767	1,100
Other liabilities	581	29	147	30	45	42	30
Total Liabilities	**$88,643**	**$4,565**	**$21,074**	**$4,743**	**$6,932**	**$6,795**	**$5,482**
Paid in capital	702	33	185	36	63	36	47
Surplus	702	33	185	36	63	36	47
Ratio fo gold reserves to F.R. note and deposit liability	--						

Legal requirements removed 3/3/65 & 3/18/68.

Item	Chicago	St. Louis	Minneapolis	Kansas City	Dallas	San Francisco
Assets						
Total Gold reserves	$2,210	$469	$161	$424	$199	$1,046
Special Drawing Rights	70	15	7	15	14	49
Cash	92	44	37	55	55	144
Discounts & Advances	227	----	----	3	----	----
Total U.S. Gov't Securities	9,785	2,279	1,218	2,427	2,815	8,769
Cash items in process	2,327	671	467	929	874	1,333
Bank Premises	17	12	12	18	8	8
Other assets	125	29	17	32	39	110
Total assets	**$14,853**	**$3,519**	**$1,919**	**$3,903**	**$4,004**	**$11,459**
Liabilities						
F.R. Notes	$9,003	$1,951	$ 875	$1,878	$1,946	$6,237
Deposits-member banks	3,430	885	623	1,104	1,257	3,814
- U.S. Treasurer	103	74	49	96	57	130
Other deposits	301	15	8	18	22	87
Deferred availibility cash items	1,714	525	320	724	617	930
Other liabilities	91	21	12	23	26	85
Total Liabilities	**$14,642**	**$3,471**	**$1,887**	**$3,843**	**$3,925**	**$11,283**
Paid in capital	$105	$24	$39	$30	$39	$88
Surplus	105	24	39	30	39	88
Ratio fo gold reserves to						
F.R. note and deposit liability	-- Legal requirements removed 3/3/65 & 3/18/68.					

Source: Annual Report of Board of Governors, Federal Reserve System.

Item	All banks	Boston	New York	Philadelphia	Cleveland	Richmond	Atlanta
Assets							
Total Gold reserves	$11,161	$577	$3,013	$560	$847	$961	$465
Special Drawing Rights	2,518	128	665	121	201	229	79
Cash	397	27	24	19	49	42	38
Discounts & Advances	1,809	106	663	54	202	189	81
Total U.S. Gov't Securities	131,368	5,849	36,612	5,558	9,673	10,517	4,640
Cash items in process	15,504	403	2,351	425	479	3,035	2,041
Bank Premises	457	100	20	53	24	89	35
Other assets	8,281	185	4,984	-491	386	726	144
Total assets	**$171,495**	**$7,375**	**$48,332**	**$6,299**	**$11,861**	**$15,788**	**$7,523**
Liabilities							
F.R. Notes	$124,241	$6,191	$35,601	$5,276	$9,463	$10,786	$3,670
Deposits–member banks	27,456	743	6,521	576	1,529	1,637	1,852
– U.S. Treasurer	3,062	---	3,062 all balances on this date at New York				
Other deposits	1,028	21	582	22	46	42	35
Deferred availability cash items	11,037	257	1,384	237	437	2,989	1,667
Other liabilities	2,265	97	570	96	196	210	119
Total Liabilities	**$ 159,089**	**$7,309**	**$47,720**	**$6,207**	**$11,671**	**$15,664**	**$7,343**
Paid in capital	$1,203	$33	$306	$46	$95	$62	$90
Surplus	1,203	33	306	46	95	62	90
Ratio of gold reserves to F.R. note and deposit liability --	Legal requirements removed 3/3/65 & 3/18/68.						

Item	Chicago	St. Louis	Minneapolis	Kansas City	Dallas	San Francisco
Assets						
Total Gold reserves	$1,722	$465	$225	$501	$572	$1,253
Special Drawing Rights	411	106	42	111	132	293
Cash	23	24	12	44	30	65
Discounts & Advances	186	51	34	138	47	58
Total U.S. Gov't Securities	20,119	5,145	2,287	6,000	7,599	17,369
Cash items in process	1,730	656	699	1,521	1,370	794
Bank Premises	16	14	28	22	13	43
Other assets	179	-139	-204	270	852	1,389
Total assets	**$24,386**	**$6,322**	**$3,123**	**$8,607**	**$10,615**	**$21,264**
Liabilities						
F.R. Notes	$19,437	$4,835	$1,807	$5,758	$7,198	$14,219
Deposits-member banks	3,495	742	655	1,350	2,312	6,044
- U.S. Treasurer	all balances on this date at New York					
Other deposits	91	20	16	27	40	86
Deferred availibility cash items	672	569	529	1,269	790	237
Other liabilities	337	84	40	99	127	290
Total Liabilities	**$24,032**	**$6,250**	**$3,047**	**$8,503**	**$10,467**	**$20,876**
Paid in capital	$177	$36	$38	$52	$74	$194
Surplus	177	36	38	52	74	194
Ratio of gold reserves to						
F.R. note and deposit liability	--	Legal requirements removed 3/3/65 & 3/18/68.				

Source: Annual Report of Board of Governors, Federal Reserve System.

Item	All banks	Boston	New York	Philadelphia	Cleveland	Richmond
Assets						
Total Gold Reserves	$11,060	$ 680	$ 3,310	$ 389	$ 655	$ 917
Special Drawing Rights	5,018	314	1,489	162	314	461
Cash (coin)	395	20	14	29	25	62
Discounts & Advances	2,170	42	34	168	890	122
U.S. Gov't Securities *	247,489	14,604	89,097	6,821	13,900	18,683
Cash Items in Process	8,739	480	1,235	421	244	459
Bank Premises	750	92	32	46	32	124
Other Assets	18,053	1,218	4,574	1,080	234	4,033
Total Assets	$293,674	$17,450	$99,785	$9,116	$16,294	$24,861
Liabilities						
Fed. Res. Notes	$229,640	$ 14,322	$78,077	$6,655	$13,704	$ 20,096
Deposits: Depository						
Institutions	39,347	2,386	9,199	1,777	1,894	3,836
Other deposits	9,551	25	9,203	13	22	54
Deferred Availability cash items	7,453	373	795	375	266	387
Other Liabilities	3,457	194	1,379	90	178	242
Total Liabilities	$289,448	$ 17,300	$98,653	$8,910	$16,064	$ 24,615
Paid in Capital	$2,113	$ 75	$ 566	$103	$ 115	$ 123
Surplus	2,113	75	566	103	115	123

Item	Atlanta	Chicago	St. Louis	Minneapolis	Kansas City	Dallas	San Francisco
Assets							
Total Gold Reserves	$ 584	$1,394	$ 368	$168	$ 490	$676	$ 1,429
Special Drawing Rights	203	656	160	66	216	307	670
Cash (coin)	36	44	29	11	30	28	67
Discounts & Advances	35	44	95	12	30	688	10
U.S. Gov't Securities*	11,220	29,213	7,080	3,428	9,051	13,496	30,896
Cash Items in Process	721	774	422	383	1,542	696	1,362
Bank Premises	59	100	21	24	47	22	151
Other Assets	1,436	2,470	1,154	1,381	1,284	-728	-83
Total Assets	$14,294	$34,695	$9,329	$5,473	$12,690	$15,185	$34,502
Liabilities							
Fed. Res. Notes	$8,889	$29,658	$ 847	$ 4,124	$ 9,758	$11,664	$ 24,846
Deposits: Depository Institutions	4,189	3,413	874	807	1,122	2,401	7,449
Other deposits	18	126	12	7	10	13	48
Deferred Availability cash items	657	565	389	353	1,507	616	1,170
Other Liabilities	149	387	91	48	119	173	407
Total Liabilities	$13,902	$34,149	$ 9,213	$5,339	$ 12,516	$14,867	$33,920
Paid in Capital	$ 196	$ 273	$ 58	$ 67	$87	$ 159	$ 291
Surplus	196	273	58	67	87	159	291

*Includes Agency Issues and repurchase agreements.
Source: Annual Report of Board of Governors, 1988.

Bibliography

Bryant, Ralph C. *Controlling Money: The Federal Reserve and Its Critics.* Washington, D.C.: The Brookings Institute, 1983.

Burgess, W. Randolph. *The Reserve Banks and the Money Market.* New York & London: Harper & Brothers Publishers, 1946.

Chandler, Lester V. *Benjamin Strong.* Washington, D.C.: The Brookings Institute, 1958.

Conway, Thomas, Jr., and Patterson, Earnest M. *The Operation of the New Banking Act.* London & Philadelphia: J.B. Lippincott Co., 1914.

DeRosa, Paul, and Stern, Gary H. *In the Name of Money.* New York: McGraw-Hill Book Co., 1981.

de Saint Phalle, Thibaut. *The Federal Reserve, An International Mystery.* New York: Praeger Publishers, 1985.

Glass, Carter. *An Adventure in Constructive Finance.* New York: Doubleday & Co., Inc., 1927.

Groseclose, Elgin E. *America's Money Machine.* Westport, Conn.: Arlington House Publishers, 1980.

_____. *Fifty Years of Managed Money: The Story of the Federal Reserve, 1914-1963.* New York & Washington, D.C.: Books Inc., 1965.

Hadjimchalakis, Michael G. *The Federal Reserve, Money, and Interest Rates.* New York: Praeger Publishers, 1984.

Harding, William Proctor Gould. *The Formative Period of the Federal Reserve System.* Boston: Houghton Mifflin Co., 1925.

Harris, Seymour E. *Twenty Years of Federal Reserve Policy, Including an Extended Discussion of the Monetary Crisis, 1927-1933.* Cambridge, Mass.: Harvard University Press, 1933.

Hollingsworth, J.B., and Whitehouse, P.B. *North American Railways.* Hong Kong: Bisson Book Limited, 1977.

Johnson, Roger T. *Historical Beginnings — The Federal Reserve.* Boston: Federal Reserve Bank of Boston, 1977.

Jones, David M. *Fed Watching and Interest Rate Projections.* New York: New York Institute of Finance, 1986.

Kemmerer, Edwin Walter. *The ABC of the Federal Reserve System.* Princeton, N.J.: Princeton University Press, 1920.

Kettl, Donald E. *Leadership at the Fed.* New Haven & London: Yale University Press, 1986.

Laughlin, James Lawrence. *The Federal Reserve Act: Its Orgin and Problems.* New York: Macmillan Publishing Co., 1933.

Livingston, James. *Origin of the Federal Reserve System.* London & Ithaca, N.Y.: Cornell University Press, 1986.

Melton, William C. *Inside the Fed; Making Monetary Policy*. Homewood, Ill.:
  Dow Jones-Irvin, 1985.
Moore, Carl H., and Russell, Alvin E. *Money—Its Orgin, Development and
  Modern Use*. Jefferson, N.C. & London: McFarland & Company, Inc., 1987.
Newton, Maxwell. *The Fed*. New York: Times Books, 1983.
Prochnow, Herbert V. *The Federal Reserve System*. New York: Harper & Row,
  1960.
Rowe, J.Z. *The Public-Private Character of United States Central Banking*. New
  Brunswick, N.J.: Rutgers University Press, 1965.
Timberlake, Richard Henry. *The Origin of Central Banking in the United States*.
  Cambridge, Mass.: Harvard University Press, 1978.
Warburg, Paul M. *The Federal Reserve System: Its Origin and Growth*. New York:
  Macmillan Co., 1930.
West, Robert Craig. *Banking Reform and the Federal Reserve, 1863–1923*. Ithaca,
  N.Y.: Cornell University Press, 1977.
Willis, Henry Parker. *The Federal Reserve System*. New York: The Ronald Press
  Co., 1923.
Wooley, John T. *Monetary Politics; The Federal Reserve and the Politics of
  Monetary Policy*. Cambridge: Cambridge University Press, 1984.

Annual Report of Board of Governors. Washington, D.C.: Federal Reserve
  System, 1936–1988.
Annual Report of the Comptroller of the Currency. Washington, D.C.: Govern-
  ment Printing Office, 1915.
Annual Reports of the Federal Reserve Board. Washington, D.C.: Federal Reserve
  Board, 1914–1935.
Banking and Monetary Statistics, 1914–1941. Washington, D.C.: Board of Gover-
  nors, Federal Reserve System, 1943.
Banking and Monetary Statistics, 1941–1970. Washington, D.C.: Board of Gover-
  nors, Federal Reserve System, 1971.
Banking and Monetary Statistics, 1970–1979. Washington, D.C.: Board of Gover-
  nors, Federal Reserve System, 1982.
*The Federal Reserve Act and Other Statutory Provisions Affecting the Federal
  Reserve System*. Washington, D.C.: Board of Governors, Federal Reserve
  System, 1983.
The Federal Reserve System—Purposes and Functions. Washington, D.C.: Board
  of Governors, Federal Reserve System, 1974.
Historical Statistics of the United States—Colonial Times to 1970. Washington,
  D.C.: Government Printing Office, 1975.
Notable Names in American History. Clifton, N.J.: James T. White & Co., 1973.
Statistical Abstract of the United States, 1984, 104th Edition. Washington, D.C.:
  Government Printing Office, 1983.

Index